3 —

BEER

TAP INTO THE ART AND SCIENCE OF BREWING

BEER

TAP INTO THE ART AND SCIENCE OF BREWING

Charles Bamforth

Foreword by

Dave Thomas

American Society of Brewing Chemists
and Coors Brewing Company

 INSIGHT BOOKS

PLENUM PRESS • NEW YORK AND LONDON

Library of Congress Cataloging-in-Publication Data

Bamforth, Charles W., 1952-
    Beer : tap into the art and science of brewing / Charles Bamforth.
        p.   cm.
    Includes bibliographical references and index.
    ISBN 0-306-45797-0
    1. Brewing--Amateurs' manuals. 2. Beer.   I. Title.
TP570.B18   1998
641.8'73--dc21   98-5697
                                                                         CIP

ISBN 0-306-45797-0

© 1998 Plenum Press
Insight Books is a Division of Plenum Publishing Corporation
233 Spring Street, New York, N.Y. 10013-1578

http://www.plenum.com

An Insight Book

10 9 8 7 6 5 4 3 2 1

Printed in the United States of America

For Diane, Peter, Caroline, and Emily

CONTENTS

FOREWORD

It is significant, to me at least, that I read Professor Bamforth's (Charlie's) manuscript quite easily on a cross-country flight to deliver a speech as the current President of the American Society of Brewing Chemists (ASBC) on the occasion of the 110th Anniversary of the Master Brewers Association of the Americas (MBAA). While 65 years of ASBC and 110 years of MBAA seem like a considerable time, both organizations are actually junior members of the worldwide brewing community, which in cooperation with the Institute of Brewing, European Brewery Convention, and other organizations, have invested many millions of hours conferring, conversing, and otherwise hobnobbing with our fellow brewing wizards about the history, art-science, humor, and enjoyment of beer. Charlie has managed to elegantly combine many of the most fascinating and memorable facts that arise from the study of beer and brewing within the pages of this text while making it an enjoyable read.

This book introduces some of the biology, biochemistry, and physical chemistry that determine final beer quality characteristics like color, foam, flavor, and drinkability. Charlie explains why beer that smells faintly like a dead skunk on a country road is caused by improper glass packaging and unique hop chemistry. He explains why maltsters have a white thumb, why brewing and maybe not baking, as previously assumed, was the activity of ancient civilizations elucidated in recent archeological digs, and why publicans in the Middle Ages would sit in their beer to determine strength before paying good brass for it! I have studied barley, malt, and beer for more than 20 years and have not read a better, more readable account of the organoleptic (beer aroma and flavor) effects of some of the macromolecules from malted barley, nor have I heard some of them aptly described as "wobbly" before.

While it is certainly true that state, federal, local, provincial, and imperial regulations prohibit brewers from advertising or labeling the nutritional content of beer today, Charlie points out that this was not always so, and he revives many strange provincial truths about the healthful aspects of beer. Brewers typically remind friends who travel widely that beer is oftentimes safer to drink than the local water, but I did not know that beer was also good for your teeth!

As I read through the manuscript I was thinking of the appropriate audience. The first that came to mind was anyone who has entered into discussion, wagers, or friendly arguments in the local bar or pub about the art and science of brewing, the virtues of a particular beer style, or the critical determinants of aroma and flavor of a favorite beer (this grouping pretty well includes everyone I know!). This book provides a handy introduction, review, and reference. Also, for my colleagues in various support industries or segments of the brewing industry who need to understand a little about brewing and malting but don't really know where to start (read marketing folks!), this book is an excellent place to start and a useful reference during discussions with brewers.

Charlie's position is strong, based on many years of experience in practical brewing, quality control, and research in the United Kingdom and intimate knowledge of the U.S. brewing industry, including the recent explosion of pubs and microbreweries. His historical accounts run the gamut from prehistoric consumption of Neolithic beers to a brief history of beer in the United States to current and future brewing technologies like the can widget and inevitable genetic manipulation of yeast and barley for making better beer. He has effectively stepped across the Atlantic by using his European brewing experience and research on worldwide brewing history to introduce the art and science of brewing in layman's terms for the United States. Armed with the information presented herein, I am confident that pub discussions, friendly differences of opinion on beer style, or technical discussions with marketing can be conducted in a more educated, fact-based manner and will expand on the enthusiasm expressed by Friar Tuck in the hit movie, *Robin Hood, Prince of Thieves*, to wit:

> *This is grain, which any fool can eat, but for which the Lord intended a more divine means of consumption. Let us give praise to our maker and glory to his bounty by learning about . . . Beer!*

—Dave Thomas
President, American Society
of Brewing Chemists
Director, Brewing Research & Development
Coors Brewing Company

PREFACE

A year or two ago I was idly flicking between television channels when I chanced upon a couple of people sipping beer and discussing their findings. One of these people has established a reputation as something of a wine connoisseur and appears to take particular pride in pinpointing the exact vintage of the bottle and the winery in which it was produced. For all I know, that person may be able to name the peasant who had trod the grapes and to predict their shoe size. With rather more certainty, however, I was able to conclude that their knowledge of beer was mediocre, or worse.

From time to time, too, I come across articles in the general press that pontificate about beer in a manner not dissimilar to the aforementioned wine buff. I applaud the efforts of some of these authors for their help in maintaining beer in the collective consciousness. I deplore it, however, when they attempt to pontificate on the rights and wrongs of brewing practice. It is galling when they dress up the taste and aroma of beer in ridiculous terminology. Personally, I have enormous difficulty reconciling the language they use with the tastes of the myriad of beers that I have had the great good fortune to consume across the world.

An analogous situation exists in my own "other life." While research into the science of brewing and beer pays my mortgage and puts food in the mouths of my children, my hobby is to write articles about soccer. I hope (and believe) that they help contribute to the pleasure of the fans who read them, but I hope I would never be accused of trying to tell the professionals within the game how to do their jobs. I might fairly articulate the views of an outsider—the fan's eye view—but I trust that it's the coaches and the players within soccer who know their specialization and can deliver a product that will thrill and delight me.

Rather more is written about beer in the nonspecialist press by "fans" than by "professionals." There is room for both. And that is why I decided to write this book, in an attempt to partly redress the balance. In it, I have attempted to capture the proud history of brewing, which stretches back to a time when articles on the merits of beer would have been written on papyrus or scrawled in hieroglyphics on walls of clay. I have attempted to convey the somewhat complex science of brewing in straightforward terms, with particular emphasis on why the properties of beer are as they are. I have endeavored to show the sensible and meaningful ways in which beer quality can be described. And I have tried to entertain, without trivializing a proud and distinguished profession.

I like beer, and, like the majority of people working in the brewing industry, I care about it and about the people who drink it. In this book I draw attention to a myriad of recent studies that suggest that beer (and other alcoholic drinks) are beneficial components of the adult diet, provided they are consumed in moderation. I certainly have no intention of encouraging the irresponsible to abuse the pleasure that comes from drinking beer in moderation, at the right time, in the right place.

I want people to understand and appreciate their beer and gain an insight into the devoted labors of all those whose combined efforts bring it to the glass: the farmer who grows the best barley, the hop grower cultivating a unique crop, the maltster who converts barley into delicious malt, the brewer who combines malt and hop to feed a yeast that he or she will have protected for perhaps hundreds of years, and the bartender who keeps the beer in top condition.

This book is about facts. Where there is scope for expressing opinions, they are my own, and not everyone in the brewing trade will necessarily agree with them. They have, however, been arrived at over a 20-year career in the brewing profession. I hope reading this book will help you form a considered opinion about brewing and about beer—and to become rather better acquainted with its art and science.

ACKNOWLEDGMENTS

No book is ever written without help. I had a lot of help—directly from people providing information, advice, diagrams, or photographs, and indirectly from those who encouraged me or who simply tolerated the emotional highs and lows that authorship unavoidably brings. For this, nobody deserves my gratitude more than my family, for this has been an out-of-hours partaking.

The photographs in this book have diverse origins, and their source is acknowledged within the captions. Many of the drawings were by George Brown, but others came from Paul Hughes, Sarah Bennett, Ian Curtis, Chandra Gopal, and Miles Schofield. John Hammond, Denise Baxter, Mike Proudlove, Derek Laws, Rob Reed, Bill Lancashire, Geoff Buckee, and Renton Righelato willingly gave of their time to read parts of the manuscript, while Barbara Kelly kindly drew attention throughout to some of my worst flights of literary fancy. The excellent brewing historian Ray Anderson brought to notice various fascinating facts, and Sue Henderson furnished plenty of valuable background literature. I appreciate, too, valuable conversations with Dr. Delwen Samuel. The help of all of these people is sincerely acknowledged. Any errors of fact, however, are purely my own.

My editors at Plenum, Frank Darmstadt in New York and Joanna Lawrence in London, have been variously patient and pushy, but always extremely helpful and supportive. My secretary Sue Tomlinson ensured that a regular dialogue was maintained with them, no matter where I was in the great world of brewing.

I thank Dave Thomas sincerely for his generous Foreword and also the Brewers and Licensed Retailers Association, Briggs of Burton, Pauls

Malt, and the Carlsberg Laboratory for so generously allowing me to reproduce published material. Miller Brewing Company and Stroh Brewery Company provided valuable background information.

It is 20 years since I joined the brewing industry. In that time I have learned from a great many people. I know that all of them will understand when I say that, above all, I learned the way and made my way thanks in the main to three of them: John Hudson, Tony Portno, and Bernard Atkinson. I acknowledge them sincerely and I hope that they will regard this book as a tribute to them. In turn, from knowing me, they will understand why this book is dedicated to my wife and children.

For a quart of ale is a dish for a king.

—William Shakespeare,
   The Winter's Tale, Act IV, Scene 3

BEER

TAP INTO THE ART AND SCIENCE OF BREWING

INTRODUCTION

Ralph Waldo Emerson (1803–1882), the great American essayist, poet, and one-time Unitarian minister, penned many learned thoughts. The reader will forgive me if I select just 13 words from the great man: "God made yeast . . . and loves fermentation just as dearly as he loves vegetation."

Beer, surely, is a gift of God, one that brings together yeast and vegetation (in the shape of barley and hops) in a drink that has been drunk for 8,000 years, a beverage that has soothed fevered brows, nourished the hungry, coupled friendly and unfriendly alike—it's even seen men off into battle.

"No soldier can fight unless he is properly fed on beef and beer," said John Churchill, the first Duke of Marlborough (1650–1722), a great British tactician and a forebear of the even more celebrated Winston.

Queen Victoria (1819–1901) was another who recognized the merit of beer: "Give my people plenty of beer, good beer and cheap beer, and you will have no revolution among them."

With these sentiments, the redoubtable monarch echoed the enthusiasm of the Athenian tragedian Euripides (484–406 B.C.):

> The man that isn't jolly after drinking
> Is just a driveling idiot, to my thinking

This book is not an exercise in trying to convince you, the reader, of the merits and demerits of drinking beer. I assume that as you have picked it up, and are starting to read, you have an interest in beer. The aim of this book is to bring to the nonspecialist an appreciation of the science and technology which underpin a truly international beverage. I use the word *international*, knowing that to do justice to the entire world of beer would

1

have demanded more than a single volume. Markets differ considerably from country to country, but the scientific principles of brewing are constant the world over. It is the science and the technology about which I particularly wish to inform the reader, for the processes involved in the brewing of beer are as fascinating as they are, in some ways, unique.

I have several audiences in mind for this book. First, and perhaps foremost, are the laypersons who want to know, in reader-friendly terms, what goes into their beer. Such people seek the magic that underpins this supreme alchemy, namely the conversion of barley and hops, by yeast, into something so astonishingly drinkable. My desire is to reinforce the pleasure that people have in responsibly drinking beer by informing them about the myriad of biochemical and chemical reactions involved in the production of their favorite drink and to expose them to the enormous reservoir of science and technology that make the malting and brewing processes two of the great "traditional" industries. It is my earnest hope that, by reading this book, beer drinkers will appreciate the care that goes into making every pint of beer. I will be describing a science, or rather, a range of sciences, and so cannot avoid using scientific terms. I hope I have achieved this in a way readily understandable to those without an understanding of chemistry, biology, chemical engineering, and the other scientific disciplines upon which brewing is founded. I have provided a simple explanation of underpinning science and also a comprehensive glossary at the end of the book.

A second group of people who should benefit from reading this book are those joining the brewing industry and who wish to have a friendly introduction to humankind's oldest biotechnology. Among these readers will be those entering in nontechnical roles: sales, marketing, finance, and—chief executives!

A third group are those who interact professionally with brewing, either as suppliers or retailers, and who need to know why Brewers are so demanding in their requirements and so very proud of their heritage.

A valued colleague has extremely strong views on the use of language in books and lectures about the brewing business. I well recall having finished giving a lecture in Canada that I thought had gone across very nicely, when she stormed up to me, asking darkly whether I had a view on whether women as well as men drank beer. Puzzled, I replied, "Of course they do." "Then why," she replied, acidly, "did every reference to the beer drinker in your talk consist of 'he this,' and 'he that.'" I had meant no offense by it, using "he" in the generic sense, but I haven't made the mistake since. For this reason, I intersperse the words *he* and *she* through-out this book. As we will see in Chapter One, it is the female of the species that was once primarily responsible for brewing the ale. She was the *brewster*, and I use the term from time to time.

Another problem I had to confront was the matter of units. Brewers in different countries have their own units of measurement. Even when the same name is used for a unit, it doesn't necessarily mean the same thing in different countries. Thus, a barrel in the United States comprises 31 gal-lons, whereas a barrel in the United Kingdom holds 36 gallons. Just to complicate matters further, a U.S. gallon is smaller than a U.K. gallon. I have used both types of barrel at various points and have indicated whether it's a U.S. or a U.K. variant. The international unit for volume, however, is the liter or the hectoliter (100 liters). By and large, this and other metric terms are employed, as Brewers across the world do tend to use them as well as their own parochial preferences. A gallon equals 3.7853 liters in the United States, hence a U.S. barrel holds 1.1734 hectoliters (hl). A U.K. barrel, on the other hand, contains 1.6365 hl because 1 U.K. gallon equals 1.201 U.S. gallons.

I also had the thorny question of which currency to use. As this book's publisher is American, I have chosen to use dollars and cents. Finally, when presenting statistical data, I have used the most recent information available to me. I regret that much of the trend information takes rather a long time for researchers to collect, so some details are a year or two old now.

When I talk about the alcoholic strength of beer it is always as % vol./ vol., which many people refer to as "alcohol by volume" (ABV). Thus a strength of 5% ABV indicates that there are 5 ml of alcohol (ethanol, previously known as ethyl alcohol) per 100 ml of beer. Although Brewers in the United States still frequently use the Fahrenheit scale, I have used degrees Celsius throughout, as it is generally understood in all parts of the world as the unit of temperature and is increasingly employed in Ameri-can brewing literature. (Those of you who find Celsius a mystery will need to apply the correction factor $°F = °C \times 9/5 + 32$.) Finally in connection with units, from time to time I talk about the levels of other molecules in beer, especially the substances that contribute to flavor. By and large these are present at quite low concentrations. You will find mention of ppm, ppb, and ppt: These refer to parts per million, parts per billion, and parts per trillion, respectively. A substance present at 1 ppm exists as 1 mg (milli-gram) per liter of beer. One ppb equates to 1 μg (microgram) per liter of beer, while 1 ppt means 1 ng (nanogram) per liter of beer. One milligram is a thousandth of a gram; one microgram is a thousandth of a milligram; one nanogram is a thousandth of a microgram. Just in case the metric system still leaves you cold, I had better point out that there are 28.35 g per ounce and 128 fluid ounces per U.S. gallon.

Finally, a brief word about convention. I use Brewer (or Maltster) with a capital letter when referring to a brewing (or malting) *company*, but brewer and maltster in the lower case when describing an individual practitioner of the art.

Enjoy the book. And enjoy the beer that is the end result of so much care and devotion.

Chapter One

FROM MESOPOTAMIA TO MILWAUKEE

The World of Beer and Breweries

THE WORLD BEER MARKET

Beer is drunk all over the world. In some places, such as parts of Germany, it is *the* drink of choice for accompanying food. Almost everywhere, though, beer is the great drink of relaxation—and moderation. It is consumed in bars, clubs, sports grounds—in fact anywhere adults congregate. Surely nowhere typifies this better than the English public house, or pub, which remains, alongside the church, the essential ingredient of any self-respecting community.

Yet is it clearly not essential to have company to pursue one's favorite tipple. In the United Kingdom, for instance, the last 10 years have seen more than a 60% growth in the proportion of beer sold in cans and more than a 170% increase for sales in nonreturnable bottles (NRBs). The volumes involved remain small compared with the amount of beer retailed on draft, which is two-thirds of the total. U.K. sales of beer on draft are surpassed only by sales in Ireland and Cuba. There is, however, a clear shift in the U.K. toward beer drinking at home. As we shall see later, developments in technology have enabled traditional beers hitherto sold only in casks to be packaged in cans, leading to a major growth in so-called draft beer in a can. The growth in volume of NRBs perhaps reflects nothing more than the emerging preferences of the younger drinker, for whom the right label on the right bottle in the right hand in the right location are the primary factors in beer selection.

In the United States, 26% of beer is purchased on premises, that is, in bars, restaurants, and hotels. Although this is a lower proportion than in, say, the United Kingdom, such establishments sell the most beer in the

United States. Otherwise, beer is retailed by convenience stores and gas stations (20%), supermarkets (19%), liquor stores (17%), neighborhood accounts (7%), home distributors (5%), drugstores (4%), and warehouse clubs and supercenters (2%).

It would be impossible in a book of this size to fully explain the evolution of the brewing industry in each of the many countries where beer is produced. I could devote page after page to the many political forces that have come to bear on a commodity that will always attract all shades of public opinion. A classic example is the pressure which led to Prohibition in the United States between 1919 and 1933 (see Box). This obliged their great Brewers to display considerable ingenuity. They made nonalcoholic products such as near beers, malted milk, ice cream, and much more—innovative abilities that remain characteristic to this day and that have ensured the survival of two of the top three Brewers in the world in their home bases in St. Louis and Milwaukee (Table 1.1).

One-third of the 1.25 billion hectoliters of beer brewed worldwide in 1996 came from just 10 companies. It is striking, too, that there are major brewing companies located in countries that do not have a large indigenous beer-drinking population. In France, for example, personal beer consumption is 39.1 liters per head—less than a third of that drunk in Germany—yet the Danone group has sales over 200% higher than Germany's biggest producer. Brazil's beer consumption per capita is also far lower than Germany's, yet it has one Brewer in the world top 10 and

Table 1.1. The world's biggest Brewers

Company	Country	Worldwide sales in 1995 (million hl)
Anheuser-Busch	United States	107.0
Heineken	Netherlands	64.3
Miller	United States	54.2
South African Breweries	South Africa	36.4
Brahma	Brazil	36.4
Kirin	Japan	33.7
Carlsberg	Denmark	31.6
Interbrew*	Belgium	28.8
Foster's	Australia	26.9
Danone	France	26.6

Source: *Statistical Handbook*, Brewers & Licensed Retailers Association, London, 1997.
*Interbrew owns Labatt, which has sales of 10.9 million hectoliters in Canada.

Prohibition

The temperance movement began in the United States in the early nineteenth century, with 13 states becoming "dry" between 1846 and 1855, with Maine leading the way. Ironically, 1846 also marked the birth of Carry Nation (1846–1911), a doyenne among prohibitionists, whose prayers and lectures in Kansas developed into more physical acts of objection to drink when she and her followers started to smash beer containers with hatchets hidden beneath their skirts. Widespread prohibition was largely precipitated by claims that extensive drunkenness severely hampered production during World War I and, on January 17, 1920, Congress enacted the Eighteenth Amendment to the U.S. Constitution. This amendment forbade the "manufacture, sale and transportation of intoxicating liquors" and was approved by all but two states. The Volstead Act of the same year was the basis of the federal government's ban on all intoxicating liquor, defined as a drink containing in excess of 0.5% alcohol.

Of course, for as many as were ardent in their antialcohol beliefs, there were those who enjoyed a drink. Unsurprisingly, the introduction of official prohibition prompted the growth in illegal home-brewing and of the bootlegging and speakeasy culture colorfully portrayed in the movies. Before Prohibition there were 15,000 saloons in New York. One year after the Volstead Act there were more than twice as many speakeasies! Gangsters grew rich at a time when federal authorities convicted 300,000 people of contravening the law. Drink-related crime surged: For example, there was an almost 500% increase in drunk-driving offenses in Chicago.

By 1933, opinion in the United States had changed (the slogan of Franklin Delano Roosevelt's Democrats was "A New Deal and a pot of beer for everyone"), and the Twenty-First Amendment to the Constitution repealed the Eighteenth. Whether to enforce prohibition or not became a state issue, but it took until 1966 for Mississippi to end its status as the last dry state.

The United States is not the only country to have embraced prohibition. The first attempts to control the sale of beer occurred in Egypt as far back as 4,000 years ago because it was felt that drinking interfered with productivity. Strong temperance movements grew up in Great Britain, largely in response to the perceived excesses of drink in the burgeoning industrial cities. People were urged to sign a pledge not to drink, but for many the soul was weaker than some of the ale! Until the 1950s in Canada, one was obliged to purchase an annual permit to buy alcoholic drinks. Prohibition was total in Finland for exactly the same period as in the United States.

A particularly vigorous temperance campaign was waged in the nineteenth and early twentieth centuries in New Zealand, where the first alcoholic drink had been brewed by the Englishman who "discovered" that land in 1769, Captain James Cook. A referendum after the First World War, which ended 51% to 49% in favor of continuance of the liquor trade (thanks largely to the vote of the military), enabled the beer business to continue.

Perhaps the most curious of the antidrink movements was that in Germany in 1600. The Order of Temperance said that adherents should drink no more than seven glasses of liquor at one time and that there should be no more than two such sessions each day!

another, Antarctica, in 11th place, with sales of 26.4 million hectoliters (it is 10% owned by Anheuser-Busch!).

The brewing industry in Germany is somewhat traditional. A strict law, the *Reinheitsgebot*, dating from Bavaria in 1487, restricts the raw materials for brewing beer to malted barley, yeast, hops, and water. The German brewing world is characterized by many relatively small brewing companies; there were 1,234 breweries in Germany in 1996, most producing individual products for relatively local consumption. The biggest Brewer in Germany produced some 7 million hectoliters. There are not many truly international German brewing brands, as indeed is the case for many other countries. It is largely the brands of some of the big ten Brewers that stand alongside the great colas on the international stage— brands such as Budweiser, Heineken, Miller, and Carlsberg. Guinness is another great world brand, produced by a company with an output which only marginally excludes it from being among the Big Ten.

As can be seen from Table 1.2, beer production and consumption statistics differ enormously among countries. The United States brews 33% more beer than the next largest producer, China. The United States, though, has a very sizable population. If the statistics are viewed on the basis of beer brewed per head, then Ireland and Denmark lead the way. Man for man, woman for woman, people drink more in Dublin and Cork, Copenhagen and Odense than they do in New York and Chicago.

The Czech Republic lays claim to the highest per capita consumption of beer: 21 more liters pass down the throats of each Czech than those of their nearest challengers, the Germans. By contrast, the Chinese drink only 12.6 liters per head, but because of the enormous population of that country, they are the second biggest producer of beer after the United States. Even more startling is the rate at which the Chinese beer industry has grown (Table 1.3). The volume of beer brewed in China has increased by over 2,000% since 1980. Major brewing companies from other countries have formed joint ventures with local companies in China and have revolutionized the technology there.

At the other end of the scale it is apparent that the Australian and British brewing industries have suffered a substantial decline in their production volumes. In part this reflects a tightening of the belt of the consumer and perhaps a change in drinking habits, but it also reflects the recognition that drinking even moderate amounts of alcohol is unacceptable when driving. The authorities are particularly vigorous in their monitoring of drink and driving in Australia.

There has been tremendous rationalization in the brewing industry in all countries, with beer production tending to be concentrated in fewer, larger breweries. For instance, in the United Kingdom there were 6,447 breweries in 1900 but only 499 in 1996. Among those 499, however, are a number of smaller brewing companies, so-called microbrewers, that have sprung up to produce beers of a traditional and distinctive character, generally for consumption on the premises. So if we look back to 1980 we find only 191 breweries in the United Kingdom. New ones spring up every year.

The same trend has occurred in the United States and has been a very welcome development. In 1983 there were fewer than 100 breweries in the States. Now there are more than 1,000—and they're still coming, many with a capacity of just a few barrels. They are generating a healthy consumer interest in beer and the art of brewing. Whether on street corners, dispensing full-flavored beers of diverse character to accompany good-value meals, or in baseball stadiums, adding to the sublime pleasure of the ball game, these tiny breweries greatly enrich the beer-drinking culture.

Table 1.2 reveals several more intriguing statistics. For example, the average strength of beer ranges from a high of 5.2% alcohol by volume (ABV) in Austria to a low of 3.9% in the Slovak Republic. This disguises, of course, a myriad of beer types of diverse strengths, which in the United Kingdom, for instance, ranges from alcohol-free beers to the so-called superlagers of 9% alcohol or above. Nonetheless, national preference is reflected in the strengths indicated in Table 1.2.

The great beer-exporting countries of the world, with the exception of Germany, feature major brewing companies. The Netherlands, home of Heineken, exports more beer than any other country, some 45% of its production. Denmark, where Carlsberg is based, exports 31% of its beer. Ireland, famed for Guinness ("the black stuff"), exports 44% of its production.

Table 1.2. Worldwide brewing and beer statistics (1995)

Country	Population (millions)	Production (million hl)	Imports (million hl)	Exports (million hl)	Consumption (l per head)	Draft (%)	Av. strength (%ABV)
Argentina	34.6	10.4	0.49	0.022	31.5	1	4.8
Australia	17.9	17.9	0.11	0.68	95.0	25	4.4
Austria	8.1	9.7	0.33	0.68	115.6	33	5.2
Belgium*	10.5	15.4	0.56	4.5	103.5	39	5.1
Brazil	161.8	84.0	0.25	1.12	51.4	2	—
Bulgaria	8.4	4.3	0.029	0.105	50.7	—	—
Canada	29.9	22.8	0.66	3.6	66.5	12	5.0
Chile	14.3	4.1	0.029	0.021	28.9	8	4.5
China	1,221.5	154.6	0.90	1.3	12.6	3	—
Colombia	35.1	17.8	0.047	0.054	50.7	1	4.2
Croatia	4.8	3.2	0.246	0.261	66.0	5	5.0
Cuba	11.0	1.2	0.06	—	11.1	70	5.0
Czech Republic	10.3	17.8	0.05	1.4	159.1	44	4.3
Denmark	5.2	10.1	0.118	3.1	124.4	7	4.6
Finland	5.1	4.8	0.082	0.31	81.3	25	4.5
France	58.0	20.6	3.5	1.4	39.1	23	5.0
Germany	81.6	117.4	2.6	7.6	137.7	20	5.0
Greece	10.0	4.0	0.23	0.23	40.0	5	5.0
Hungary	10.3	7.8	0.18	0.17	83.0	18	4.5
Iceland	0.29	0.082	0.046	—	44.8	17	4.5
Ireland	3.6	7.4	0.49	3.3	112.7	80	4.2

Italy	57.3	11.9	3.0	0.44	25.4	17	5.0
Japan	125.6	67.3	2.7	0.33	56.2	12	4.9
Korea (Rep.)	45.1	17.6	0.037	0.28	38.4	13	4.0
Mexico	93.7	44.4	0.21	3.9	43.5	1	4.0
New Zealand	3.6	3.6	0.16	0.20	99.5	44	4.0
Netherlands	15.4	23.1	0.61	10.4	86.0	30	5.1
Nigeria	111.7	4.5	0.007	0.005	4.0	0	4.5
Norway	4.3	2.3	0.067	0.01	52.5	27	4.3
Peru	23.8	7.9	0.004	0.013	33.3	1	—
Philippines	67.6	14.0	0.01	0.08	20.6	1	4.7
Poland	38.6	15.2	0.053	0.166	39.0	—	4.3
Portugal	9.9	6.9	0.23	0.72	64.7	30	5.1
Romania	22.7	8.6	0.42	0.001	39.2	—	5.0
Russia	147.0	17.8	2.0	—	13.5	—	5.0
Slovak Republic	5.3	4.4	0.8	0.21	93.8	39	3.9
Slovenia	2.0	2.1	0.051	0.29	92.8	—	—
South Africa	43.2	24.5	0.05	0.45	55.8	1	5.0
Spain	40.5	25.3	2.0	0.36	66.6	35	5.1
Sweden	8.8	5.3	0.38	0.06	64.5	12	4.5
Switzerland	7.2	3.8	0.7	0.03	61.6	32	4.9
Ukraine	51.3	7.1	0.16	0.06	14.0	36	—
United Kingdom	58.6	56.8	5.2	3.1	100.9	65	4.0
United States	262.8	233.7	13.2	9.8	83.5	11	4.6
Venezuela	21.8	16.3	0.09	0.35	73.7	1	—

Source: *Statistical Handbook*, Brewers & Licensed Retailers Association, London, 1997.
*Includes Luxembourg, because of inaccuracies introduced by cross-border trading.

Table 1.3. Growth or decline in beer volume over 15 years

Country	Beer production 1995 (million hl)	% change from 1980
China	154.6	2,477
Argentina	10.4	357
South Africa	24.5	195
Brazil	84.0	184
Philippines	14.0	100
Portugal	6.9	92
Mexico	44.5	63
Colombia	17.8	50
Japan	67.3	48
Netherlands	23.1	47
Denmark	10.1	23
Republic of Ireland	7.8	21
Canada	22.8	6
United States	233.7	3
Belgium	14.4	3
Germany	117.4	1
New Zealand	3.6	−6
Australia	17.9	−8
United Kingdom	56.8	−12

Source: *Statistical Handbook*, Brewers & Licensed Retailers Association, London, 1997.

The export of beer first took off with British imperialism in the nine-teenth century and with the shipping of vast quantities of so-called India Pale Ale (I.P.A.), a product still available from several Brewers in the home market today. This beer was of relatively low strength, to suit drinkability in hotter climes, but was well hopped, as hops have preservative qualities. The advent of pasteurization, and the attendant destruction of potential microbial contaminants, enhanced the market for such exports, as it meant that shelf lives could be lengthened still further.

Beers are still exported from country to country, a principal driving force being the opportunity to make marketing claims concerning the provenance of a product. However, most major Brewers realize how illogi-cal it is to transport vast volumes of liquid across oceans—after all, water is by far the major component of beer! They have either established their own breweries to supply specific market regions or have entered into franchise agreements in target countries with Brewers who brew their beer for them, generally under extremely tight control. For example, beers from major American Brewers are brewed locally in the United Kingdom, with each of these companies insisting on the adherence to brewing recipes, yeast strain, and the various other features that make their brands distinctive. Companies operating franchise agreements may insist on key technical personnel being stationed in the host brewery in order to maintain responsibility for a brand.

There are, of course, circumstances when a franchise brewing approach is impractical and when it is also not possible to ship finished product. For instance, during World War II a British ship, HMS *Menestheus*, transported its own brewery to make beer for far-off troops!

All Brewers are well aware that they not only compete with one another in the marketplace but also with producers of other drinks, both alcoholic and nonalcoholic. In the United States average consumption each year (per head) is over 50 gallons of soft drinks, 30 gallons of coffee, and 25 gallons of milk. Beer, in fourth place, amounts to 22.4 gallons per head, but if you consider that the legal drinking age in this country is 21, it is clear that beer commands a significant position in the league of drinks consumed.

For wines and spirits, just as for beers, there are distinct national statistical differences in consumption (Table 1.4). In most countries more beer than wine is consumed (although we should remember that wines generally contain two to three times more alcohol than beer, volume for volume). However, the French drink considerably more wine than beer, while in Portugal there is almost an equivalence between consumption of the two beverages.

One significant factor influencing the respective amount of beer and wine drunk in different countries is the relative excise tax (duty) raised on them (Table 1.5). In seven member states of the European Community (EC), including Italy, wine attracts no duty whatsoever. The tax levy on wine in France is very low, whereas duty rates on wine (but also on other types of alcoholic beverage) are very high in Sweden, Finland, and Ireland.

There are major differences in the excise rates for beer across the EC. This issue has been brought to the fore in the United Kingdom, since France is now just a 30-minute train ride away through the Channel Tunnel. As beer is so much cheaper in France because it attracts less than one-sixth of the excise duty levied in the United Kingdom, a growing number of people make trips across the English Channel to buy stocks. Currently, some 1.3 million pints of beer a day are coming across the

Table 1.4. Drinks consumption (per capita, 1995)

Country	Beer*	Wine*	Spirits*
Australia	95.0 (−4.0)	18.2 (−0.3)	1.4 (+0.1)
Belgium	103.5 (−3.7)	21.9 (+0.7)	2.2 (−0.1)
Brazil	51.4 (+12.6)	1.8 (0)	—
Canada	66.5 (−1.7)	8.2 (+0.4)	1.8 (0)
China	12.6 (+1.1)	0.2 (+0.1)	2.8 (+0.1)
Czech Republic	159.1 (−2.0)	15.0 (0)	3.1 (−0.7)
Denmark	124.4 (−2.3)	27.6 (+1.4)	1.1 (0)
Finland	81.3 (−1.6)	8.2 (−0.6)	1.8 (0)
France	39.1 (−0.2)	62.5 (0)	2.5 (0)
Germany	137.7 (−1.8)	17.4 (−0.1)	2.2 (−0.2)
Republic of Ireland	112.7 (−0.1)	6.0 (+0.4)	1.7 (0)
Italy	25.4 (−0.8)	15.8 (−0.2)	0.5 (0)
Japan	56.2 (−3.7)	1.1 (−0.1)	2.3 (−0.1)
Netherlands	85.8 (−0.2)	15.8 (−0.2)	1.8 (0)
New Zealand	99.5 (−3.2)	16.9 (+0.1)	1.1 (−0.1)
Norway	52.5 (+2.0)	7.1 (+0.3)	0.8 (0)
Portugal	64.7 (+2.4)	52.5 (0)	1.0 (0)
Russia	13.5 (−2.1)	6.8 (−0.1)	3.7 (0)
Slovak Republic	93.8 (+0.5)	13.1 (−1.3)	3.8 (+1.8)
South Africa	55.8 (+0.3)	8.1 (0)	1.0 (−0.1)
Spain	66.6 (+0.4)	31.1 (−1.2)	2.5 (+0.1)
Sweden	64.5 (−2.8)	12.6 (−0.5)	1.3 (−0.2)
United Kingdom	100.9 (−2.8)	14.7 (+0.3)	1.3 (−0.3)
United States of America	83.5 (−1.7)	6.8 (+0.1)	1.9 (−0.1)

Source: *Statistical Handbook*, Brewers & Licensed Retailers Association, London, 1997.
*Values in parentheses indicate growth or decline from previous year; values are given as liters or, for spirits, as liters of pure alcohol.

Channel into England and, thence, to the rest of the U.K. There are no limitations on the amount of beer you can bring back into England, providing it is for personal consumption, but the retail of such purchases is forbidden. Yet probably half of this imported beer is intended for illegal resale. From the numbers of vans returning to the United Kingdom packed to the roof with beer, it would appear either that there are some fun parties to attend in Britain, or else the law is being flouted big time! The latter is, of course, the case: For beer alone, it is estimated that some £75 million ($112 million) of tax revenue has been evaded through smuggling operations into the United Kingdom. It seems unlikely that the duty imbalance will change substantially, particularly as beer duty contributed almost 60% of

Table 1.5. Rates of excise duty and value added tax
in the European Community

Country	Beer (cents per pint at 5% ABV)	Wine (cents per 75 cl bottle at 11% ABV)	Spirits ($ per 70 cl bottle at 40% ABV)	VAT %
Austria	9.8	0	2.01	20.0
Belgium	11.6	35.0	4.61	21.0
Denmark	25.2	74.7	10.25	25.0
Finland	82.2	217.2	14.31	22.0
France	7.2	2.6	4.00	20.6
Germany	5.0	0	3.62	15.0
Greece	8.9	0	2.63	18.0
Ireland	60	217.8	8.25	21.0
Italy	9.6	0	1.82	19.0*
Luxembourg	5.4	0	2.90	15.0*
Netherlands	12	36.3	4.19	17.5
Portugal	8.1	0	5.63	17.0*
Spain	4.8	0	1.92	16.0
Sweden	47.4	231.3	15.92	25.0†
UK	46.1	158.1	7.98	17.5

Source: *Statistical Handbook,* Brewers & Licensed Retailers Association, London, 1997. *Original data was quoted in Pounds Sterling. An exchange rate of £1 = $1.50 has been employed.*
*VAT rates for wine lower.
†Rate for beer <3.5% ABV is lower.

the £77 billion ($115 billion) receipts of Her Majesty's Customs and Excise in 1995–1996. This sum was almost matched by receipts from value added tax (VAT) on beer. No other member state of the European Community collects anywhere near as much revenue from Brewers. France, ironically, is the next biggest drawer on Brewers but levies less than 30% of the tax taken in the United Kingdom, most of that being VAT.

In the United States matters are complicated by the three layers of government that levy taxes on beer. Congress first placed an excise tax on beer in 1862. The federal rate of excise tax in 1997 for the large Brewer is $18 per barrel (U.S.). State excise tax varies, but the current median is $5.74.

Although production costs associated with the brewing industry vary enormously from company to company, I would estimate that excise tax probably accounts for approximately 27% of the cost of beer in the United States. Estimates for other expenditures would be malt (3.5% of costs), adjuncts (1.5%), hops (0.2%), packaging materials (26%), production costs

(20%), and sales costs (21%). Hence excise duty is one of the single most costly elements of a can of beer.

Brewing makes a major economic impact in the States. Apart from tax contributions, it is a major employer, with over 2.5 million people working directly in the production, marketing, and selling of the product or indirectly in the industries that supply to the Brewers. These include farming, malting, and the production of packaging materials. For instance, 56 billion beer bottles and cans are produced each year.

Despite the competition that beer faces from wine, there has been a steady growth in world beer production in recent years (Table 1.6). The volume of beer brewed has almost doubled since 1970, in which time the world population has increased by 54%. As Tables 1.3 and 1.4 show, there has been formidable growth in the quantity of beer brewed and consumed in a number of countries. China, in particular, stands out as a country where an increasing number of people in an increasingly favorable economic climate have acquired access to beer. Similar stories have unfolded over recent years in countries in South America and Africa. Beer consumption worldwide now averages some 21 liters per head.

Returning to the United States, and before we leave this statistical survey, we might analyze the drinking habits of the individual states of the Union. It seems that the good folk of Nevada are well above the national average in their consumption of beer at 48.2 gallons per head each year (incidentally, they lead the way with wine and spirits, too). This reflects the greater disposable income and the lower tax base of that state. The national

Table 1.6. Trends in world
beer production

Year	World beer production (million hl)
1970	648.1
1980	938.6
1990	1168.5
1991	1177.6
1992	1184.4
1993	1195.3
1994	1227.8
1995	1253.3

Source: Statistical Handbook, Brewers & Licensed Retailers Association, London, 1997.

average is 32.6 gallons per head. The most abstemious state is Utah, at 20.8 gallons per head. In Utah the state tax amounts to $11 per barrel, which is relatively high when compared to the 62 cents per barrel in Wyoming but much less than the $23.80 imposed in South Carolina. In Nevada the state tax on beer is $2.79 per barrel, which can be compared with the rate in the states that are home to the headquarters of the four great American brewers: Missouri ($1.86), Wisconsin ($2.00), Colorado ($2.48), and Michigan ($6.30).

A BRIEF HISTORY OF BEER

Most historical accounts of brewing cite ancient Babylon of some 8,000 years ago as the birthplace of beer. Beer was consumed throughout the Middle East but, as a drink, it would hardly have borne much resemblance to what most of the world today regards as beer. According to Delwen Samuel, a distinguished researcher from the University of Cambridge, England:

> beer, together with bread, was the most important item in the diet of the ancient Egyptians. Everyone, from Pharaoh to farmer, drank beer and no meal was complete without it. Beer was much more than just a food stuff. In a cashless society it was used as a unit of exchange, its value fluctuating just as currencies do today. Furthermore, beer played a central role in religious belief and ritual practice. Offerings to the gods or funerary provisions included beer, either real or magical.[1]

Samuel's archaeological pursuits have unveiled the remains of beer solids crusted to the inside of ancient vessels, and among these solids were found fragments of grain. She has painstakingly examined these remains using techniques such as scanning electron microscopy and has made proposals as to how beer was brewed in Egypt 3,000 years ago from malted barley and a primitive type of wheat called emmer (Fig. 1.1). The recipe was used by the Brewers Scottish & Newcastle to make 1,000 bottles of a beer called Tutankhamun Ale—and it sold out from the prestigious Harrods' store in Knightsbridge, London, within three weeks of going on sale.

The techniques applied in the brewing of beer by the Egyptians seem to have been quite refined. How the first beer was developed several thousand years prior to this is unclear, but it might be anticipated that its origins were founded on serendipity and were linked to the baking of bread. Most commentators suggest that batches of barley must have gotten

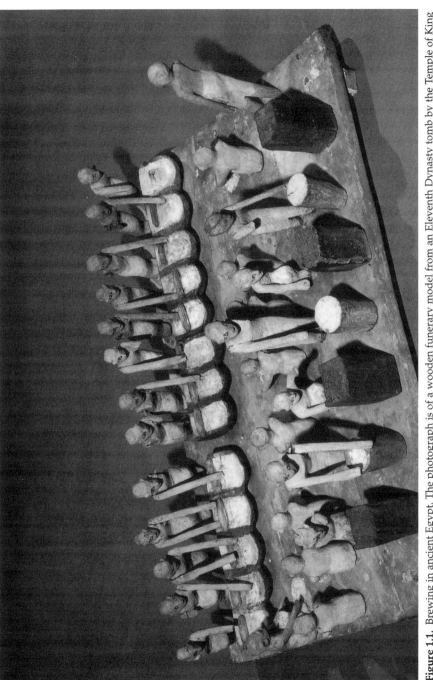

Figure 1.1. Brewing in ancient Egypt. The photograph is of a wooden funerary model from an Eleventh Dynasty tomb by the Temple of King Nebhetepre Montuhotep (approximately 1980 B.C.). The model shows the grinding of grain, the sieving of the resultant flour, the mixing of dough, the stoking of ovens, and the putting of the bread into fermenting vats to turn it into beer (© *The British Museum*).

wet through inadequate storage (rain was more plentiful thereabouts than it is now) and, as a result, the barley began to germinate. Presumably it was found that drying stopped this germination, and, logically, the ancients would have discovered that this "cooking" improved the taste of the grain. Neither would it have taken them long to realize that malt is more nutritionally advantageous than raw barley; those eating malt would have been healthier than those whose diet included barley and, for certain, they would have found their meals to be tastier.

It is assumed that the sprouted barley (forerunner to today's malt) was made into a dough before bread making and that batches of the dough then spontaneously fermented through the action of yeasts living on the grain and in cracks and crevices in vessels. Soon the ancient brewers would have realized that the dough could be thinned with water and strained as a precursor to fermentation and that the process could be accelerated by adding a proportion of the previous brew. A range of plants would have been used to impart flavors, among them the mandrake, which has a flavor much like leek. The use of hops came much, much later.

The work of archaeologists has suggested that in Mesopotamia and Egypt the characteristic tool of the brewer was an earthen vat. Certainly hieroglyphics depict people stooped over such vessels in pursuit of their craft. It has been suggested that the Pharaoh Ramses had a brewery that furnished 10,000 hl of beer each year free of charge to those employed in the temple.

In ancient Greece and Rome wine was the drink of the privileged classes, with beer consumed by the rest. Beer was not foremost among the developments bestowed by the Romans in the lands that they conquered. Pliny the Elder (23–79 A.D.), a Roman author, was almost contemptuous in his view that "the whole world is addicted to drunkenness; the perverted ingenuity of man has given even to water the power of intoxicating where wine is not procurable. Western nations intoxicate themselves by means of moistened grain."

It seems that it was through a more northerly route that the Celts brought westward their ability to brew. Perhaps this related to the mastery over wood of the people of Northern and Central Europe and their ability to fashion it into brewing vessels and barrels. Whereas the Greeks and others in the South were drinking wine from pottery, the German tribes were drinking barley- or wheat-based drinks out of wood.

As people established larger, settled communities, the malting of barley and brewing of beer developed into larger concerns, no longer focused on the home. As the brewers' art began to be perfected, it was passed on to apprentices. By now, humans had learned how to smelt and subsequently fashion metal into vessels. Readily cleaned, flameproof but easily heated brewhouse equipment made of copper emerged. Metal would have been used, too, to secure wooden fermenters, enabling bigger vessels to be constructed.

Much of the history of the world's brewing industry is tied up with the Church, to the extent that the monks in the Middle Ages were even convinced that the mortar used in the building of their churches and monasteries was better if mixed using ale rather than water. To this day, the strong Trappist beers of Belgium are brewed by monks, and bona fide travelers in England are still entitled to lay claim to ale and bread if they care to visit a cathedral church. The Domesday Book (1086) tells that the monks of St. Paul's Cathedral in London brewed almost 70,000 gallons (U.K.) of ale that year. They would have learned that it was safer to drink ale than water—for which reason the whole family in medieval society would have consumed ale as a matter of routine. Within the home, brewing was the preserve of the wife, or the brewster.

Despite the fact that beer could now be made on a larger scale and, doubtless, with enhanced efficiency and consistency, it was still very much more an art than a science. By the end of the seventeenth century only one textbook on brewing had been produced. In 1691 Thomas Tryon provided the text *A New Art of Brewing Beer, Ale, and Other Sorts of Liquor so as to render them more healthful . . . To which is added the art of making malt . . . Recommended to All Brewers, Gentlemen and others who brew their own drink.* Many years would elapse before the slow emergence of the science that would explain what was happening in the malting and brewing processes and how they could be modified and controlled to ensure the production of consistent products of high quality. This science, and the refined technology which developed from it, forms the heart of this book.

Long before the science developed, however, governments had recognized the opportunity that the brewing industry presented to bolster their coffers. Hlothhere, King of Kent in the seventh century, proclaimed: "If one man takes away the stoup (drinking cup) of another . . . he shall pay . . . a shilling to him who owns the house, six shillings to him whose stoup has been taken away, and twelve shillings to the king." The first specific tax on beer (or rather its principal ingredient) came in 1614, when a financially embarrassed James I of England levied fourpence a quarter on malt. (A quarter is 28 pounds or 12.7 kg.) Wars have been fought on the strength of moneys contributed from the brewing industry. In the English Civil War, which started in 1641, Parliament was quick to raise a duty of two shillings on all beer costing in excess of six shillings a barrel. When royalty was restored with Charles II, Brewers were optimistic the excise duty would be abolished. They were disappointed then—and ever since.

A BRIEF HISTORY OF BREWING SCIENCE

It was in 1680 that a 48-year-old draper from Delft in Holland, Antonie van Leeuwenhoek (Fig. 1.2), reported to the Royal Society in London how he had developed a microscope that had enabled him to inspect a drop of fermenting beer and reveal therein something we now recognize as yeast cells. One hundred and fifty years later Charles Cagnaird La Tour in France and Theodor Schwann and Friedrich Kutzing in Germany independently claimed that yeast was a living organism that could bud. They were ridiculed by the Germans Justus von Liebig (Fig. 1.3) and Friedrich Wöhler, who insisted (we believe with sarcasm) that yeasts consist of eggs that turn into little animals when put into sugar solution. Liebig and Wöhler, who clearly had little sympathy with matters biological, suggested that these animals

> have a stomach and an intestinal canal, and their urinary organs can be readily distinguished. The moment these animals are hatched they begin to devour the sugar in the solution, which can be readily seen entering their stomachs. It is then immediately digested, and the digested product can be recognized with certainty in the excreta from the alimentary canal. In a word, these infusoria eat sugar, excrete alcohol from their intestinal canals, and carbonic acid from their urinary organs. The bladder, when full, is the shape of a champagne bottle, when empty it resembles a little ball; with a little practice an air-bladder can be detected in the interior of these animalculae; this swells up to ten times its size, and is emptied by a sort of screwlike action effected by the agency of a series of ring-shaped muscles situated in its outside.[2]

It was another Frenchman who sorted the matter out. Louis Pasteur (1822–1895; Fig. 1.4) became professor of chemistry at Lille University and was urged by the local Brewers to sort out the difficulties they were having with beer going sour after fermentation. He demonstrated that the infection was due to airborne organisms that he could trap in guncotton and that then could be inactivated by heat. By 1860, this tanner's son from Dole was able to conclude that "alcoholic fermentation is an act correlated with the life and organization of the yeast cells."[3]

Figure 1.2. Antonie van Leeuwenhoek. Microscopy was just a hobby for van Leeuwenhoek. He made his own microscopes out of the magnifiers used by his father-in-law, a cloth merchant. Van Leeuwenhoek studied a range of samples: red blood cells, spermatozoa, aphids, and the bacteria in the scrapings from between his teeth! He didn't, of course, know what they were—he simply referred to them as "flora of the mouth." (*Reproduced courtesy of the Library & Information Center, Royal Society of Chemistry.*)

Figure 1.3. Justus von Liebig. Von Liebig was born at Darmstadt, Germany, in 1803 and was only 19 when he earned his doctorate. In 1824, King Ludwig I of Bavaria provided von Liebig with a laboratory at the University of Giessen, and he taught there until 1852, when he moved to Munich. It is surely ironic that von Liebig was expressing his eccentric opinions on fermentation from one of the great homes of brewing. (*Reproduced courtesy of the Library & Information Center, Royal Society of Chemistry.*)

Figure 1.4. Louis Pasteur. Pasteur was only mediocre as a student of chemistry at the Sorbonne. But he developed—and in 1876 he penned a book, *Etudes sur la Biere* (*Studies on Beer*). (*Reproduced courtesy of the Library & Information Center, Royal Society of Chemistry.*)

The informed brewing historian Ray Anderson has eloquently described how Pasteur's role, while pivotal in the history of brewing science, was not absolute. As Anderson says:

> Pasteur's genius—and make no mistake he was a genius—was in bringing together disparate elements and making the whole greater than its parts. What sets Pasteur apart is the rigor of his scientific method, the clarity of his vision in recognizing the significance of his results and in applying his findings to practice.[4]

Anderson, then, emphasizes the contribution of those such as Carl Balling, who spoke in the 1840s of the living nature of yeast in his lectures to Brewers in Prague. There were James Muspratt and Heinrich Bottinger (the latter head brewer of a brewery in Burton-on-Trent), who disagreed with their teacher Liebig and who also recognized the criticality of live yeast. There was Jean Chaptal, a French chemist who, in 1807, recognized the association between films of vegetation that formed on wine whenever it was sour. In fact, the present shape of the brewing industry as a well-controlled, highly efficient and reliable multi-billion-dollar industry is testimony to the researches of diverse eminent scientists working not only on yeast, but also on the germinative properties of barley, the composition of hops, and the refinements of the malting and brewing processes in their entirety.

A seminal moment in the shaping of the modern brewing industry came in 1883. Emil Christian Hansen (Fig. 1.5), head of the Physiological Department of the Carlsberg Laboratory in Copenhagen, proposed that the all too frequent occurrence of brews that produced an unsaleable product were not necessarily due to infection by bacteria, as Pasteur had proposed, but rather to wild yeasts. The term *wild yeast* persists to this day and refers to any yeast strain other than the one that the Brewer intends to be used to ferment his beer, for it is that yeast that largely determines the beer's unique character. It was Hansen who perfected a system for purifying yeast into a single, desired strain—a system that forms the basis for the efficiency and brand-to-brand individuality of beers to this day.

In the ensuing 100-plus years, technology for the malting of barley and brewing of beer has advanced remarkably, building on the scientific explorations of many gifted scientists worldwide. The processes are enormously more efficient now than they were even 50 years ago. For instance, the malting process is now completed in less than a week, whereas it took twice as long half a century ago. Brewing can take as little as one to two

Figure 1.5. Emil Christian Hansen. Hansen (1842–1909) was the son of a house painter from Ribe in Southern Jutland. His father was quite a character; among his exploits was a stint in the French Foreign Legion. Young Emil Christian was struck by his father's words: "a person can do everything as long as he has the will to do it." Academically, the boy developed slowly, becoming a house painter at the same time he was painting pictures (he was rejected by the Danish Royal Academy of Arts) and writing stories. His attention then turned to science, and he became something of an authority on peat bogs before turning his attention to the physiology of yeast under Professor Panum in Copenhagen in 1877. It was at this time that he joined Carlsberg. (*Reproduced courtesy of Carlsberg, from "The Carlsberg Laboratory 1876–1976."*)

weeks, although many Brewers insist on longer processing times. Brewers take pride in their products and, while striving for efficiency, won't take short cuts if quality would be jeopardized.

Brewing scientists have bequeathed to society many concepts beyond beer that are now accepted as commonplace. For instance, James Prescott Joule was employed in a laboratory at his family brewery in Salford, England, when he contemplated the research that led to the First Law of Thermodynamics. Sørensen (Fig. 1.6), working in the Carlsberg Laboratories, explained the concept of pH (the universal scale for measuring acidity and alkalinity) and its importance in determining the behavior of living systems, notably through an impact on enzymic activity. W. S. Gosset, who was breeding new varieties of barley and hops for Guinness, published under the pseudonym Student, a name familiar to statisticians everywhere who apply the T-test. The impact of Pasteur on modern society extends, of course, far beyond beer.

A BRIEF HISTORY OF THE NORTH AMERICAN BREWING INDUSTRY

To be worthwhile, of course, scientific principles must have technological application. The Industrial Revolution centered on Victorian Britain, and it is there we must look to find the major advances that spawned the malting and brewing industries of today. Such industrialization was founded on the great inventions of the likes of Trevithick and Watt, who gave us the steam engine. James Watt's name is perpetuated to this day in the title of Heriot-Watt University in Edinburgh, Scotland, which has for many years had a prestigious brewing school.

It was the British that brought beer to North America. Sir Walter Raleigh is said to have malted corn in Virginia in 1587 (and in South America malted corn had been fermented by the Incas many years before Spanish settlers founded a brewery near Mexico City in the mid-sixteenth century), but it was the Pilgrim Fathers arriving at Plymouth Rock in December 1620 who shipped the first beer into the country. The first brewery in the United States was opened in Lower Manhattan by the Dutch West India Company in 1632.

It has been claimed that advertisements were soon being placed in London newspapers inviting experienced brewers to emigrate to America

Figure 1.6. Soren Sørensen (1868–1939). Sørensen, a farmer's son from Slagelse in Denmark, began to study medicine but soon shifted to chemistry. He became Head of the Chemical Department of the Carlsberg Laboratory in 1901. (*Reproduced courtesy of Carlsberg, from "The Carlsberg Laboratory 1876–1976."*)

America. And the first paved street in America was laid in New Amsterdam in 1657 to aid the passage of horse-drawn beer wagons, which hitherto tended to get stuck in the mud.

By the eighteenth century, New York and Philadelphia were the principal seats of brewing, and at the turn of the next century, there were over 150 breweries in the United States, with one-third of them in each of the above two locations. Production, though, was less than 230,000 barrels (U.S.). George Washington had recently died, leaving his own brewery on his Mount Vernon estate in Virginia. Earlier, in the War of Independence, American troops each received a quart (2 pints) of beer per day. For that luxury the soldiers had perhaps to thank Samuel Adams, the Massachusetts-based leader of the early independence movement, who was himself a brewer. Boston *Tea* Party, indeed! Thomas Jefferson composed the Declaration of Independence at the Indian Queen Tavern in Philadelphia, but time does not record what he had in his glass.

We must move on to the mid-nineteenth century, though, to find the beginnings of the great brewing dynasties of the States. Bernard Stroh, from a Rhineland family with two centuries of brewing pedigree, opened his brewery in Detroit in 1850. Five years later, Frederick Miller bought out Best's Brewery in Milwaukee. In 1860, Eberhard Anheuser purchased a struggling St. Louis Brewery and, after his daughter married a supplier, Adolphus Busch, an émigré from Mainz, the mighty Anheuser-Busch company was born. And then, a dozen years later, another immigrant from the Rhineland, Adolph Coors, set up shop in Colorado.

By 1873 there were over 4,000 breweries in the United States; outputs averaged some 2,800 barrels each. In all countries, brewing undergoes rationalization, so by the end of World War I there were half as many breweries, each producing on average 20 times more beer than 45 years earlier. By the time World War II had run its course, there were just 465 breweries in the United States, their output averaging some 190,000 barrels. Compare those volumes with the output of the gigantic Coors Brewery in Golden, Colorado, which by the early 1990s was producing over 19 million barrels of beer each year.

Before 1850, the standard brew in North America was ale, produced along similar lines to the traditional product of Britain. The production of lager (a style that the likes of Busch, Miller, Stroh, and Coors would have been more familiar with in their homeland) demanded ice. Accordingly, such beer had to be brewed in winter for storage (*lagering*) until the greater summer demand. Such protocols were possible in Milwaukee, Wisconsin,

Frederick Miller

Frederick Edward John Miller was born on November 24, 1824, into a wealthy family from Riedlingen in Germany. For seven years, from the age of 14, he studied in France and, prior to returning to Germany, he visited an uncle in Nancy. That uncle, fortuitously, was a brewer, and Frederick liked what he saw so much that he decided to stay and learn the trade. Soon he was in a position to brew his own beers, so he leased the royal brewery in Sigmaringen, back in his home country. With the Germanic Confederation of states in some turmoil, Miller became one of many to seek a new life in the United States of America, where he arrived in 1854 with his young wife Josephine and their infant son Joseph Edward. They had in their possession $9,000 worth of gold.

The Millers spent a year in New York before settling in Milwaukee. It is said that on arriving Miller exclaimed, "A town with a magnificent harbor like that has a great future in store." Before long, Frederick had bought the Plank-Road Brewery from Frederick Charles Best for $8,000. Beer at the time retailed at less than 5 cents a glass in the taverns of Milwaukee. In its first year the brewery produced 300 barrels of lager-style beer. By the time Miller died in 1888 the annual production was 80,000 barrels.

Miller clearly knew his business. The brewery in the Menomonee Valley had a good water supply and had ready access to excellent barley grown locally. Frederick Miller was a kindly employer, opening a boarding house next to the brewery for unmarried staff and, in addition to the free meals (four per day) and lodging, paid them salaries of up to $1,300 a year. They had to work, though, with just a one hour break in days that started at 4 A.M. and finished at 6 P.M.

Sadly for such a generous man, Frederick Miller had a tragic domestic life. Josephine died in April 1860, having borne six children, most of whom did not survive infancy. Miller married Lisette Gross the same year, and they had many children, of whom five survived beyond their fledgling years. It was these children that carried forward the name of the Miller Brewing Company, notable among them being Frederick C. Miller, the grandson of the founder and a Notre Dame football star in his college days. In 1954 Miller was the ninth biggest brewing company in the United States with production of 2 million barrels. In 1969 Philip Morris Co. acquired a 53% controlling share in the company, buying the remaining shares a year later. In 20 years production increased eightfold, making Miller Brewing Company today the second largest Brewer in the United States, with breweries in Milwaukee; Eden, North Carolina; Fort Worth, Texas; Trenton, Ohio; and Irwindale, California; as well as the subsidiary Leinenkugel Brewing Company in Chippewa Falls, Wisconsin.

Anheuser-Busch

The story of the world's largest Brewer really begins in 1860, when 55-year-old Eberhard Anheuser bought the Bavarian Brewery in St. Louis from George Schneider. There were 40 breweries in the great Missouri city at the time: Anheuser's ranked 29th. A year later, Eberhard's daughter Lilly married Adolphus Busch, age 22, who, three years thereafter, joined his father-in-law's company.

By now output was 8,000 barrels a year. In 1876 a new brand was introduced that would go on to become the world's best-selling beer: Budweiser. Eberhard Anheuser lived just four more years, Adolphus Busch becoming president of the new Anheuser-Busch. Subsequently the presidency has passed successively through the Busch line: August Busch, Sr. (born December 29, 1865), Adolphus Busch III, August Busch, Jr. (born March 28, 1899), and August A. Busch III (born June 16, 1937). In 1992 August A. Busch IV became vice-president of Budweiser Brands, thus continuing the great brewing family tradition.

Stroh

Bernhard Stroh sailed from Germany to the United States in 1849. His family had been brewing in Kirn since the late 1700s, and Bernhard delivered this pedigree to Detroit in 1850, applying the traditions of his grandfather Johann Peter Stroh. Since then the brewing baton has been successively carried with distinction by Bernhard Jr., Julius, Gari, John, and Peter, with Peter's son John III succeeding in the chief executive role in 1997.

The Stroh Brewery Company is one characterized by both tradition and innovation. An example of the former is the continuing use for some beers (Stroh's, Stroh Light, and Signature) of direct heating of the wort boiling process using fire, rather than steam, which is used elsewhere. Julius Stroh introduced this direct firing at the start of this century.

It was in the tenure of John W. Stroh that the company rapidly expanded, moving into the six million barrel range by the late 1970s. Under Peter Stroh the company grew still larger, notably through strategic acquisitions such as Goebel, Schaefer, Schlitz, and, most recently, Heileman, which itself had grown by merger and acquisition, bringing in such notable names as Rainier in Seattle, Lone Star in Texas, and Schmidt's of Philadelphia. The Stroh empire, with headquarters still centered by the Detroit River, now brews in Lehigh Valley, Pennsylvania; Winston-Salem, North Carolina; St. Paul, Minnesota; Longview, Texas; Tampa, Florida; La Crosse, Wisconsin; Seattle, Washington; and Portland, Oregon.

Coors

Adolph Coors Company, the United States' third largest brewer, is another founded on German brewing traditions. Adolph Coors founded his brewery in the foothills of the Rocky Mountains at Golden, some 20 miles west of Denver, in 1873. Like Anheuser-Busch and Stroh, the company is still characterized by strong family involvement. William K. Coors is chairman of the company, the brewing subsidiary of which (Coors Brewing Company) has Peter H. Coors as vice-chairman and chief executive officer.

The Coors operation differs from that of the other big Brewers in the United States in that it is concentrated on just two sites, the enormous Golden plant at which Adolph Coors first brewed 124 years ago and, since only 1990, a brewery at Memphis, Tennessee. For 10 years Coors has packaged its product at Shenandoah Valley in Virginia, the beer being shipped there from Golden in refrigerated tanks on rail cars.

---

using the ice from Lake Michigan and local caves for storing the beer. Milwaukee rapidly emerged as the great brewing center of the States, with Pabst and Schlitz among those competing with Miller. Once machines were developed to produce ice, lager could be brewed any time and anywhere. And the application of Pasteur's proposals for heat-treating beer to kill off spoilage organisms meant that beer could be packaged in bottles and consumed almost anyplace after shipment nationwide in refrigerated railcars. The American taste rapidly swung toward the pale, brilliantly clear, relatively dry, and delicately flavored products that are now the norm and which represent two-thirds of beer sales in the United States. The top four brands in the United States (1996) are Budweiser, Bud Light, Miller Lite, and Coors Lite, with combined sales of some 92 million barrels. Over $350 million is spent on advertising them.

*   *   *

This chapter has given us a feel for the magnitude of the world beer market, the pressures that come to bear on it and that influence production outputs, and how its shape today is a direct reflection of a long-standing pedigree. It's now time for us to understand the essence of the remarkable processes involved in converting barley and hops into the world's favorite alcoholic drink.

ENDNOTES

1. D. Samuel, "Fermentation Technology 3,000 Years Ago: The Archaeology of Ancient Egyptian Beer," *Society for General Microbiology Quarterly*, February 1997, pp. 3–5.
2. J. W. Sykes, "The Indebtedness of Brewers to M. Pasteur," *Journal of the Federated Institutes of Brewing*, 1897, pp. 498–525.
3. L. Pasteur, "Memoire sur la fermentation alcoholique," *Annales de Chimie et de Physique*, 58, 1860, 323–426.
4. R. G. Anderson, "Highlights in the History of International Brewing Science," *Ferment* 6, June 1993, pp. 191–198.

Chapter Two

GRAIN TO GLASS

The Basics of Malting and Brewing

To start our journey through the art and science of brewing, we will begin with an overview of the entire process, from barley to beer. In subsequent chapters the individual stages are covered in more detail.

The staple ingredients from which most beers are brewed are malted barley, water, hops, and yeast. The nature of beer derives from these raw materials and from the two separate (but related) processes that have been used to make this drink for thousands of years. In Germany, legislation decrees that beer production will involve these materials *alone*. Excellent beers are produced in Germany, but they are also produced in the rest of the world, where there is greater flexibility in the materials available to the Brewer. The ability to use a variety of adjuncts, for instance, enables the Brewer to provide the consumer with a splendid selection of beers for every drinking occasion. The opportunity, too, to use process aids such as clarifying agents and stabilizers ensures the Brewer's capability to produce beer that will have good shelf life and to do it economically—benefits that are passed on to the consumer. The Brewer is not unrestricted in what can be used: In all countries legislation dictates what may be legitimately employed in making beer, what the label has to declare, and how beer may be advertised. In some countries, such as the United Kingdom, the package must indicate the date by which a beer should be consumed. At present, though, U.K. Brewers do not have to provide an ingredients label on the container, whereas in some countries they do. In the United States, the Food and Drug Administration (FDA) and the Bureau of Alcohol, Tobacco and Firearms (BATF, which is within the Treasury Department) regulate all aspects of wholesomeness of beers.

At the simplest level, malting and brewing are the conversion of the starch of barley into alcohol. Brewers are interested in achieving this with maximum efficiency and thus seek to produce the highest possible alcohol yield per unit of starch. At the same time, though, they insist on consistency in all other attributes of their product: foam, clarity, color, and, of course, flavor.

When we speak of barley in a brewing context we are primarily concerned with its grain, the seeds growing on the ear in the field; it is these that are used to make beer (Fig. 2.1). Barley grains are hard and difficult to mill. Try chewing them if you will—but have a good dentist on hand! They also don't taste particularly pleasant; they dry the mouth and leave a harsh, astringent, and extremely grainy aftertaste. Indeed, beer brewed from raw barley is not only troublesome in processing, but it also has a definite grainy character. It must have been pure serendipity when the process of malting was discovered some 100 centuries ago, but from such happenstance has sprung a mighty industry responsible for converting this rather unpleasant cereal into a generally satisfying malt.

MALTING

Figure 2.2 is a simple representation of the malting process. Barley is first steeped in water, which enters the grain through the micropyle and then moves through the food reserve (the starchy endosperm; Fig. 2.3). The water also enters the embryo, which springs into life. The embryo is the infant plant; it produces hormones that journey to the tissue (called the aleurone) that immediately surrounds the starchy endosperm. These hormones switch on the production of enzymes; they first chew up the walls of the cells in the aleurone and then move into the starchy endosperm, digesting its walls and some of its protein (Fig. 2.4). As these are the materials that make barley hard, it is this hydrolysis that renders the grain friable, easily chewed, and, subsequently, more readily milled in the brewery. The experienced maltster will evaluate how well this modification process is proceeding by rubbing or squeezing individual grains between his fingers. Happily, in the relatively short periods of time needed to soften grain (typically four to six days), only 5% to 10% of the starch in the endosperm is removed, although the starch-degrading enzymes produced in the aleurone do bore holes in it. The starch is the material that the Brewer will subsequently use as a source of fermentable sugars to make beers. The more starch that survives malting, the better!

Figure 2.1. Barley. The grain develops on the ear. Each grain is generally referred to as a corn. The whiskers (awns) are distinctive of barley.

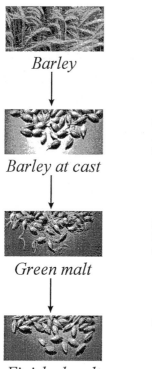

(11–12% moisture)
steep in water for 48–72 hours
at 14–18°C

Barley

(43–46% moisture)
germinate for 4–6 days
at 16–20°C

Barley at cast

(42–45% moisture)
kiln for 24–36 hours at temperatures
over the range 50°C–220°C

Green malt

(2–3% moisture)

Finished malt

Figure 2.2. The malting process.

The cell wall and protein polymers are degraded into small, soluble molecules, which migrate to the embryo to provide it with nourishment. Using this food, the embryo starts to germinate and produce rootlets and a shoot (acrospire). Excessive production of these tissues is not desirable, as this consumes material that can otherwise to be sold to the Brewer.

When the germination stage is deemed to have proceeded for a long enough period, it is stopped by heating the grain in a process referred to as kilning. The aim is to drive off water until the moisture level in grain is below 5%, the point when barley metabolism stops and the product stabilizes. The heating process needs to be conducted carefully. If the Brewer is to have access to the starch in the grain, she will need to use the enzymes (the amylases) that are present in the grain and that are mostly produced during germination. Enzymes are for the most part susceptible to death by heat, and they are particularly sensitive at higher moisture levels. For

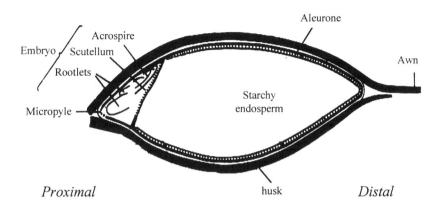

Dorsal

Proximal   *Distal*

Ventral

Figure 2.3. The basic structure of the barley corn.

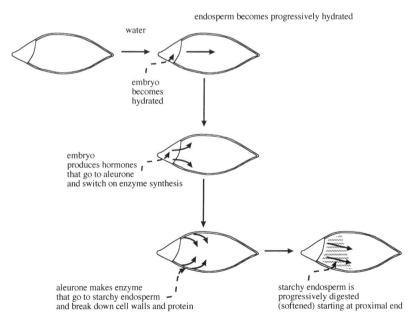

Figure 2.4. A schematic depiction of events during barley steeping and germination.

this reason, the kilning process is started at quite a low temperature (perhaps 50°C). When about half of the water has been removed, the temperature can be raised, and this ramping will continue according to a preset regime, depending on the nature of the malt required.

Malts destined to produce ales are kilned to a higher temperature. This has two implications: The first is that these malts will be darker. In the kilning process, the breakdown products (amino acids and sugars) released from proteins and carbohydrates during germination combine to form melanoidins, which are colored. The higher the temperature (and the more breakdown products in the first place, i.e., the more extensively modified is the grain), the darker the color (Fig. 2.5).

The second implication of higher kilning temperatures is the development of complex flavors. The pleasant flavors that we associate with malt and that enter, for instance, into malty bedtime drinks, are produced during the kilning process and from the interactions between the breakdown products from protein and carbohydrate. If malt is kilned to particularly high temperatures it is possible to make especially dark products (the sort that are used to color stouts) and to develop flavors described as burnt and smoky.

Malts destined for lager-style beers are generally less extensively modified than are those aimed at ale production (i.e., they contain less amino acid and sugar), and they are kilned to a relatively mild regimen.

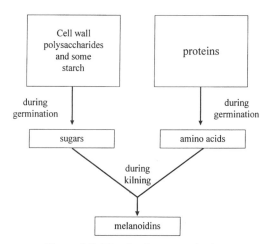

Figure 2.5. The development of color.

They therefore develop less color and produce quite pale straw- or amber-colored beers. They may also deliver a wholly different kind of flavor into beer, one that tends to be more sulfury.

BREWING

It is unusual for a maltings and a brewery to be on the same site, even for so-called brewer-maltsters, which are brewers that produce their own malt.

The first step in brewing (Fig. 2.6) is the milling of the malt. The phrase *grist to the mill* is, of course, an accepted part of the English language. Malt is the principal grist material used for brewing, but there may be others, such as roasted malt or barley, corn, and rice.

All of the unit operations within the brewery must be performed correctly if the process is to be efficient and trouble-free. Milling is as

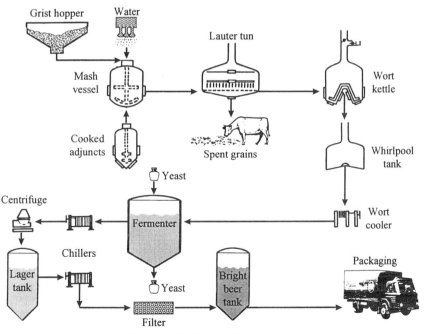

Figure 2.6. The brewing process.

important as any stage that follows in the brewery. The aim in milling is to produce the distribution of particles best suited to subsequent processes in the brewhouse. In large part the malt should be converted to a flour with particles small enough to enable access of water. This will hydrate the particles and activate the enzymes in the malt. It will also solvate the substrate molecules (principally starch) that the enzymes are targeting. For most brewhouses, though, it is important for the husk component of the malt to remain as intact as possible after milling, because it will be used to form the filter bed through which the solution of sugars produced in the mashing operation will be recovered in as "bright" a condition as possible.

The milled grist is stored briefly in the grist case before going to the mash mixer (mash tun, conversion vessel). Here it is mixed with warm water to commence the hydrolysis process. Mashing often begins at a relatively low temperature (say, 50° C) to enable the more heat-sensitive enzymes to do their job. These include the enzymes that degrade any cell-wall polysaccharides that survive the malting process. Then, after perhaps 20 minutes, the temperature is raised to at least 65° C, for it is at this temperature that the starch is gelatinized. This process can be likened to melting. It involves the conversion of starch from a crystalline, difficult-to-digest structure to a disorganized state readily accessed by the amylase enzymes responsible for chopping it up into fermentable sugars. Happily, the amylases largely survive this higher temperature. The mash is held for perhaps an hour before the temperature is raised once again, this time typically to 76° C. This stops most enzymatic activity and reduces viscosity, thereby improving the fluidity of the mash.

In most breweries the sugar solution produced (wort) is separated from the spent grains in a vessel called a lauter tun. The bed depth is relatively shallow, and rakes are used to loosen the bed structure. Efficient lautering is a skilled operation, the aim being the recovery of as clear a wort as possible (bright wort) containing as much as possible of the soluble products of mashing (the sum total of which is called extract). It is also generally important that the recovered wort be relatively concentrated—so-called high-gravity wort—if production throughput in the subsequent fermentation stage is to be maximized. To facilitate washing of the break-down products (made from carbohydrate and protein) out of the mash bed, hot water is used to sparge the grains. Clearly, too much water will excessively dilute the wort. The aim, though, is extraction of as much of the fermentable material as possible from the grains within the restricted time available; the more rapidly the wort can be recovered from the residual grains, the more brews can be performed per day. Almost without exception, the spent grains are sold off as cattle food.

Wort flows directly (usually) from the lauter tun (or one of the other wort separation processes that we will come to in Chapter Six) to the kettle (sometimes called the copper, even though these days they are mostly fabricated from stainless steel).

Wort boiling serves several functions. Foremost among these is the extraction of bittering materials and of aroma components from hops. Traditionally, hopping meant adding whole cone hops, and this is still the practice in a good many breweries. The hop residue will remain after the boil and, as in malt husk and wort separation, the residual hops are used in a so-called hop back to form the filter medium through which the bittered wort is separated. More frequently these days, hops have been preprocessed. It is common for hops to be milled and pelletized before entering the brewery, in which case vegetative matter does not survive intact and the postkettle vessel is the whirlpool (see page 134). Alternatively, liquid extracts of hops are used.

Hops contain resins that are extracted in the wort boil and converted into more soluble (and more bitter) forms. Hops also possess a complex mixture of essential oils, and it is these that provide the different types of hoppy character associated with different beers. These molecules are quite volatile and will evaporate to a greater or lesser extent in the boil. Hops added at the start of a boil, which typically lasts for 1 hour, will lose essentially all of their oils. For this reason, in traditional lager brewing in Europe, a proportion of the hops is held back and added during the final few minutes of the boil, thereby enabling a proportion of the essential oils to survive and provide a distinctive character. This procedure is called late hopping. In traditional ale brewing in the United Kingdom, a handful of hops is added to the cask prior to its leaving the brewery. This makes for a much more complex hop character in a beer, as there is no opportunity for any of the oils to evaporate.

Apart from extracting substances from hops, wort boiling concentrates wort to a greater or lesser degree (depending on the rate of evaporation allowed, which can range from 4% to 12%), driving off unwanted flavor molecules, inactivating enzymes that might have survived mashing and wort separation, and sterilizing the wort. (Because of boiling and because antimicrobial bitter compounds are introduced during boiling, there was a time when beer was far safer to drink than the local water, which carried diseases such as cholera and typhoid. For this reason, in some countries, beer should be your preferred drink.) Most importantly, boiling also coagulates much of the protein from the malt, a process that is promoted by tannin materials extracted from the malt and hops. This precipitation, which forms an insoluble complex called trub, is important, as these proteins, if not removed here, will be capable of dropping from solution in the subsequent beer to form unsightly hazes and sediments.

In most breweries the next stage involves the whirlpool. The boiling wort is passed tangentially into a large vessel and allowed to swirl there for an hour or so. By centripetal forces the trub collects in the central cone at the base of the whirlpool, leaving a bright wort above it. The removed trub is often mixed in with the spent grains (and mixed well, because of its intense bitterness!) before sale for cattle feed.

The wort is now almost ready for fermentation, but first it must be cooled before yeast is added. This is achieved using a heat exchanger, commonly referred to as a paraflow, in which the wort flows through channels against a flow of cold water or other coolant in adjacent channels. Heat transfers from the wort to the water, the latter now being recovered for cleaning duties. The wort will have been cooled to the desired temperature for fermentation, which may be as low as 6°C for traditional lager brewing in mainland Europe, or to 15° to 20°C for ale brewing in England.

Prior to the addition of yeast, a little oxygen (or air) is bubbled into the wort. Although the fermentation process leading to the production of alcohol is anaerobic, yeast does require some oxygen, which helps it to make certain parts of its cell membrane and allows it to grow.

The traditional distinction between brewing yeasts divides them into two types: top fermenters and bottom fermenters. The first type was traditionally used for ale brewing in open fermenters in the United Kingdom, and such strains have their name because they migrate to the surface of the beer during fermentation. Bottom fermenters, as the name suggests, settle to the base of the fermentation vessel, and they are traditionally associated with the production of lager-style beers. These days the distinction is blurred, insofar as ales and lagers are frequently fermented in the same type of vessel. Although traditional fermenting systems survive, the most common system is the cylindroconical tank, within which the distinction between different flotation characteristics of yeasts becomes blurred.

Fermentation is primarily concerned with the conversion of sugars into alcohol; the rate at which this occurs is in direct proportion to the temperature and to how much yeast is "pitched" into the fermenter. Ale fermentations can take as little as two or three days, whereas traditional lager fermentations can take more than a fortnight to be completed. The process, however, represents more than simply an alcohol production factory—otherwise the temperature employed would be substantially greater. Brewery fermentation is also about producing a subtle mix of flavor compounds. The balance of these will depend on the yeast strain involved, which is why Brewers jealously guard and protect their own strains: The character of a beer depends as much as anything else on the yeast.

All shades of opinion govern what happens next. The traditional Brewer of lager beers will insist that a beer must be stored (lagered) in a decreasing temperature regimen from 5° to 0° C over a period of months. Others are convinced, however, that no useful changes in beer quality occur in this time and that this period can be substantially curtailed. All are agreed, however, about the merits of chilling beer to stabilize it. For most Brewers this involves taking the beer to as low a temperature as possible, short of freezing it. In practice this means −1° C for a few (perhaps three) days. Whereas heat-precipitable proteins are removed in the boiling and whirlpool operations, it is the cold-sensitive proteins that drop out at this conditioning stage. The colder the better: −1° C for three days is far better than 1° C for two weeks. Of course, not all beer is chilled. Traditional English ale, for instance, is clarified using protein preparations known as isinglass finings, which are extracted from the swim bladders of certain types of fish. The isinglass promotes the settling of solid materials from beer.

Clarification of beer in the brewery can be achieved using various types of filter. Generally clarification will be assisted by the use of a so-called filter aid, such as *kieselguhr*, which serves to keep an open bed through which beer can flow and also to provide pores that will trap solids. Kieselguhr is a diatomaceous earth: a mined substance consisting of the skeletons of primitive organisms.

At this stage, too, various materials may be added to promote the stability of the beer. Some of these materials remove the protein or polyphenols that cause hazes. Others are antioxidants that prevent beer from staling. Some Brewers employ an agent such as propylene glycol alginate, derived from seaweed, to promote foam stability.

The beer is filtered into the so-called bright beer tanks, where it awaits packaging. The Brewer will ensure that it has the correct carbon dioxide content. CO_2 is, of course, a natural product of fermentation, but its level in bright beer may have to be increased to meet the specification. Or it may have to be lowered; some beers should contain less carbon dioxide than that which develops in deep fermenting vessels. Some beers have nitrogen gas introduced into them at this stage to enhance foam stability.

Finally the beer is packaged into cans, bottles (glass or plastic), kegs, casks, or bulk tanks. The packaging process must be fast but must also ensure quality: There should be no oxygen pick-up in the beer, for this will cause the product to go stale. Consistent fill heights must be achieved to satisfy weights and measures legislation, no foreign bodies must enter the package, and, last but not least, the container must be attractive and undamaged during the filling process, which, in the case of cans, might be at rates as fast as 2,000 cans per minute.

BEER STYLES

Fundamentally, beers may be divided into ales, lagers, and stouts. Traditionally, ales and stouts were brewed with *top-fermenting* yeasts, those that migrate to the surface of the fermenting vessel. They were brewed in open vessels from which the yeast was scraped as a means of collection. They were dispensed at relatively warm temperatures (10° to 20°C). Lagers, on the other hand, were traditionally produced using *bottom-fermenting* yeasts, which formed sediment during the process and were collected from the base of the vessel, and were served cool (0° to 10°C).

In the late twentieth century, however, there is considerable blurring of the boundaries that divide these beer styles. Successful brewing companies are characterized by strong new product development programs, from which have emerged some remarkable beers that don't fall easily into any recognized classification. Where, for instance, would you pigeonhole a stout containing oysters, ales tasting of heather, or lagers with just a hint of citrus or a whole chili? Even more fundamentally, beers that may fall into an obvious genre in one market may be slotted into an entirely different category elsewhere. For instance, a beer that an Australian might describe as a bitter ale, an Englishman might perceive as having the characteristics of a lager.

Table 2.1 gives a breakdown of the principal beer types. Some would maintain that this is too abbreviated a list and would cite many more examples of lagers (for instance, Dortmunder, Vienna, and Munchner), further categories of ales (Kolsch or Dalsons, for instance), or Porter as another class of stout. Certainly the Brewers native to the places where

Table 2.1. Types of beer

Type of beer	Origin	Typical range of alcoholic strength (% by vol.)	Characteristics
Ales and stouts			
Bitter (pale) ale	Britain	3–5	Hoppy, bitter, estery, malty, low carbonation, copper color
Alt	Germany	4+	Some esters, bitter, copper color
Mild	Britain	<3.5	Dark brown, sweet
Stout	Ireland	4–7+	Roast, bitter, black
Sweet stout	Britain	3.5–4	Sweet, dark brown/black
Barley wine	Britain	8–10	Estery, copper/brown
Lagers			
Pilsner/Pils	Czechoslovakia	5–5.5	Late hop, full-bodied, amber color
Bock	Germany	6	Sulfur, malty, colors ranging from straw to dark brown
Wheat beers			
Weizenbier	Germany (Bavaria)	5–6	Cloves, cloudy, straw color
Weissen	Germany (Berlin)	2.5–3.0	Light, acidic, straw color

such beer styles developed will insist on the individuality of their product genres.

It is a fact, sad or otherwise depending on your point of view, that it is increasingly difficult to pigeonhole beers. This difficulty has been exacerbated by the tremendous surge of new product development ideas that has characterized the brewing industry in recent years. The British market has seen (and rejected) black lagers. A similar fate befell a colorless lager in the United States. In both instances, perhaps, the problem was a discontinuity for the drinker between what the appearance of a beer told them and what the label said. A black lager? A beer that looks like water (apart from the head)?

In appearance, most new products have adhered to established convention. Modern technology, though, has permitted the extension of the list of beer categories to light beer, ice beer, dry beer, non- or low-alcohol beer—and the opportunities don't end there. A beer is increasingly characterized by a technological story told about it (e.g., ice beer), an image (e.g., dry beer), or a particular property that the consumer expects from it (e.g., light beer or low-alcohol beer). It is a fact that many beers in the world are referred to as "Pilsners" or "Pils" despite falling beyond the definition given in Table 2.1. A beer nowadays seems to be what you choose to call it. For most of us that still breaks down to ales, lagers, and stouts.

Ice Beers

The ice beer story is a fascinating example of how an entirely new beer concept emerged from a technology that failed in the purpose for which it was originally intended. In the 1980s, many Brewers had decided that, rather than ship finished beer around the countryside to its destination, it would make economic sense to transport the beer in a concentrated form and then reconstitute it at the point of sale. They experimented with a technique called freeze concentration, which took advantage of the fact that, if you freeze beer, the first thing to come out of solution is almost pure water—in the form of ice. Most of the beer components remain in solution in a concentrated form.

Labatt, a major Canadian Brewer, was one company that experimented with the technique. They quickly realized that it wasn't going to be a winner for the purpose for which it was intended. Fortunately for Graham Stewart, their Technical Director at the time, and his colleagues, they hit upon an even more exciting use for freeze concentration. They were looking for a new angle on beer marketing and identified *ice* as being a powerful concept that associated extremely well with beer in the perception of Canadian drinkers. It didn't take long for the intellectual leap to be made: "Hey, let's chill out our beer and position a new beer genre as ice beer." As Professor Stewart says, "After all, Canadians already knew all about putting beer out onto the window ledge in the winter, freezing ice out from it, thereby increasing the alcohol content!"

By the early 1990s a new and exciting beer story was being told, and most major Brewers developed their own ice brands. In 1996 some 24 million barrels of ice beer were brewed in the United States, with the market share for such beers increasing by almost 4% over the previous year.

Dry Beers

The mid 1980s saw the emergence of dry beer and, through it, the astonishing growth of the Japanese Brewer, Asahi. They launched a new brand called Super Dry and saw their market share increase 25% within three years. As the name suggests, it is a product analogous to dry wine: a lager with a relatively low proportion of residual sugar. Clever marketing, and the characteristic outstanding package quality associated with Japanese Brewers, made it a clear winner. In no time it was followed by other dry beers, and a dozen countries contributed over 30 new brands of dry beer. Such beers were launched in the United States, too, but in 1996 had just 0.1% of the market share, which represented a 50% fall from the previous year.

Light Beers

Premium light beers constituted the most popular beer category in the United States in 1996, occupying 27.9% of the market, with other premium beers at 27.5%. These beer styles are differentiated by their content of residual carbohydrate: standard premium beers contain a proportion of carbohydrate that survives the fermentation process, whereas a light (or lite) beer has most or all of this sugar removed by techniques we will visit in Chapter Seven. These beers therefore have lower calorie contents, provided they don't contain extra alcohol, which contributes to calorie intake. It is perhaps no surprise that in a market (U.S.) where 24% of all beer consumed is by women, the proportion of light beers drunk by women increases to 30%.

Draft Beers

The word *draft* (draught in the British Isles) can refer to two entirely distinct beer types. Traditionally it refers to beer dispensed from kegs or casks via pipes and pumps or straight from the cask—as is still the case for some traditional English ales. It is also used, however, to describe canned beer that has been sterile-filtered rather than pasteurized. The marketers' new angle for canned beer was beer "as nature intended."

From Cask-Conditioned to Nitrogenated Beers

The big growth market for beers in the United Kingdom is in nitrogenated products. Their emergence is an informative lesson in how modern technology can transform products whose origins are in traditional practice.

The classic beer style in England is nonpasteurized ale of relatively low carbon dioxide content. Happily, many famous brews of this type continue to be produced. Traditional English ales pass directly from fermentation into casks, to which are added hops, sugar, and finings materials that help the residual yeast to settle out. That yeast uses the sugar to carry out a secondary fermentation, which carbonates the beer to a modest extent. The product is not pasteurized and must be consumed within a few weeks. It is characterized by a robust hoppy flavor but also by much less gas fizz than other product types.

Again in the mid-1980s, marketers decided they wanted to sell this type of beer in cans for domestic consumption. The problem was the low CO_2 content, for the gas is required to pressurize and provide rigidity to cans and also to put a head on beer. For cask beers, it is the handpump of the English pub that does the work of putting a head on the beer. For "normal" canned beers, the relatively high gas content does the job for you on pouring. So how could the foaming problem be overcome for canned beers containing relatively little carbon dioxide? The answer was the widget, a piece of plastic put into the can that flexes when the can is opened and causes bubbles to come out of solution (see Chapter Three). This technology had been invented by Guinness, a Brewer with a long tradition of producing stouts with superbly stable heads. Another innovation pioneered by Guinness and taken advantage of by many Brewers to enhance the heads on their draft beers was the use of nitrogen gas, which makes vastly more stable foams than does carbon dioxide. So nitrogen was included in the cans—dropped in in its liquid form during canning. Not only does the nitrogen improve the foam, it also smoothes out the palate and enhances the drinkability of beers that contain it. The sales of canned beer with widgets zoomed and, seeing this, Brewers recognized the potential for so-called nitrokeg beers, where the beer is on draft dispense but is characterized by low CO_2 and the presence of N_2.

Nonalcohol and Low-Alcohol Beers

"Normal" beers range in their alcohol content from 2.5% to 13%. To a Bavarian used to beers possessing 6% alcohol or more, the regular tipple of the English ale drinker at, say, 4% might be viewed as low alcohol. Non- and low-alcohol beers (NAB/LABs) can be classified in many ways. For our purposes I define them as beers containing less than 0.05% or less than 2% alcohol (by volume), respectively.

While there are a few successful NAB/LABs in the world, they are the exception rather than the rule. For many people it is a contradiction in terms to associate beer with low alcohol content. After all, what is a beer if it doesn't deliver a kick? The rationale behind developing such beers in the first place is an interesting one and is largely based on the proposal that peer pressure convinces some people of the need to be seen to be drinking a product indistinguishable (by sight) from a normal beer, but one that has reduced alcohol content, thereby enabling them to drive more safely after drinking. Increasingly, it has been appreciated that this peer pressure phenomenon was overstated and that educated consumers will happily drink an established nonalcoholic product, say a juice or a cola, if the circumstances demand it. It seems that the only justification for purchasing a beer of low alcohol content is if it is pleasing to the palate, a characteristic that certainly hasn't been applicable to many such beers. The shortage of quality products in this genre is reflected in the statistics: In the United Kingdom NAB/LABs grew to occupy 1.1% of beer sales in 1989, but this had declined to 0.3% of sales just six years later.

This type of product has been made in many ways, and we will touch on some of them here. Perhaps the most common techniques are to limit alcohol formation in fermentation or to strip out the alcohol from a normal beer. In the first case the yeast can be removed from the fermenting mixture early on, or indeed the wort with which the yeast is furnished may be produced so that its sugars are much less fermentable. Alcohol can be removed by reverse osmosis, or by evaporating the alcohol using vacuum distillation. Not surprisingly, attempts to remove alcohol also strip away desirable flavors. Equally, if fermentation is not allowed to proceed to completion, these very flavor compounds are not properly developed and undesirable components derived from malt are not removed. Either way, flavor will be a problem. Considering that ethanol itself influences the flavor delivery of other components of beer, as well as contributing to flavor itself, it is evident why good NAB/LABs are few and far between.

*   *   *

In Chapter Four we will start our more in depth step-by-step investigation of the various stages that are involved in going from barley to beer. First, though, we really need to get a feel for the product that the Brewer is painstakingly brewing and for the quality parameters that make beer such a refreshing and wholesome drink.

Chapter Three

EYES, NOSE, AND THROAT

The Quality of Beer

The consumer of beer drinks as much with his eyes as with his mouth. This can be demonstrated by a simple experiment. Try adding a few drops of a flavorless dye—food coloring—to a lager so that the color darkens to that more typical of ale. People presented with this beer will judge its flavor to be closer to an that of an ale than a lager, although if they are blindfolded they won't be able to distinguish the taste of the beer before and after the dye has been added.

Color is just one visual parameter of beer. Most people prefer their beers to be sparkling bright, with no suggestion of cloud or haze; however, there is greater variation in the extent to which drinkers like a head of foam on beer. In some countries a copious delivery of foam on dispense is essential. For instance, it is traditional in countries such as Belgium for as much as half the contents of the glass to comprise froth. In the United Kingdom, there are distinct regional differences. In some places, for example London and the Southeast, foam seems frequently to be regarded as an inconvenience. By contrast, a stable head, perhaps 2 inches deep, is generally required in the north of England. But unlike, say, the Belgian, many an Englishman appears to want foam *and* a full measure of beer. Matters reached a head (one might say) when the status of beer foam was challenged in the courts of law. Landlords who dutifully dispensed the beer with a head were challenged by those insisting on a full pint of liquid. The most recent High Court judgment was that a reasonably sized head *should* be regarded as an integral feature of the beer, but that the customer is within her rights to insist on a full measure of liquid beer. Such concerns are only relevant, of course, for draft beer. For beer in cans and bottles the unit of volume is fixed by what is present in the container. Whether a head is generated is more often in the hands of the customer than the bartender. Indeed, that's if the beer gets poured at all. Some prefer their booze directly out of the bottle or can, in which case foam (and color and clarity, for that matter) assume a more academic dimension.

Just as color influences the perception of the flavor of a beer, so does the head seem to affect a drinker's judgment. Again there is likely to be a psychological component at work. It is, however, likely that the presence of foam does directly affect the release of flavor components from the beer. In other words, a beer smells differently depending on whether it does or does not have a head of foam on it. Not only that, but there are also substances in beer that have a tendency to move onto the surfaces, such as the bubble walls in foam and that are therefore called surface-active compounds. These include the bitter compounds, which make the foam more bitter than the rest of the beer.

You can see, then, that long before a drinker raises the glass to her lips, she will have already made some telling judgments about its quality, drawn from visual stimuli alone: the quality of the can or bottle, the font if the beer is on draft dispense, the appearance of the foam, the color, and whether the beer is cloudy. And all this is quite apart from the effect of other stimuli associated with the place in which the beer is being drunk: the lighting, the background music, the attractiveness of the bar layout, and even the company being kept! Beer flavor is important, of course, but even the most delicious of beers won't be enjoyed if all the other elements of the drinking experience are flat.

FOAM

Typically a packaged beer contains between 2.2 and 2.8 volumes of carbon dioxide (that is, for every milliliter of beer there are between 2.2 and 2.8 milliliters of CO_2 dissolved in it). At atmospheric pressure and $0°\,C$, a beer will dissolve no more than its own volume of CO_2. Introduction of these high levels of CO_2 demands the pressurizing of beer, yet if you take the cap off a bottle of beer the gas normally stays in solution. The beer is said to be supersaturated. To produce a foam you must do some work.

Foaming depends upon the phenomenon of nucleation, that is, the creation of bubbles. Bubble growth and release occurs at nucleation sites, which might include cracks in the surface of a glass, insoluble particles in beer, or gas pockets introduced during dispense. Pockets of gas are introduced whenever beer is agitated, as anyone who has tried to open a dropped can of lager will tell you.

The physics of bubble formation is far from completely understood and is astonishingly complicated. Brewers have approached the problem as often empirically as scientifically. For instance, glasses have been scratched to ensure a plentiful and continuous release of gas bubbles to replenish the foam, a phenomenon sometimes referred to as beading. Draft dispense is typically through a tap designed to promote gas release. Most recent of all is the widget, which we came across in Chapter Two (Fig. 3.1). Widgets have now even found their way into bottles.

Although beers are generally supersaturated with CO_2, foam generation is still easier and more extensive the more highly carbonated the beer. Bubble formation is easier in liquids of lower surface tension (see Box).

Figure 3.1. Widgets.

> *Surface tension* is the force that holds drops of liquid (such as water) together. The molecules in the liquid are attracted to one another, which drives the tendency to make the surface as small as possible. Therefore drops are round. Anything that stresses a surface to become bigger (such as foaming) is in opposition to this surface tension. As soon as the driving force is removed, surface tension restores the liquid to its original condition.
>
> *Viscosity* is the resistance of liquids to flow. It is due to friction between adjacent molecules in the liquid. If the molecules next to one another interact strongly, viscosity is high. If they don't, viscosity is low. Thus honey is a highly viscous liquid, but water isn't.

Various materials can lower surface tension, among them the alcohol of beer (ethanol). Ethanol is curious insofar as it promotes foam formation when present in beer at levels below 5%; alcohol above this level is detrimental to foam. The reasons for this are unclear.

Various physical factors dictate the rate at which beer foam collapses. As soon as a foam has formed, gravity causes beer trapped between the bubbles to drain from it. Anything that increases the viscosity of the beer should reduce the rate of drainage. Since viscosity increases as temperature decreases, colder beer has better foam stability. Counter to this is the fact that foam *forms* more readily at higher temperatures because gas is less soluble.

As liquid drains, the regions between bubbles become thinner, leading to coalescence as bubbles merge into bigger ones. This coarsens the foam and makes it less attractive. Foams with smaller bubbles are whiter, with a more luscious consistency in the mouth.

The least desirable set of circumstances occurs if the bubbles in a foam are of assorted sizes. The gas pressure in a small bubble is greater than that in a larger one. If two such bubbles are next to one another, gas will pass from the small bubble to the larger one until the smaller bubble disappears. The result, once again, is a shift to a "bladdery" and unattractive foam. This phenomenon, called disproportionation, happens more quickly at higher temperatures, but to a lesser extent if the gas pressure above the liquid is increased. Try covering your beer glass—you'll find that the foam survives longer. This is the principle of the German beer stein, although as steins are generally opaque and the beer can't be seen the objective is rather defeated!

The rate of disproportionation is also less for gases of lower solubility. For instance, nitrogen is only sparingly soluble in water. Adding just 30 to 50 mg of nitrogen gas per liter of beer creates foam with very small bubbles that is therefore extremely creamy and stable.

Of course, when bubbles form in a liquid, surface area increases. This phenomenon opposes the forces of surface tension and is the reason pure liquids can't give stable foams. Materials are needed that get into the bubble wall and stabilize it. In beer, the backbone material for bubbles is protein, which comes from the malt. Those proteins which have a relatively high degree of hydrophobicity (water-hating character) preferentially migrate into the head. There they encounter other substances with highly hydrophobic character, notably the molecules from hops which give beer its bitterness (see page 112). The interactions between the proteins and the bitter substances hold the bubbles together. This interaction takes several minutes. As it happens, the texture of the foam changes from liquid to almost solid, in which state foam can adhere to the glass surface, a phenomenon known as lacing, or cling.

Just as there are materials in beer which promote foam, so there are other substances which interfere with it, primarily lipids (which include fats), and which, like the proteins, can originate from the malt. However, good brewing practice should ensure that very low levels of lipids survive into the beer. These types of substance are much more likely to get into the beer and destroy the foam when it is in the drinking glass. Any grease or fats associated with food are bad news for beer. If you eat potato chips, the oils associated with them easily kill foam. Lipstick contains waxy substances that will pop bubbles, and the detergents and rinse-aids used to wash glasses also tend to be foam-negative. When beer glasses are washed, the detergent must always be washed from the glasses using clean water, the glasses should be allowed to dry by draining. If the glasses are wiped on a kitchen cloth, it must be a clean one.

Before we leave foam we should remember that it isn't always good news. From time to time foaming occurs spontaneously when a can or bottle is opened. In extreme examples, as much as two-thirds of the contents spew forth in a wild and uncontrollable manner. Most people find this to be somewhat irritating! There may be several reasons for the phenomenon, which is called *gushing*. The first, of course, is that the package has been ill-treated—dropped or shaken. Brewers take great care when shipping beer to avoid unnecessary agitation of the product. If a container is given an hour or two to settle after being dropped or shaken, the beer won't be wild when the can or bottle is opened.

Unfortunately, gushing is sometimes due to substances which promote the phenomenon and which originate in the raw materials. Barley grown in wetter climates is susceptible to infection by a fungus called *Fusarium*. This organism produces a very small protein molecule which gets into malt and, from there, into beer, where it acts as a very active nucleation site for bubble formation. Another type of molecule which can act in the same way is an oxidation product of hops which is from time to time to be found in certain preparations used to bitter beer.

COLOR

An enormous range of colors is found in beers: there are exceedingly pale, strawlike lagers, copper-colored ales, rich brown milds, and the blackest of stouts. This wonderful range is seldom achieved by the addition of coloring materials, although caramels have and continue to be used in some quarters for this purpose. Generally, the color of beer is determined by the malt and other solid grist materials which are used in the brewhouse. (Recently, a new method of coloring beers has been introduced in which the color of dark malts is extracted and separated from the flavor-active molecules in those malts and added as a liquid late in the brewing process. This process involves making an extract of the dark malt in water and fractionating it according to the size of the substances it contains. This can be achieved using special membranes that allow small molecules to pass through, but big molecules to be retained. The components responsible for flavor are small, but the coloring materials are large. Using this technique, then, preparations have become available that enable a beer to be made darker without introducing the smoky-burnt characteristics typical of a roast malt and, conversely, to introduce such flavors into pale beers without making them dark. This presents splendid new product development opportunities to Brewers, as well as an opportunity for introducing color without the use of caramel.)

The color-forming materials in grist are primarily the melanoidins, complex molecules produced when sugars and amino acids are heated. Heating is an integral feature of the process by which malt is produced (Chapter Four). The more intense this kilning, the darker the malt. Also, the more sugars and amino acids present, the greater the potential for making melanoidins. Sugars form during the germination of barley, when complex carbohydrates (primarily starch) are broken down. Similarly, the amino acids are the end point of protein breakdown. A malt destined for lager production tends to have had relatively limited germination and, more significantly, is kilned to modest temperatures, so its color contribution is low. Ale malts are more extensively modified during germination and are kilned to a higher temperature, so they are darker. If the malt is kilned to ever more intense extremes, then profoundly dark malts are obtained (Fig. 3.2). Such materials are traditionally employed in the production of darker ales and stouts.

A second source of color in brewing is the oxidation of polyphenol or tannin materials. These molecules originate from both malt and hops and are prone to oxidation if large amounts of oxygen are allowed to enter into the brewhouse operations. The reaction involved is exactly analogous to the browning of sliced apples. If this source of color is to be eliminated, it is

Figure 3.2. Malts with different colors resulting from different intensities of kilning. (*Photograph reproduced courtesy of Pauls Malt, Kentford, U.K.*)

essential to exclude oxygen from the mash mixer and, especially, the wort kettle (see Chapter Six).

HAZE

Oxidation of polyphenols is much more important for another reason: It forms haze. In the oxidation process the individual tannin units associate to form larger molecules that associate with protein to form insoluble particles that cause haziness in beer. The reactions involved are similar to those responsible for the tanning of leather.

Other materials may cause cloudiness in beer. For instance, if the complex carbohydrates of barley—chiefly the starch or the polysaccharides that make up the barley cell walls—are not properly digested in malting and brewing, they can precipitate out of beer as hazes or gels, particularly if beer is chilled excessively. Another natural component of malt is oxalic acid, which brewers should ensure is removed in the brewhouse operations by having enough calcium in the water to precipitate it out. If they fail in this task, the oxalic acid will survive into beer. This is primarily a problem for draft beer because oxalate will precipitate out in the dispense lines and clog them. This is so-called beer stone.

FLAVOR

The flavor of beer is no simple affair. There are the obvious tastes one associates with the product, in particular the bitterness imparted by hops. And, as for most foodstuffs, the characters of sweet and salt play a part, although few desirable beers have sourness among their attributes. A wide range of volatile substances contribute to the aroma of beers, including esters, sulfur-containing compounds, and essential oils from hops. Ethanol itself provides a warming effect and seems to influence the extent to which other molecules contribute to a beer's character. Even carbon dioxide has a role to play.

To complicate matters further, it should be appreciated that the flavor of beer is not static. From the time that fermentation is complete to the moment that the beer is packaged, changes occur in its taste and aroma. And it doesn't stop there. Just as for wine, the character of beer changes in the package. Only rarely are these changes for the better in beer, as we shall see.

The Nature of Beer Flavor

The flavor of a beer can be broken down into its taste, smell (aroma), and mouthfeel (texture or body). Brewers also talk about flavor stability in reference to the deterioration in quality as the beer ages in the package.

Taste.   The bitterness of beer is due to a group of compounds called the iso-α-acids, which originate from hops (see Chapter Five). There are six iso-α-acids that differ in their relative bitterness impact. The perceived bitterness of a beer, therefore, depends not only on the overall level of these iso-α-acids in the product but also upon the relative proportions of each of the six isomers. These proportions, in turn, depend on the variety of hop from which the bitterness is obtained and on the manner by which the hop is processed before it is used in the brewery. To add to the complication, a drinker's perception of bitterness changes after he has taken a sip of beer. There is an initial surge in perceived bitterness, followed by a gradual subsidence of the effect (Fig. 3.3). The shape of this time-intensity curve differs among iso-α-acids—but it also differs among tasters.

In fact, the ability of a drinker to estimate the bitterness of a beer is generally fairly poor. A well-trained taster may be able to address the problem, but nonprofessionals tend to have their judgment clouded by other features of the beer, most notably sweetness.

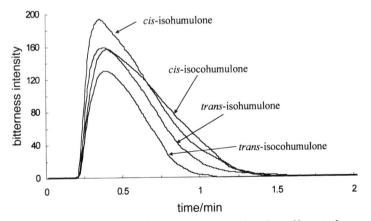

Figure 3.3.   A time-intensity plot. Drinkers are armed with a glass of beer and a computer. They take a sip of beer and then indicate the intensity of a flavor character in that beer by moving the computer mouse away from them as the intensity increases on their palate and then back toward them as it subsides. Software in the computer translates this mouse movement into a graph, as shown here. The compounds named on the graph are iso-α-acids.

The sweetness of beers is due to residual sugars that have not been fermented into alcohol. Frequently the Brewer adds sugar (primings) to the beer before packaging. Beers vary enormously in their relative sweetness—indeed in their bitterness–sweetness balance.

Although *salty* is not a word that many people would use to describe beer, certain salts do contribute to beer flavor. In particular, the ratio of chloride to sulfate is important. Sulfate increases the dryness of a beer, while chloride is said to mellow the palate and impart fullness. Other ions are also significant. For example, traces of iron, which might be picked up from the materials used to filter beer, give an unacceptable metallic character to a product.

Aroma.   People often refer to the taste and the smell of a foodstuff such as beer. In fact, these are very closely related sensory phenomena. What a drinker generally describes as the flavor of a beer is in reality character that is actually detected in the nasal passages. It is strictly speaking defined as aroma. If you have suffered from a head cold and have blocked nasal passages, you will appreciate the effect that this can have in eliminating the sense of taste.

Whereas relatively few substances contribute to the true *taste* of beer (bitter, sweet, salt, sour), many different types of molecules influence aroma. Lots of these are produced by yeast during fermentation. There are alcohols other than ethanol, which can impart coconut or solvent-type character, and there are aldehydes, which give aromas like green leaves. Principally, though, there are the esters, the short-chain fatty acids, and many of the sulfur compounds. The pH of beer also depends largely on fermentation, as yeast acts to lower the pH of wort from approximately 5.5 to 3.8–4.5.

The pH of beer has enormous influence on product quality. Many of the molecules in beer can exist in charged and uncharged forms, the relative proportions of which depend directly on pH. For instance, the bitter compounds exist in both uncharged and charged states, and the former is more bitter than the latter. The hydrogen ions that cause a beer to be acid (low pH; see Appendix One) impart sourness. That is, if a beer has a low pH (say 3.8) it will be more sour than one of pH 4.5.

A selection of esters is present in beers. Esters vary in the type of flavor that they impart (Table 3.1). It is the mix of esters and other volatile compounds that determines the aroma of beer. Drinkers might say that a beer is *fruity* or even *bananas*, but its true character is seldom so simple as

Table 3.1. Some of the esters found in beer

Ester	Flavor descriptor	Approximate flavor threshold* (ppm)
Ethyl acetate	Solvent, fruity	30
Butyl acetate	Banana, sweet	7.5
Isoamyl acetate	Banana, apple	1
Ethyl valerate	Papaya	1
Isoamyl propionate	Pineapple, aniseed	1
Ethyl nicotinate	Medicinal	6
Phenylethyl acetate	Roses, honey	4
Methyl caprate	Coconut	1
Octyl caproate	Orange peel	5
Isoamyl caprate	Tropical fruits	3

*The flavor threshold is the concentration of a substance that must be present in a beer before it can be detected.

to be traceable to just one or even a very few types of flavor molecules. Rather, it is the combined effect of a complex mixture that determines overall "nose." Such complexity ensures that individual beers are unique, but it also makes considerable demands on the brewster if she is to ensure consistency.

Esters, then, have a range of individual aromas in the pure state that aren't simply related to the character these substances impart to the complex matrix that is beer. The same applies to other classes of compound found in beer. For instance, various sulfur compounds may be present (Table 3.2). Comparison of the flavor descriptors and flavor thresholds of the sulfur compounds with those of the esters indicates why Brewers are often rather more worried about the former!

One prominent sulfur compound, present in many lager-style beers, is dimethyl sulfide (DMS). DMS is a remarkable molecule, found throughout nature. Apart from finding it in lager, you might detect it in baby's breath and cat's urine! It is also prominent in the smell of parsnips, tomato ketchup, black currants, and sweet corn.

Brewers differ in their preference for having DMS in their lagers. Some like it, generally in the range of 40 to 100 ppb, and there are certainly a good many lagers across mainland Europe that have a character substantially determined by DMS at these levels. Other Brewers are adamant that DMS is an "off" character that must be maintained at levels below its flavor threshold of around 30 ppb.

Table 3.2. Some of the sulfur compounds found in beer

Sulfur compound	Descriptor	Approximate flavor threshold (ppb)
Ethyl mercaptan	Rotting leek, onion, garlic, egg	2
Dimethyl sulfide	Cooked vegetable, corn, black currant	30
Diethyl disulfide	Garlic, burnt rubber	0.5
Tertiary amyl mercaptan	Rotting guava; cat urine	0.0001
Methional	Mashed potato	250

To control DMS in lager to a defined level is a remarkable feat (see Chapter Six). However, even if DMS is controlled to the desired level, there is still a problem—one that illustrates nicely the thesis that the aroma of beer is the net result of the contribution of a whole range of compounds. It has been shown that even expert tasters given a wide range of beers to taste can't correlate perceived DMS character with the level of DMS measurable in those beers. Amazingly, they *could* detect a decrease in perceived DMS character as the level of phenylethanol (rose flavor) in beers increased. For beers of similar phenylethanol content, there is a direct link between actual DMS and the ability of tasters to detect it. In other words, some compounds are able to suppress the extent to which other compounds can be detected. Equally, it is believed that other compounds interact cumulatively in their effect on flavor. For example, several compounds may individually be present in beer at levels below their flavor thresholds, but they "combine" to provide a discernible character, presumably because they each react at the same location in the olfactory system.

Short-chain fatty acids generally provide undesirable characters to beer. Descriptors include cheesy, goaty, body odor, and wet dog! Happily for the drinker, the Brewer's control over the process means that undesirable levels of this type of compound seldom find their way into the beer.

Just as undesirable is the character introduced by the so-called vicinal diketones. Diacetyl, the most important of these, has an intense butterscotch flavor. Few of us like our beer to taste of candy!

Diacetyl is naturally produced in all brewery fermentations. It is an offshoot of the metabolic pathways that yeast uses to make some of the building blocks it requires for growth. The diacetyl leaks out of the yeast cell and into the fermenting broth. Happily, yeast is capable of mopping up the diacetyl again. And so, toward the end of fermentation, the yeast scavenges the diacetyl and converts it into substances that do not have an intense aroma. To do this the yeast must be in a healthy state, but even then the process can take a considerable period of time. Thus the period for which a beer must stay in the fermenter depends not only on the time taken to convert sugar into alcohol, but also on the additional days required to eliminate diacetyl and take it below its flavor threshold of approximately 0.1 ppm.

Another undesirable flavor in beer is acetaldehyde, which imparts a character of green apples to a product. Surpassing all others in the undesirable flavor stakes, however, is the character due to a compound called 3-methyl-2-butene-1-thiol (MBT). This is produced through the degradation of the iso-α-acid bitter substances, a degradation brought on by light. People differ in their sensitivity to MBT, but for many it can be detected at levels as low as 0.4 parts per trillion. To put this into perspective, these poor people would have been able to detect a tenth of a gram of MBT distributed throughout the balloon of the airship Graf Zeppelin II.

The aroma that MBT imparts is referred to as *lightstruck*, or, worse still, *skunky*. Brewers have known about the problem for many years, and it is the reason beers need to be protected from light. Brown glass is better than green glass for this purpose. Clear flint glass is the worst option. An alternative strategy is to use modified (reduced) iso-α-acids that, when broken down, no longer give off MBT. The added advantage is that this reduction increases the hydrophobicity of these molecules and therefore enhances their foam-stabilizing properties.

It's high time we returned to some of the more desirable characters in beer. Generally these originate from malt and hops. Malty character is quite complex and is due to a range of chemical species. Hoppy character, too, is far from simple and may indeed take various forms. In all cases it is due to the essential oils of hops. The contribution they make to aroma, however, differs considerably among beers.

For the most part, hops are added at the start of the boiling process. The essential oils, being volatile, are comprehensively driven off during the boiling operation; the resultant beers, while bitter, have no hoppy character. Because of this volatility, some Brewers hold back a proportion of the hops and add them late in the boil. In this way some of the essential oils survive into the wort and thence into the beer. The process, for obvious reasons, is called late hopping.

In traditional ale brewing in England, with the beer dispensed from casks, it is customary to add a handful of hop cones to the beer at the point of filling. In this way all of the essential oils of those hops have the opportunity to enter into the beer, affording a complex and characterful nature to such products. This process is called dry hopping.

Flavor Balance.   This is an appropriate stage to emphasize that beer flavor is not simply a matter of introducing greater or lesser quantities of a given taste or aroma, depending on the character desired in a given product. A beer is pleasing, interesting, and, above all, *drinkable*, because it has its various organoleptic properties in balance.

If I were to have a single criticism of some of the beers being produced by microbrewers, it would be that they have failed to grasp this point. Many of these Brewers seem to have overdosed on hops, rendering their beers intensely aromatic and, of course, extremely bitter. It is perfectly satisfactory to have a very bitter beer—there are many such long-standing products in the world. Equally, there are many leading brands of lager that have pronounced late hop character but that possess modest levels of bitterness. We have seen how aroma and bitterness levels in beer can be independently adjusted, enabling a product with excellent *balance*. Along with hop-derived characters, parameters such as sweetness–bitterness, chloride–sulfate ratio, and volatiles. A high level of DMS may be utterly unacceptable in one product, whereas in another it may be warranted because is offsets or complements a characteristic introduced by a different component.

The myriad of interactions that take place in the human taste and olfactory system following the consumption of beer must be enormously complicated. Certainly there is only limited knowledge of the physiological basis for them. Yet it is perfectly possible, indeed essential, for the Brewer to design products that delight the consumer because their flavor characteristics are so carefully balanced, with or without high overall flavor impact. These are the products that a consumer will find drinkable and that he or she will be tempted to order again.

Mouthfeel.   One of the least understood aspects of beer flavor is mouthfeel, which is sometimes referred to as body or texture. It seems unlikely that the perception of body relates to one or even a very few components of beer.

Recently a vocabulary to describe what expert tasters perceive as mouthfeel has been described. One of the terms is *tingle*, which is quite clearly directly related to the carbon dioxide content of a beer. CO_2 reacts with pain receptors in the palate, and yet most people find this sensation to be pleasurable. For many beers, a relatively high concentration of CO_2 is essential to deliver this effect, which is due to an influence on the trigeminal nerve. In the United States, most beers are relatively highly carbonated (in excess of 2.6 volumes CO_2 per volume of beer). However, English ales traditionally have been of low carbon dioxide content, and a new genre of low CO_2 keg ales has sprung up in recent years. These are the nitrokegs, so named because the beer also contains nitrogen both to support foam qualities but also to impart textural smoothness long known to be associated with use of this gas. The downside for some Brewers is that the use of nitrogen suppresses hoppiness, another example of how one aspect of beer quality influences another.

Nobody is certain of all the chemical species in beer that might influence texture. Some say the long and wobbly polysaccharides (the β-glucans) originating in the cell walls of barley have a role. Certainly they increase viscosity, and some people suspect that increased viscosity is an important contributor to mouthfeel, as it alters the flow characteristics of saliva in the mouth. Others have championed proteins, chloride, glycerol, organic acids (such as citric acid and acetic acid), and even ethanol itself as determinants of mouthfeel. However, it seems certain that the polyphenols that we referred to earlier are important. They have long been known to cause astringency in ciders, and astringency is certainly one term in the mouthfeel vocabulary.

Flavor Stability.   While flavor is conveniently described in terms of the individual components of a freshly packaged beer, the quality of beer most definitely changes over time. The gross flavor changes that occur are indicated in Fig. 3.4. This is a fairly simplistic representation of the changes that occur; they may well adopt a rather different form in different types of beer.

Although all of these changes are important, and in an ideal world would be minimized, in reality the most significant and damaging effect is the development of a papery or cardboard character. Despite years of extensive research there is no consensus among brewing scientists regarding the origin of the carbonyl compounds that cause this character. Some champion the bitter compounds, the iso-α-acids, as a prime source. Others believe that certain higher alcohols produced by yeast during fermenta-

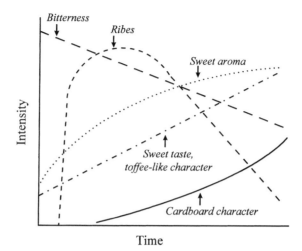

Figure 3.4. Changes in various flavors in beer as the beer is stored. For an understanding of the term "ribes" see Fig. 9.2.

tion are important. The majority believe that the staling of beer, just like that of other foodstuffs, can be traced to the oxidation of unsaturated fatty acids, notably linoleic acid, which originate in the malt.

What is known is that the degradations that lead ultimately to staleness depend on the presence of oxygen. For this reason it is essential during packaging to minimize the ingress of oxygen into the can, bottle, or keg. Furthermore, oxygen uptake into the package in trade must be avoided. This is only really significant in bottled beers, where oxygen can sneak in through the seal between the crown cork and the neck of the bottle. Recently some Brewers have used corks that have an oxygen scavenger melded into them.

Despite the precautions taken to avoid oxygen access to beer in the package, all beers stale eventually. There is increasing evidence that the tendency to form this cardboard character is built into the product during the production process, so Brewers have started to consider eradicating oxygen uptake throughout the brewery and have even started to suspect that the oxidation reaction begins in the malting operation. The reason these carbonyl compounds don't reveal themselves during the process may be because oxidation only goes as far as an intermediate, which subsequently breaks down in the package over time. Alternatively, it may be that the staling compounds are produced early in the process, bind onto other compounds (principally sulfur dioxide, which is a natural product of fermentation), and that the complex formed progressively degrades in the beer, exposing the carbonyl character.

Like other chemical processes, the staling reaction is retarded at reduced temperatures. In some markets, notably the United States, refrigerated distribution is widely employed.

BEER AS A FOODSTUFF

Is Beer Good for You?

For many years Guinness advertised their beer on a platform of *Guinness is Good For You* before changes in law decreed that this type of claim could no longer be made. Later, also in the British Isles, came claims (less overt perhaps) for another beer: *A Double Diamond Works Wonders*. A Shakesperian actor, Sir Bernard Miles, was featured in a television campaign extolling the virtues of Mackeson Stout, using the immortal lines: *It looks good, it tastes good, and by golly it does you good!* Now, in the very late twentieth century, there is little doubt that the former of those two claims, regarding appearance and flavor, could still be legitimate in a television advertisement. The problem would come with the third statement. No longer is it legitimate to claim that beer drinking is good for you, despite the scientific evidence in support of such statements.

Of course, a broad spectrum of opinion exists concerning the desirability of consuming alcoholic beverages. For millions worldwide such drinks are condemned on religious grounds. In cultures where alcohol is tolerated, right-minded individuals recognize the social unacceptability of consuming alcohol to excess, with the terrible price it can have for some through road traffic accidents and family distress and for others through the development of conditions such as cirrhosis of the liver. This is quite apart from the impairment of performance that drinking at inappropriate times can cause. Increasingly, however, it is becoming recognized that there may be some health benefits associated with the consumption of alcoholic beverages in moderation—not only by helping to reduce stress and stress-related problems such as increased excitability and heart rate.

Perhaps the most glowing reference to the benefits of drinking beer was penned by John Taylor, who kept an alehouse in London, England. In 1651 he suggested that beer is a singular remedy against all melancholic disease, tremor cordis and maladies of the spleen; it is purgative and of great operation against Iliaca passio, and all the gripings of the small guts; it cures the stone in the bladder, reines [or kidneys] and provokes urine wonderfully, it mollifies tumours and swellings on the body and is very predominant in opening the obstructions of the liver. It is most effectual for clearing of the sight, being applied outwardly it assuageth the unsufferable pain of the Gout called Artichicha Podagra or Ginogra, the yeast or barm being laid hot to the part pained, in which way it is easeful to all impostumes, or the pain in the hip called Sciatica passio . . . and being buttered (as our Gallenists well observe) it is good against all contagious diseases, fevers, agues, rheums, coughs, and catarrhs.[1]

That's quite a testimony. We can say, though, with rather more careful consideration and supportive evidence, that there are indeed potentially positive aspects to the drinking of beer.

In comparison with other alcoholic beverages, the content of alcohol is relatively low in the majority of beers. The alcohol strength of beers, which for the most part tends to be in the range of 3% to 6% by volume, is much lower than that of most other alcoholic drinks. Beer, then, is more suited to the quenching of thirst and counteraction of dehydration than is wine, for instance. In some countries (such as Germany) beers at the lower alcohol end of the spectrum are favored as sports drinks, because their osmotic pressure is similar to (isotonic with) that of body fluids. Such beers do possess some calorific value as an energy source because they contain some carbohydrate. Incidentally, all beers are, to all intents and purposes, fat-free.

It has been claimed that beer (though not the alcohol within it) stimulates milk production in nursing mothers. It may reduce the risk of gallstones and promote bowel function. It has even been claimed in Japan that materials produced during the kilning of malt and that enter into darker beers suppress the onset of dental caries!

Beer contains some vitamins, notably some of those in the B group (pyridoxine, niacin, and riboflavin), and minerals, especially magnesium and potassium. Beers generally have a low ratio of sodium to potassium, which is beneficial for blood pressure.

Recently, a number of publications have drawn attention to the importance of antioxidants in foodstuffs and the possible contribution these could make in protecting against the undesirable effects of oxygen radicals. Principal among these antioxidants are the polyphenols, which are present in beer. They may also include folic acid and selenium. Small wonder that, for generations, stouts have been recommended for the diet of nursing mothers.

Most debate in recent years has focused on the relative merits and demerits of consuming ethanol itself. Evidence emerging from the medical community that moderate drinking correlates with lower death rates due to various causes led a few years ago to the United Kingdom raising its recommended maximum for drinking by adults: Men are advised to drink no more than 26 units a week (a unit in the United Kingdom is 8 g of alcohol, which is roughly equal to half a pint of medium-strength beer) and women fewer than 21 units. Additionally, the advice is to consume no more than 4 units per day. Compare this with the recommendations of the French, whose more liberal attitude to alcohol and predilection for wine prompts them to advise men to drink no more than one bottle of wine per day, and women half as much.

In particular there seems to be evidence for alcohol protecting against cardiovascular disease. These effects may be linked to a component of beer other than alcohol itself, but ethanol may alter the balance of the high- and low-density lipoproteins in the blood by reducing the deposition of fats on artery walls. Alcohol also appears to reduce the "stickiness" of blood platelets, making them less likely to aggregate as blood clots.

Another component of beer that may have a hypocholesterolemic influence is the β-glucan, the principal component of the cell walls of barley, which can cause all sorts of problems for the Brewer (see Chapter Six). If this polysaccharide, which is soluble fiber, does survive into beer, it may have a cholesterol-lowering effect.

A wide range of clinical studies has concluded that there is a U-shaped relationship between deaths and alcohol consumption (Fig. 3.5). Modest consumption of alcohol lowers the relative risk of death, particularly through a lesser incidence of coronary heart disease. This relationship appears to hold across national boundaries and cultures and was most famously publicized as the so-called "French Paradox." A people famed for their enjoyment of fine food high in saturated fats leading to high levels of serum cholesterol nonetheless report some of the lowest frequencies of deaths from coronary heart disease. Hence we see a justification for their relatively high recommended alcohol intake, although it has also been suggested that it is not only the alcohol in drinks that has a beneficial effect but also other components of the Mediterranean diet, such as garlic.

In summary, it does seem that benefits may be associated with the

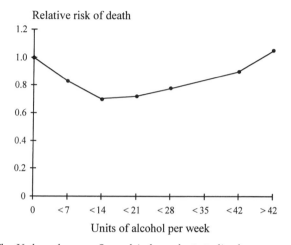

Figure 3.5. The U-shaped curve. Several independent studies have generated a profile similar to this one, which is adapted from an article by Denise Baxter (*The Brewer*, February 1996, pp. 63–66). Indeed the first report of such a U-shaped curve was made in 1926 by R. Pearl in a book entitled *Alcohol and Longevity* (New York, Alfred A. Knopf). Since that time studies in Britain, Japan, Denmark, and the United States have all demonstrated this type of response, with particular emphasis on coronary artery disease. An excellent review of this topic was penned by Dr. Tim Cooper (*Proceedings of the 23rd Convention of the Institute of Brewing, Asia Pacific Section*, 1994, pp. 32–37).

moderate consumption of alcoholic beverages, including beer, by mature and well-adjusted adults, at the appropriate time and in the appropriate place. Drinking to excess always has been and always will be antisocial, dangerous, and unacceptable.

Why Beer Can Be Safer to Drink Than Water

Beer is most inhospitable to the growth of microorganisms. The boiling stage in beer production kills most of the organisms that might have entered the process. During fermentation the pH falls to about 4.0, which is too low for most organisms to thrive, and, of course, most of the nutrients a contaminating microbe would need are efficiently consumed by yeast. At the same time, ethanol is produced, which itself protects against microbial growth. Most beer is packaged under relatively anaerobic conditions, preventing the growth of any microbe that requires oxygen. And it has been proven that those pathogenic bacteria that don't require oxygen are unable to populate beer. Above all, beer contains various substances that suppress bacterial growth. These include some of the tannins, but in particular it is the bitter compounds, the iso-α-acids, that have a profound antimicrobial influence. (What wonderful things these substances are: They make beer nicely bitter, they help provide the foam, they prevent bug infections—what a pity they are the cause of skunky flavor!)

BEER STRENGTH: ITS RELEVANCE

The strength of a beer is defined by its alcohol content. At one extreme are beers containing more than 13% alcohol by volume (ABV). At the other pole are alcohol-free beers. Obviously, variations in alcohol strength produce variable physiological impacts; these variations also influence flavor and foaming properties.

Perhaps of most importance, though, is the fact that in many countries, taxes on beer are levied on the basis of alcoholic strength. This is not the case in the United States, where fixed-rate levies are made at federal and state levels on a per barrel basis, irrespective of the strength of the beer in the container (see Chapter One).

In the United Kingdom, however, the amount of duty levied is in direct proportion to the alcohol content of the beer (see Chapter Nine). Small wonder that the precision with which alcohol content of beer can be measured is most important, both to the Brewer and to Her Majesty's Customs and Excise. Indeed, in all countries, it is most important to make careful checks and records of beer volumes because that information directly affects the size of the tax check the Brewer will be writing.

We can focus on the United Kingdom if we are to learn something of the ingenuity with which governments have ensured that duties are comprehensively levied on Brewers and the lengths to which they have gone to ensure that Brewers toed the line. In fact we can go back to 1188 to find Henry II levying a tax on all tradespeople, including Brewers, to help him fight the Crusades.

In the Middle Ages, local authorities appointed ale conners, whose job it was to test the quality of ale on sale and to ensure that it was being dispensed in the correct measure. A Brewer was obliged to announce that a beer had been brewed by putting a stake with a branch or a brush at the end of it in front of the brewery. The ale conner would come along, taste the ale, and declare whether it was suitable for drinking. If he decided it

Table 3.3. Typical alcoholic strengths of various beverages

Drink	Typical alcohol content (% ABV)	Volume of a drink constituting a unit
Premium beer	4.5	Approx. half a pint
High-strength beer	9.0	Approx. quarter pint
Wine	12.0	Approx. tenth of a 75 cl bottle
Whiskey	40.0	20 ml
Gin	40.0	20 ml
Vodka	45.0	15–20 ml
Vermouth	15.0	Appox. fifteenth of a 75 cl bottle

wasn't of the appropriate strength, he could instruct the brewer to sell the ale at a lower price. The test he applied for checking whether the sugar had been converted into alcohol was to pour some of the ale onto a bench and sit in it in his leather pants. If he stuck to the bench then he knew that there was still sugar in the ale—and woe betide the brewer!

Typical alcohol levels for a range of alcoholic beverages are shown in Table 3.3, together with the volume of that drink that constitutes a unit.

*   *   *

We have discovered in this chapter that a myriad of compounds and physical interactions influence the quality of beer. Let just one of them be out of balance, and the whole product will be ruined. Time now, then, to walk steadily through the malting and brewing processes to see how it is that the devoted Maltster and Brewer strive to ensure that the balance in your beer is indeed right, time after time after time.

ENDNOTE

1. J. Taylor, *Ale Ale-vated into the Ale-titude*, 1651, as quoted in H. S. Corran, *A History of Brewing*, Newton Abbot: David & Charles, 1975, p. 87.

Chapter Four

THE SOUL OF BEER

Malt

Barley malt is the key grist component of more than 90% of the beer brewed worldwide. True, some beers, such as the Weissbiers in Germany, are produced from malted wheat, and some beers in South Africa are based on sorghum. Many malt-based beers contain other grist materials, often for reasons of cost, but also because they may introduce distinctive characters. Thus a major international brand features rice in its recipe, and some Brewers use wheat-based adjuncts because they feel they enhance foam quality. These adjuncts will be considered in Chapter Six.

It is malted barley, however, that remains the foundation of most beers, and it seldom accounts for less than 50% of the grist. Frequently it comprises the sole source of fermentable carbohydrate. Efficient brewing to produce top-quality beer is inextricably linked to the quality of the malt. This focuses attention on the quality of the barley and on the malting operation, both of which must be right.

BARLEY

Cultivated barley (*Hordeum vulgare*) belongs to the grass family (the Gramineae) and is grown in more extremes of climate than any other cereal (Table 4.1). It has been estimated that barley emerged from its ancestor in Egypt some 20,000 years ago. Worldwide production of barley now exceeds 170 million tons, but less than 25% of that is malted for the brewing of beer.

Barley can be identified in the field by its characteristic whisker, or awn (see Fig. 2.1). Two types of barley are used for malting and brewing.

75

Table 4.1. Production of barley

Country	Barley grown (million tons)*
Russia and countries of the former USSR	48
Germany	14
Canada	13
United States	11
France	10
United Kingdom	10
Spain	9
China	6
Turkey	6
Denmark	5
Australia	4
Poland	4
Remainder	34

*Figures are rounded averages of production over a 10-year time frame.

In two-rowed barley, two rows of kernels develop, one on either side of the ear. Six-rowed barley has three corns on either side of the ear. Space is restricted on the ear, meaning that some of the corns in the latter type must be twisted in order to fit. Six-row barleys may have a higher proportion of cell wall material in their endosperms. This characteristic must be efficiently dealt with if problems are to be avoided in the brewery. These barleys are generally capable of producing higher levels of enzymes.

The barley corn consists of a baby plant (embryo) and an associated food reserve (starchy endosperm) packed within protective layers (see Fig. 2.3). It is the food reserve that is of primary interest to the Brewer (and therefore the Maltster), as this is the origin of the fermentable material that will subsequently be converted into beer. The reserve consists of starch in the form of large (type A) and small (type B) granules, packed within a matrix of protein and the whole is wrapped up in a relatively thin cell wall (Fig. 4.1). The cells of the starchy endosperm (each barley corn contains approximately a quarter of a million of them) are dead; although they contain a few enzymes, most of the significant enzymes that are necessary to digest the food reserves can't be made by the starchy endosperm.

It is the embryo that ultimately controls breakdown of the endosperm. After all, this is *its* food reserve, the true function of which is to support its growth. The endosperm wasn't designed to oblige the Maltster or

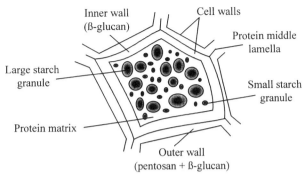

Figure 4.1. A schematic representation of a cell in the starchy endosperm of barley. The walls have inner and outer regions comprising different types of polysaccharide, while the area between cells is called the middle lamella and is made of protein. Protein is also found inside the cells, where it surrounds large and small starch granules.

Brewer! The skilled maltster takes advantage of the embryo's ability to mobilize its foodstore to enable her to furnish the brewer with good-quality malt.

The embryo itself is capable of some enzyme synthesis, through the region known as the scutellum. Primarily, though, it is believed that enzyme production is the preserve of the aleurone tissue, which is two to four cells deep and surrounds the starchy endosperm. The embryo produces a series of hormones that migrate to the aleurone, where they control the switching on or off of enzyme synthesis. The hormones called gibberellins largely promote the development and release of enzymes, which are antagonized by another hormone called abscisic acid. It seems that the balance of these different hormones regulates the extent to which the various enzymes are produced.

Before an embryo can leap into action and produce these hormones and before any enzyme can act to hydrolyze the starchy endosperm, the barley must have its moisture content increased. Whole barley from a malting store will typically contain some 10% to 13% water, with the embryo holding 18% to 20% moisture. To commence metabolism of the embryo, this moisture content must be increased. The starchy endosperm, too, must be hydrated, for enzymes act more rapidly if their substrates are solvated.

In the malting process, then, barley is first steeped in water, to bring it up to a moisture content in the region of 42% to 46%. This triggers the synthesis and migration of enzymes into the starchy endosperm. The first enzymes produced are those that open up the cell walls and hydrolyze their constituents. Following from these are the proteolytic enzymes. The last enzymes to be made are the amylases, which are responsible for degrading the starch.

The first requirement in the production of malt for brewing is comprehensive hydrolysis of the cell walls, which softens the grain and facilitates its milling and extraction. Second, there needs to be a substantial breakdown of protein. This eliminates potential haze-forming material and releases foaming polypeptide, but more importantly, the breakdown produces amino acids that the yeast requires as building blocks for it to make its own proteins and grow. What the Brewer does not want is significant degradation of the starch, for it is this that he wants to break down in the brewery to yield fermentable sugars.

The germination of barley, therefore, is carried out for a time sufficient to degrade cell walls and protein and long enough for starch-degrading enzymes to be synthesized but not long enough to cause excessive growth of the embryo. The process is generally referred to as *modification*. Once modification is completed to the required extent it is halted by kilning.

WHICH BARLEY?

Any barley, providing it is living (viable), can be malted, but the quality of the malt and the efficiency of the malting operation depend greatly on the nature of the barley. Ensuring barley quality makes certain demands of the farmer.

Barleys can be divided into malting and nonmalting (or feed) grades. The division is based on the amount of extractable material that can be obtained from their malts in a brewing operation. Malting varieties give high levels of extractable material; nonmalting grades don't. Or, more accurately, they don't when malted for conventional periods of time and brewed in a conventional manner.

The difference between barleys lies in the ease with which their endosperms can be modified during germination. In nonmalting grades substantial areas of the endosperm will remain intact after conventional periods of germination (four to six days). This may be because water doesn't get distributed evenly throughout the endosperm, which in turn must relate to their structure. Alternatively, their cell walls may be less easily degraded than those of better grades, or such barleys may be less capable of synthesizing enzymes.

Evidence suggests that all of these factors may be important. Feed-grade barleys have a relatively high proportion of corns that have "steely" endosperms, in which the components are very tightly packed, which means that neither water nor enzymes can easily gain access. Malting barleys, however, have more "mealy" endosperms, which distribute water easily and are readily accessed by enzymes.

Steely endosperms *can* be hydrolyzed—it merely takes longer than for mealy grain. Like the Brewer, the Maltster works with tight time frames and ordinarily selects barley varieties of the higher malting grades. Indeed, the Brewer is likely to insist on given varieties. Given the choice of two malts that possess identical analyses, many brewers opt for a variety they know, because unexpected problems might occur with unproven varieties.

New varieties are continually coming into the marketplace as the end product of plant breeding and, with similar rapidity, older varieties disappear. Each variety has its own name, and some rather colorful ones at that! For many years varieties such as Plumage Archer, Maris Otter, and Proctor led the way in the United Kingdom. Their popularity was relatively long-lived in that they were used year after year by Brewers who were convinced of their importance in the brewing of top-quality ales. Indeed there are still a few Brewers who swear by Maris Otter today, and malts made from this variety are very popular with microbrewers in the United States. These days you'll find many more varieties in the United Kingdom, with the likes of Halcyon, Alexis, Chariot, and Optic currying favor. It is extremely unlikely that they will have so long a life as Maris Otter, the current fashion being for change. In the States there are Robust, Morex, Harrington, Moravian, and Galena, among others.

For it to be accepted, a newly bred variety must differ demonstrably from an existing cultivar and possess some advantage over existing ones, for instance higher extractability. Not only must a new malting variety be capable of performing well in the maltings and brewery, it must also possess the necessary properties when growing in the field, such as high yield, disease resistance, relatively short stiff straw of uniform length, and early ripening.

To be accepted for malting, any barley also needs to satisfy other criteria. First of all, it should have a relatively low content of nitrogen, that is, protein. For a given size of grain it is self-evident that the more protein packed within it, the less room there is for other components. In other words, the more protein, the less starch. And it is, of course, the starch in which the Brewer is primarily interested, rather than the high protein content that is needed in feed barley. Generally speaking, nitrogen levels are lower in grain from barley grown on lighter soils. Maltsters specify the nitrogen content of barley, which in turn obliges the farmer to restrict the use of nitrogenous fertilizer. Accordingly, yields of malting barley tend to be lower than for crops grown for feed purposes. To compensate for this, a malting premium is paid for barley that meets the necessary criteria of uniformity in variety and low nitrogen.

Other specifications must be met, too. First and foremost, the barley must be living. If the embryo has been killed—which can occur all too easily, for example, if the barley has been badly dried—then it is incapable of producing the hormones that promote germination. Viability can be quickly checked by a staining test: living embryos cause a colorless tetrazolium dye to turn red.

Even if an embryo is alive, it may still not be capable of immediate germination. This dormant state is quite normal, albeit an irritation to the Maltster. What controls dormancy in plant seeds is not quite known. It tends to vary from variety to variety, and it also depends on environmental factors. The further north a barley is grown, the more it tends to display dormancy. Cool and wet conditions in the growing season promote dormancy. The phenomenon might be an irritation to the Maltster, but it's important to the barley! If dormancy didn't exist, the grain would germinate prematurely on the ear and not at the appropriate stage after leaving the parent plant. It is for this same reason that the phenomenon is actually important to the Maltster, too. In certain climatic conditions, such as high rainfall at certain stages in the growing season, grain can start to chit (sprout) on the ear. When the barley is harvested and dried, then the heat kills the growing embryo and the malting process is jeopardized.

Dormant barley must be stored to allow it to recover from this condition. Various treatments have been recommended for the release of barley from dormancy, including warm storage (for example, 30° C) or, ironically, cold storage! It is certainly the case that a Maltster might almost welcome dormancy if it was a condition that he could switch on or off at will in order to optimize barley purchasing and turnover.

A phenomenon related to dormancy is water sensitivity. All barleys to a greater or lesser extent display this trait, in which germination is inhibited by the presence of too much water. There are various plausible explanations for the effect, the most likely being the role of water in inhibiting the access of oxygen, which the embryo requires to support respiration. Recognition of the phenomenon some 40 or so years ago led directly to the introduction of interrupted steeping regimens in maltings. Previously, barley had been steeped continuously in water. Once it was realized that this would suppress embryo activity by swamping it, procedures were introduced whereby barley is steeped for a shorter period of time, followed by a draining stage and ensuing air rest. Then more steep liquor is applied, followed by another air rest, and so on. The precise regimen is optimized for each variety but seldom takes longer than 48 hours, whereas before the days of interrupted steeping the process took at least twice as long.

Barleys with larger corns are preferred by brewers, as they possess a larger ratio of starch to peripheral tissue (e.g., husk, which can amount to as much as 10% of the weight of the grain).

The reader might suspect that one barley looks very much like another. True, it is difficult to tell them apart, but an expert is able to inspect a handful of grain and pretty much identify the variety by studying things like color of the aleurone (some are white, others are blue), size of the corns, and length of the rachilla and the hairs on it (the rachilla is a remnant of the flowering stage in the development of the barley plant). If the sample is representative of the entire shipment, he will be able to tell whether he is looking at just one variety or a mixture. As barley varieties differ substantially in their performance, it is vital to malt them separately, and the buyer would be entirely justified in rejecting a batch of barley on the basis of visual assessment alone. If further evidence is warranted, a protein fingerprint can be obtained. The proteins of the grain are extracted and separated on gels, across which an electric current is passed. The proteins migrate to different extents on the gels before they are detected by staining. The patterns obtained are a characteristic of the variety (Fig. 4.2). More recently, just as in forensic science, the analogous DNA fingerprinting has been suggested for barley—one might say it's to detect the crime of fraud in barley sales. A visual inspection, though, is generally sufficient, and it also delivers a verdict on whether a barley is free from infection and physical damage. It is easy and rapid and can be performed when the barley is taken into the maltings.

COMMERCIAL MALTING OPERATIONS

There are four basic process stages in a modern malting operation: intake, drying, and storage of barley; steeping; germination; and kilning.

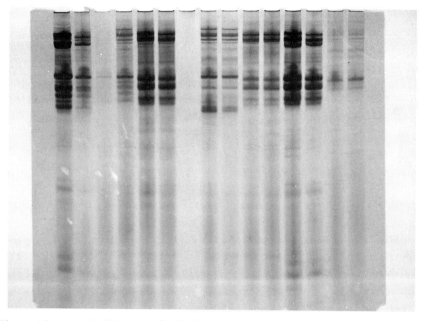

Figure 4.2. A protein "fingerprint" of barley. Proteins are extracted from barley and separated on gels by electrophoresis (the protein mixture is applied to the top of the gel and an electric current is passed through the gel). The various proteins move through the gel to different extents and are located by staining with a dye. Each of the bands seen in this photo represents a different protein, and each of the lanes has had extracts from different barleys applied to it.

Intake, Drying, and Storage of Barley

Barley can be classified into two categories based on time of sowing and harvest. Winter varieties are sown in the fall, whereas spring varieties are sown in spring and harvested a little later than the winter varieties. Generally speaking, the earlier in the year the seed is sown, the lower the protein content in harvested grain (and the higher its yield) because starch accumulates through the entire growing season.

Purchase of grain by the Maltster will be according to an agreed specification, which will include freedom from infection and infestation, nitrogen content, grain size, viability, and moisture content. A typical specification for moisture in a two-row barley in the United Kingdom would be 16%. The farmer will be paid proportionately less for batches of progressively higher water content because the Maltster will be obliged to dry them to an increased extent to prevent spoilage by insects and microorganisms. Most Maltsters don't favor the farmer taking responsibility for drying for fear of destroying the embryo. In many parts of the world, including North America, drying is unnecessary, as the barley is harvested with a sufficiently low moisture content (12% or lower).

The grain arrives at the maltings by road or rail and, as the transport waits, it is weighed and a sample is tested for the key parameters of viability, nitrogen content, and moisture. Expert evaluation also reveals the amount of weed content and whether the grain smells sweet. A few grains may be sliced in half lengthwise and their endosperms assessed as to whether they are mealy or steely. Remember: The Maltster prefers mealy endosperms. Once accepted, the barley is normally cleaned to remove everything from dust and weeds to dead rodents and screened to remove small grain and dust before passing into a silo, perhaps via a drying operation. Drying is seldom at temperatures greater than 55° C, with the grain not getting above 30° C due to the latent heat of evaporation—the heat energy consumed by water to enable it to evaporate. As the water siphons off the heat, the grain remains relatively cool. A continuous throughput of air is used, and drying may be continuous or in a batch operation.

Dry barley may be stored in various locations, ranging from steel- or concrete-framed sheds capable of holding up to 30,000 tons to steel bins holding no more than 750 tons. Whichever facility is used, it is essential to protect the store from the elements, yet also to ventilate it, because barley, like other cereals, is a generous host (see Box). The risk from different pests and diseases differs tremendously between sites and environments. Frequently no protective agents are needed, but it is essential to prevent pockets of infection by organisms such as *Penicillium* and *Aspergillus* and infestations by insects and vermin.

Barley is a hospitable vehicle for a selection of insects, including weevils, the saw-toothed grain beetle, and the quaintly named, but no less undesirable, confused flour beetle. Insecticides, approved for use on the basis of health and safety legislation, have an important role. Like anything else accumulating on the surface of barley, they are washed off during the steeping operation and don't get into the malt used for brewing.

Although successive generations of barley varieties tend to have increased resistance to fungal infection, in certain growth regions systemic fungicides are still needed in the field to prevent the development of diseases such as mildew, eyespot, and take-all. These fungicides, by keeping the barley plant free from disease, help it to produce grain that is

A Selection of Threats to Barley

Diseases

Mildew	*spread by wind from infected plants; infects grain*
Take-all	*spread by root contact; infects roots and base of stem*
Eyespot	*spread by splashing with rain; infects stem*
Fusarium	*spread by root contact; infects grain*
"Rust"	*spread by wind; infects grain*

Pests

Aphids	*cause grain to be shriveled and discolored; carry the barley yellow dwarf virus*
Leatherjackets	*plants eaten away at ground level*
Nematodes	*attack roots*
Rabbits	*nibble seedlings*
Birds	*enjoy grain*

well filled and in good condition for malting. Everybody benefits: the farmer, because he enjoys a high crop yield; the Maltster, because she has good viable, healthy, and fragrant barley to malt; the Brewer, because the malt is uniformly of excellent quality and will "behave well" in the brewery—producing excellent beer in good yield, beer that is free from infectious agents; and the consumer, because she will be purchasing a quality product with no defects that might be traced to the barley, such as a flavor problem or gushing (see Chapter Three).

Only pesticides and fungicides that have been rigorously assessed by legislative authorities and subsequently approved are used. They have received extensive screening for health and safety factors, and the assessment must have demonstrated that they will not damage the barley, the process, or the product.

In the United States pesticide regulations occur at federal (Environmental Protection Agency) and state levels. Furthermore, bodies such as the Food and Drug Administration and the Occupational Safety and Health Administration have a say in what may and what may not be done.

Steeping

The purpose of steeping is to increase the moisture content of the grain from 11% to 12% to 43% to 46% within two days. Grain will not germinate if the moisture content is below 32%. A typical steeping regimen consists of an initial water stage for 6 to 16 hours to raise the moisture content to 33% to 37%. An air rest for 12 to 24 hours follows, during which air is sucked downward through the grain bed to disturb films of moisture on the grain, expose the embryos to oxygen, and remove carbon dioxide produced by respiration, all of which is designed to prevent the embryo from being suffocated. This is followed by a second immersion of 10 to 20 hours, which will bring the moisture to the required level.

Water enters the grain through the micropyle, a small opening at the embryo end of the grain. The surface layers of the grain prevent access of water at any other point unless these tissues have been deliberately damaged (see page 86).

There are no hard-and-fast rules for steeping regimens: They are determined on a barley-by-barley basis by small-scale trials. It must be realized, too, that a barley changes its properties over time. It increases in so-called vigor (the speed of growth essential for malting), which is reflected in enhanced capability for synthesizing enzymes and, therefore, rate of modification of the endosperm. A barley, then, needs to be processed differently in the maltings as the year goes on. In some locations barley is graded according to size before steeping, because different-sized barleys take up moisture at different rates.

A schematic representation of a steeping vessel is shown in Fig. 4.3. Steeping vessels are normally fabricated from stainless steel and most recently have consisted of flat-bottomed ventilated vessels capable of holding as much as 250 tons of barley. The steep water (or liquor, as it is referred to in many parts of the world) is either from a well, where it is likely to have a relatively constant temperature within the range 10° to 16°C, or from a city water supply, in which case there may be a requirement for temperature control facilities.

The aim of steeping is to homogeneously distribute water across the entire bed of grain. The first steep water washes a large amount of material off the barley, including dust and leached tannins from the husk. It goes to drain without reuse, and leads to a significant effluent charge.

A range of process aids has been used from time to time to promote the malting operation; generally they have been introduced in a steep or on transfer from steeping to germination. A few Maltsters still employ potassium bromate to suppress the growth of rootlets within the embryo, for such growth is wasteful and can also cause matting, which leads to handling problems. Bromate also suppresses proteolysis. The use of bromate is not permitted in the United States.

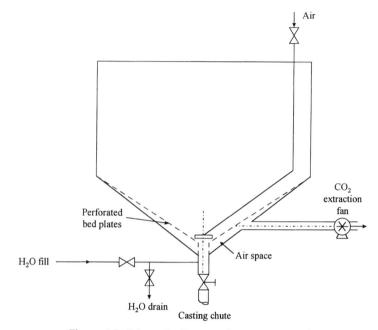

Figure 4.3. Schematic diagram of a steeping vessel.

More frequent is the use of gibberellic acid (GA), obtained from fermentations with the fungus *Gibberella fujikoroi* (see Box). GA is added to supplement the native gibberellins of the grain. Although its use is prohibited by some users of malt, GA can successfully accelerate the malting process. It tends to be sprayed onto grain at levels between 0.1 and 0.5 ppm as it passes from the last steep on its way to the germination vessel. Some Maltsters couple the use of GA with a scarification process, whereby the end of the grain furthermost from the embryo is abraded. This enables water and GA to enter the distal end of the grain, triggering enzyme synthesis and modification in the region that is normally the last part of

Gibberella fujikoroi derives from the Japanese term *foolish seedling* and was so named because infection of rice with this fungus led to bolting and production of very tall plants that tended to fall over. More than 80 gibberellins are known, of which the most frequently employed in malting is GA_3.

the corn to be degraded. Because these events are also being promoted "naturally" by the embryo, the resultant effect is called two-way modification. It is an opportunity to accelerate the germination process and to deal with barleys that are more difficult to modify.

Germination

The aim of germination is to develop enzymes capable of hydrolyzing the cell walls, protein, and starch and to ensure that these soften the endosperm by removing the cell walls and about half of the protein while leaving the bulk of the starch behind.

Traditionally, steeped barley was spread out to a depth of up to 10 cm on the floors of long, low buildings and germinated for periods up to 10 days, with men using rakes to thin out the grain ("the piece") or pile it up, depending on whether the batch needed its temperature lowered or raised. The aim was to maintain it at 13° to 16° C.

Very few floor maltings survive because of their labor intensity. A range of designs of pneumatic (mechanical) germination plants are now used. The earliest such germination vessels were rectangular, fabricated from brick or concrete and known as Saladin Boxes (Figs. 4.4 and 4.5). They are still widely used and generally have a capacity of up to 250 tons. The

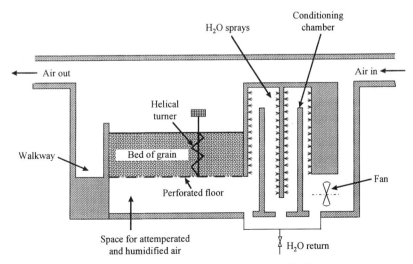

Figure 4.4. Schematic diagram of a Saladin Box.

Figure 4.5. A germination box. (*Photograph courtesy of Pauls Malt.*)

floors of these vessels are made from perforated stainless steel to allow air to pass through the bed of grain. A mechanical turning system, such as a helical screw, is used to turn the grain and prevent matting of the rootlets. Newer germination vessels are circular, of steel or concrete, with capacities as much as 500 tons and are microprocessor controlled (Fig. 4.6). They may incorporate vertical turners located on radial rotating booms, but just as frequently it is the floor itself that rotates against a fixed boom.

The modern malting plant is arranged in a tower format, with vessels vertically stacked and steeping tanks uppermost (Fig. 4.7).

Germination in pneumatic plants generally occurs at 16° to 20° C. In this process some 4% of the dry weight of the grain is consumed to support

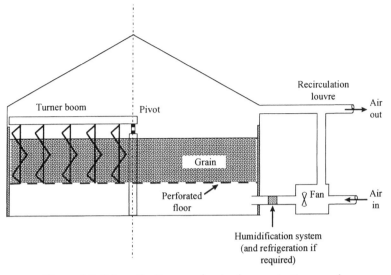

Figure 4.6. Schematic diagram of a circular germination vessel.

the growth of embryonic tissues, and much heat is produced. Dissipating this heat demands the use of large amounts of attemperated air, the oxygen of which is needed by the embryo for respiration; the carbon dioxide produced is flushed away by the air flow.

Take a walk through a malting plant with an experienced maltster and you will see him grab a handful of germinating grain and spread it on the palm of one hand, glance at it, and then rub a few corns between the thumb and first finger. If the whole endosperm is readily squeezed out and if the shoot initials (the acrospire) are about three-quarters the length of the grain, then the green malt is ready for kilning.

Kilning

Kilning dries the malt to such a low level of moisture that it is stabilized, germination is arrested, and enzymatic digestion is halted. The enzymes of the malt, though, must not be destroyed. It is always important that the starch-degrading enzymes survive into malt, for the Brewer needs those to generate fermentable sugars in the mash. Often it is important that the cell wall and protein-degrading enzymes survive, too, because they

Figure 4.7. A tower malting plant. (*Illustration courtesy of Albrew Maltsters.*)

may not have completed their job in the maltings—and they may be needed to deal with proteins and polysaccharides present in nonmalted adjuncts that the Brewer may use in mashing.

Kiln designs vary greatly, but most modern kilns feature deep beds of malt. They may be rectangular, but more frequently they are circular in cross-section and are likely to be made from corrosion-resistant steel. They have a source of heat for warming incoming air, a fan to drive or pull the air through the bed, together with the necessary loading and stripping systems. The grain is supported on a wedge-wire floor that permits air to pass through the bed, which is likely to be up to 1.2 m deep. Figure 4.8 depicts a double-decker kiln, while Figure 4.9 illustrates the loading of a kiln.

Of course, kilning is an extremely energy-intensive operation, so modern kilns incorporate energy conservation systems such as glass tube air-to-air heat exchangers. Energy usage has been halved by such systems, but can still amount to 2.85 gigajoules per ton of malt (see Box).

Newer kilns also use indirect firing, in that the products of fuel com-

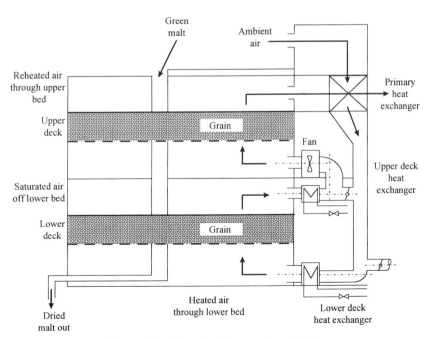

Figure 4.8. Schematic diagram of a malt kiln.

Figure 4.9. Loading a malt kiln. (*Photograph courtesy of Pauls Malt.*)

bustion don't pass through the grain bed but are sent to exhaust, the air being warmed through a heater battery containing water as the conducting medium. Indirect firing arose because of concerns with the possible role of oxides of nitrogen in kiln gases in promoting the formation of nitrosamines in malt.

Although the temperatures used in malt kilning are much higher, the physics of the drying of malt is very similar to that of the drying of barley and, in both cases, are somewhat complicated! There are, in fact, four phases to the drying process (Fig. 4.10).

Stage one consists of free drying. Air flows of up to 6,000 $m^3 min^{-1} t^{-1}$ are used, with the air entering the grain bed at 50° to 60°C (the air-on temperature). At this stage the moisture content of the grain drops readily to approximately 23%. The remaining water is now more resistant to driving off and, indeed, is largely associated with grain components. Because water is not now being easily volatilized and is not keeping the temperature of the bed down by latent heat of evaporation, the temperature of the air leaving the kiln (air-off) starts to rise. The air-on temperature is increased and, at this intermediate stage, moisture in the bed falls to 12%.

Kilning of Malt Consumes a Lot of Energy

James Prescott Joule (1818–1889) might have emulated his dad and become a brewer! Instead he was fascinated by chemistry (he studied in Manchester, England) but soon turned his attention to physics, performing his experiments at home because of severe invalidity. In particular he was interested in the amount of heat that equated to mechanical energy, and in his most famous investigation he studied the extent to which water was warmed by vigorously spinning paddles in it. Joule found that the work done by a 1-pound weight (0.45 kg) falling through a distance of 9 inches (23 cm) raises the temperature of 1 g of water by 1°C. This quantity of work has henceforth been referred to as a joule, which is now the standard unit of heat.

Giga means one billion, so we can see that the kilning of each ton of malt burns up nearly three billion joules. That sounds like a lot, and it is—as a glance at the following table reveals:

Activity	Energy consumed
Playing an hour's tennis	about 1,500,000 joules
Eight hours' very active work	about 7,500,000 joules
Eight hours' sleep	about 2,000,000 joules
Washing dishes for half an hour	about 200,000 joules
Kilning malt	*approximately 100 joules for every grain of barley*

Or, picture it this way: The amount of energy involved in kilning one ton of malt is equivalent to the recommended daily energy intake of 40 men.

All of the water is now bound, the temperature is raised again, and the fan speed is reduced until the water level in the bed is approximately 6%. Finally, we reach the curing phase, designed to lower the moisture to final specification, which is typically 4% or lower. At this stage the air-on temperature may be anything between 75° and 110° C, depending on the type of malt required. Lower temperatures will give malts of lighter color and will tend to be employed in the production of malts destined for lager-style beers. Higher temperatures, apart from giving darker malts, also create a wholly different flavor spectrum. Lager malts give beers that are relatively rich in sulfur compounds, including dimethyl sulfide. Ale malts have more roasted, nutty characters. For both lager and ale malts, kilning

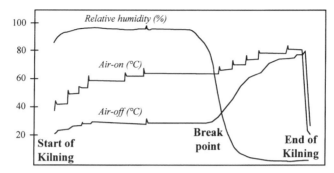

Figure 4.10. Changes in moisture and malt bed temperature during kilning.

is sufficient to eliminate the unpleasant raw, grassy, and beany characters associated with green malt.

When kilning is complete, the heat is switched off and the grain allowed to cool before it is stripped from the kiln in a stream of air at ambient temperatures. On its way to steel or concrete hopper-bottomed storage silos, the malt is "dressed," which involves mechanical removal of dried rootlets (referred to as culms), aspiration of dust, sifting out of loose husk and incomplete kernels, and the elimination of any large contaminants.

Specialty Malts

Some malts are produced not for their enzyme content but for use by the Brewer in relatively small quantities as a source of extra color and distinct types of flavor. They may also be useful sources of natural antioxidant materials. There is much interest in the opportunities these products present for brewing new styles of beer. Table 4.2 describes some of these malts, which are produced in small drum kilns equipped with water sprays—for obvious reasons! Those specialty malts produced with the least extra heating (e.g., cara pils and crystal malt) can be used to introduce relatively sweet, toffeelike characters. Those produced with intense heating (e.g., black malt) deliver intense burnt and smoky notes.

What the Brewer Looks for in a Malt

As the years have unfolded and the links have progressively been established between malt composition, the behavior of a malt in the brew-

Table 4.2. Colored malts

Type	Color (°EBC)	Production regime
Cara pils	15–30	The surface moisture is dried off at 50°C before stewing over 40 minutes with the temperature increase to 100°C, followed by curing at 100°–120°C for less than 1 hour.
Crystal	75–300	As for cara pils, but first curing it at 135°C for less than 2 hours
Chocolate	500–1200	Lager malt is roasted by taking temperature from 75°–150°C over 1 hour, before allowing temperature to rise to 220°C
Black	1200–1400	Similar to chocolate malt, but the roasting is even more intense

Based on C. W. Bamforth and A. H. P. Barclay, *Malting Technology and the Uses of Malt*, eds. Alexander W. MacGregor and Rattan S. Bhatty, St. Paul, Minn., American Association of Cereal Chemists, 1993, pp. 297–354.

ery, and the quality of the finished beer, more and more demands have been placed on the Maltster by the Brewer. There has been a tendency, still prevalent among the traditionalists, for the Brewer to blame the poor old Maltster whenever things go wrong. The trend, too, has been for the Brewer to place more and more specifications on the malt. In many cases, this is rather unfair because the demands are often contradictory. For instance, a Brewer may insist on the malt being well modified, with very little cell wall material surviving while also demanding that it contain very little dimethyl sulfide (DMS) precursor. However, prolonged germination periods, which enable better cell wall breakdown, go hand in hand with high DMS precursor. The Maltster could suppress DMS precursor development by using bromate but, as often as not, the Brewer will stipulate that the malt should be additive-free. Understandably, all this can leave the Maltster in a quandary.

Brewers apply a wide range of specifications to malt. Many Brewers, applying quality assurance principles, look to the Maltster to provide documentation with the malt shipment that details all the required analyses on a batch of malt, certifying that the malt meets the required tolerances. The Brewer will spot check occasional batches. Woe betide the transgressing Maltster! From time to time, too, the Brewer audits the Maltster (as, indeed, he will audit most of his raw material suppliers). I don't believe that there is a Brewer today who applies the sliced bread test for auditing maltings hygiene. Time was when the Brewer would visit the maltings, wipe the inside of a vessel with a piece of bread, and invite the Maltster to eat it for breakfast. Crude certainly, but a powerful incentive for the Maltster to keep the plant spotless! Thankfully, most of the analytical methodology applied to assess malt quality is somewhat more sophisticated than this.

The most important parameter is the hot water extract, which is a measure of the total material that can be solubilized from the malt in a mashing operation. As such, it reflects the extent to which the endosperm is solubilized during germination of barley and also that portion that is released by enzymes during mashing. The higher the value, then potentially the more alcohol that will be derived by the Brewer per unit of malt and the more valuable the malt—if other relevant specifications are met. The hot water extract is typically measured on 50 g of malt, which is milled, mixed with water at 65° C, and stirred for an hour in a beaker. The liquid portion is then filtered off from the spent grains and its specific gravity measured: The higher the specific gravity, the more dissolved material.

Brewers realize, however, that, while material may be readily extracted from a batch of malt in a small-scale test, this may not be the case in a full-scale brewery operation. There are various reasons for this. Most importantly, a batch of malt with a large proportion of relatively under-modified kernels will give large particles after roller-milling, and these particles cannot be readily extracted. Brewers may therefore insist on some measure of modification being applied to the malt. The most common of these involves the fluorochrome calcofluor. A typical procedure is for 50 grains to be embedded in plastic and, literally, partly ground down using the sort of electric sander that you might use in home decorating. This exposes the starchy endosperm, which can be examined longitudinally. Calcofluor, a material originally developed for use in domestic washing powders, is added. Calcofluor can bind to the cellulose fibers in shirts and emit a strong fluorescence, rendering the shirts "whiter than white." Of more interest to the brewer (at least for testing his malt if not for his sartorial elegance) is the fact that the calcofluor also latches on to the β-glucan in the endosperm cell walls of barley. Inspection of a calcofluor-stained sanded malt sample therefore highlights whether the cell walls in the malt have or have not been efficiently removed during germination and with what consistency between corns. High levels of fluorescence indicate high levels of residual wall and associated poor malt extractability.

The small-scale mash used to measure hot water extract is also analyzed for the level of protein it contains, higher levels indicating more
extensive modification. Actually, it is total nitrogen that is measured, not
protein. For many years the nitrogen was measured using a method
developed by Johan Kjeldahl (Fig. 4.11) in 1883 at the Carlsberg Laboratories, a standard procedure for measuring bound nitrogen that has long
since been applied far beyond malting and brewing (see Box). More recently, a safer method, devised by Dumas, has superseded Kjeldahl's
procedure.

More useful to the Brewer than the measure of total soluble nitrogen is
that of free amino nitrogen (FAN)—the level of amino acids in the wort.
Apart from influencing whether a wort will or will not be fermented by
yeast, the FAN levels also influence the extent to which a yeast produces
flavor compounds such as esters, and therefore it affects beer flavor.
Furthermore, if the FAN level is too high, there will be more than enough
for the yeast to use during fermentation. Any FAN left over in beer is a
hazard, because it could make a tasty meal for spoilage organisms.

Figure 4.11. Johan Kjeldahl. (*Reproduced courtesy of Carlsberg, from "The Carlsberg Laboratory
1876–1976."*)

Johan Kjeldahl (1849–1900)

Few names in the world of analytical chemistry are better recognized than that of Kjeldahl. His method for measuring the level of nitrogen contained in all types of sample, notably foodstuffs, became the accepted standard from the time it was first developed in 1883. Nitrogen in this context is not gaseous nitrogen, which occupies some 79% of the earth's atmosphere, but the nitrogen that is a component of chemical compounds. In particular, nitrogen is a key component of two types of substance that comprise the architecture and working elements of living matter, namely proteins and nucleic acids. Indeed, when Maltsters and Brewers refer to the nitrogen content of a barley, malt, or wort they are really using this as a measure of the amount of protein in that sample.

Working at the Carlsberg Laboratories, which he joined on May 1, 1875, Kjeldahl developed a procedure employing the hydrolysis of proteins to release ammonia, which can be readily measured colorimetrically. The more ammonia was released, the more protein was indicated to be present. A standard relationship was demonstrated that showed that the amount of protein equated the amount of nitrogen multiplied by a factor of 6.25. Kjeldahl did research on many other topics, but his name will forever be associated with protein measurement.

Tragically, Kjeldahl suffered from severe depression and exhaustion, which are said to have interfered with his experimental work, yet he was also understood to be the life and soul of many a party.

The wort from the small-scale mash is also used to assess color, generally by measuring the amount of light absorbed at 430 nm, and wort viscosity is also taken as an indicator of potential wort separation and beer filtration problems. High-viscosity liquids flow more slowly.

The level of moisture in a malt is measured by oven drying of the malt itself. The level of various enzymes in the malt may be measured, too. If the hot water extract, viscosity, FAN, and modification form part of the specification, it should seldom be necessary to quote specific enzyme levels, as these parameters will only be within specification if the appropriate starch-, cell wall- and protein-degrading enzymes are present. A Brewer may, however, require a measure of the major cell wall-degrading enzyme, β-glucanase, to confirm that kilning has not been excessive, especially if the malt is to be used as the enzyme source for dealing with adjuncts.

Brewers will specify that the nitrosamine content must be below a certain level (typically less than 1 ppb). As we have seen, it is very likely that a Brewer will place a specification for DMS precursor in lager malts, either a level below 2 ppm if they believe that their lager suffers from the presence of DMS, or 5 to 6 ppm if they believe that DMS in reasonable quantities makes a positive contribution to lager flavor.

*   *   *

DMS, as we have seen, is just one of the flavors of beer that can originate in malt. Rather more flavor is contributed by yeast, as we shall see in Chapter Six. When most people think of beer flavor, however, they automatically summon up a picture of hops. It's time for us to do the same.

Chapter Five

THE WICKED AND PERNICIOUS WEED

Hops

When many people consider beer, they automatically think of hops. Many misguided people believe it is hops alone that are the basic raw materials for making beer and that all the alcohol and flavor in beer flows from them. Of course, it is the starch in malted barley and adjuncts that serves as the fermentation feedstock that yeast uses to make alcohol. Hops are simply a flavoring material, albeit one that has other key impacts on beer and brewing. However, as we shall see (and have seen in Chapter Three), the chemistry of hops and hopping is anything but simple.

THE HISTORY OF HOPS

Hops were cultivated in Babylon as far back as 200 A.D., but the earliest reference to hops in Europe is to a garden in the Hallertau in the year 736. Not until 1079 do we hear of hops being used to make beer. Indeed beers at that time were flavored with all manner of herbs, including rosemary, yarrow, coriander, and bog myrtle, which were added in mixtures known as *gruit*. The use of caraway, pepper, pine roots, spruce, potato leaves, and tobacco in beer has been recorded.

It was in the thirteenth century that the hop started to threaten gruit as a flavoring for beers in Germany. "Threaten" is a word I use advisedly, for growers in all countries of the hitherto traditional flavorings fought vigorously against the introduction of hops. The plant was banned from use in the brewing of beer in Norwich, England, in 1471, and in 1519 hops were condemned by the English as a "wicked and pernicious weed."

101

Medieval adherents of ale (a term then restricted to unhopped beer) would also have rebelled, but not necessarily the brewers. The ales to which drinkers were accustomed were strong and sweet—and deliberately so, for high concentrations of sugar and alcohol suppress the growth of the microorganisms that can ruin beer. Hops, though, have strong antiseptic properties. Using them in beer would have enabled brewers to "thin out" the drink and make it weaker. Reynold Scot, writing in 1574, says that "whereas you cannot make above 8–9 gallons of very indifferent ale from a bushel of malt, you may draw 18–20 gallons of very good beer."[1] The first hopped beer wasn't seen in England until 1400, when it was imported from Holland through Winchelsea.

Hops were first grown in southeast England in 1524, 100 years before they were first cultivated in North America. Just as the Yakima Valley in Washington State is famed for its hops, so too is Kent, the Garden of England and the verse runs:[2]

> *Hops, Reformation, Bays and Beer*
> *Came to England in one bad year*

The tirade against hops was relentless. Andrew Boorde wrote in 1542

Bere is made of malte, hoppes, and water; it is the natural drynke for a Ductheman, and nowe of lete days it is much used in England to the detryment of many Englysshe people; specially it kylleth them the which be troubled with the colyke; and the stone and the strangulion; for the drynke is a colde drynke, yet it doth make a man fat, and doth inflate the bely, as it doth appere by the Dutche men's faces and belyes. If the bere be well served and be fyned and not new, it doth qualify heat of the liver.[3]

Not a particularly supportive reference. Happily a somewhat different view of hops and their contribution to beer quality now exists and, these days, very little malt-based beer is devoid of hops. However, the manner by which the unique bitterness and aroma of the plant is introduced into the beverage is often very different than that which was practiced six centuries ago.

A SOLITARY OUTLET

The hop is remarkable among agricultural crops in that essentially its sole outlet is for brewing, apart from a somewhat limited market for its oils in aromatherapy and for whole cones in hop pillows. It is said that if you sleep on such a pillow you will not only sleep well but will also dream about your true love.

Although hopping accounts for much less than 1% of the price of a pint of beer, it has a disproportionate effect on product quality and, accordingly, much attention has been lavished on the hop and its chemistry.

Hops are grown in all temperate regions of the world (Table 5.1). Over 100,000 tons are grown each year, approximately one-third of those in Germany. The United States is the next largest producer, with over 25,000 tons produced from three major sites: Washington, Oregon, and Idaho. Hops are grown in the southern hemisphere as well as the northern, with significant crops in Australia and, to a lesser extent, New Zealand and South Africa.

There are two separate species of hops: *Humulus lupulus* and *Humulus japonicus*. The Romans called hops *Lupus salictarius*, *Lupus* meaning *wolf* and the hop being likened to a wolf among sheep because it grew wild amidst the willow. *H. japonicus* contains no resin and is merely ornamental. Hops for brewing use are *H. lupulus*, which is rich in resins and oils, the former being the source of bitterness, the latter the source of aroma.

The genus *Humulus* is within the family *Cannabinaceae*; a close relative of the hop is *Cannabis sativa*, Indian hemp, better known as marijuana or hashish. A key point of distinction is in their respective resins: Those from

Table 5.1. Production of hops

Country	Hop production*
Germany	35
United States	27
Czech Republic	11
Russia and former states of USSR	9
China	8
England	5
Yugoslavia	4
Poland	2
Australia	2
Japan	2
Spain	2
Romania	2

*Figures are rounded in terms of thousand tons. Total world production was approximately 120,000 tons.

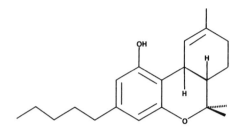

(-)-tetrahydrocannabinol

Figure 5.1. The active ingredient of cannabis resin.

hops (page 113) make beer bitter, those from marijuana (Fig. 5.1) have hallucinogenic effects. I don't advocate smoking either!

CULTIVATION

Hops are hardy climbing herbaceous perennial plants. They are grown in gardens using characteristic string frameworks to support them (Figs. 5.2 and 5.3). Their rootstock remains in the ground year after year and is spaced in an appropriate fashion for effective horticultural procedures (for example, spraying by tractors passing between rows). In recent years, so-called dwarf varieties have been bred, which retain the bittering and aroma potential of traditional hops but which grow to a shorter height (6 to 8 feet as opposed to twice as high). As a result they are much easier to harvest, and there is less wastage of pesticide during spraying. Dwarf hop gardens are also much cheaper to establish, at a typical cost of $2,000–$2,500 which is a third lower than for nondwarf varieties.

Hops are susceptible to a wide range of diseases and pests (see Box). The most serious diseases are *Verticillium* wilt, downy mildew, and mold, with the damson-hop aphid an especially unwelcome visitor. Varieties differ in their susceptibility to infestation and have been progressively selected on this basis. Nonetheless, it is frequently necessary to apply pesticides, which are always stringently evaluated for their influence on hop quality, for any effect they may have on the brewing process and, of course, for their safety. A Brewer will not use hops or hop preparations (or,

Figure 5.2. An English hop garden early in the season.

indeed, any other raw material) unless absolutely convinced that they will be entirely hazard-free for process, product, and consumer.

Some hop-growing regions present more of a problem in terms of diseases and pests than do others. For instance, whereas downy mildew has regularly been of concern in Europe, it has been virtually unheard of in the United States since it was first observed in 1909 in hop gardens on the East Coast. The hop-growing business subsequently shifted to the opposite coast, where the disease was unheard of until 1997, when in excess of

Figure 5.3. Harvesting hops.

Diseases and Pests in Hops

Downy mildew is due to a fungus, *Pseudoperonospora humuli*. The disease is rapidly transmitted between parts of plants and separate plants. Infection may prevent the development of cones and, where cones do develop, may reduce the yield of the α-acid precursors of bitter compounds. Infected stock must be burnt; mycelia may persist in rootstock and demand attention in subsequent years.

Hop mold is caused by the fungus *Sphaerotheca macularis*, which reveals itself as red patches on leaves and cones. One effective treatment involves spraying with sulfur.

The third fungal disease of hops, wilt, is due to *Verticillium albo-atrum*. This infestation can spread rapidly and demands urgent attention if it is to be contained. For instance, in the United Kingdom, growers are legally required to report the discovery of wilt immediately. Infection demands the burning of plants and infected rootstock. Small wonder that hop growers are extremely cautious about allowing outsiders to visit their gardens.

The most significant pest infecting hops is the hop-fly, more commonly referred to as the damson-hop aphid because its eggs spend the winter in the bark of the damson (or sloe or plum), with the hatched flies subsequently migrating to the hop.

50% of the hop crop in the Yakima Valley in Washington succumbed to downy mildew.

The components of the hop required by the Brewer—the resins and the oils—are located in the cones of female plants (Fig. 5.4). More particularly, they are found in the lupulin glands, which are alongside the seeds at the base of the bracteoles (Fig. 5.5).

Internationally, there are different preferences for seeded as opposed to unseeded hops. In the United Kingdom, male plants are included alongside female plants, leading to fertilization and seed levels of up to 25%. Hops are perennial, however, and can be propagated from cuttings, so unfortunately for the male of the species, his services can be readily dispensed with. Indeed, in the rest of Europe and the United States (with some exceptions in Oregon), male hops are not planted, and the hops supplied for brewing are seedless. On a weight-by-weight basis the content of resin and oil is greater in seedless hops, but horticultural yield is lower. It is believed by some that seedless hops make for easier downstream processing of beer.

A typical hop-grower's year in the hop-growing district of Yakima, Washington, begins in March with some shallow plowing to lower the weed count and to mulch into the ground residual leaves and vines from the previous crop, as well as some fertilizer. In the following month, the wirework is established on 3 m wooden poles at a spacing of 2 m × 2 m prior to training new shoots from the rootstock onto the strings. In June, plowing is undertaken to control weeds, and spraying occurs in July and August to control pests. Harvest commences in mid-August and lasts for a month.

Hops are harvested within a similar time span in the Kent and Hereford-and-Worcester hop gardens of England, but through the month of September. Traditionally this has been a most labor-intensive operation, demanding short-term labor bussed in from the city, but now machine picking is universally employed.

The principles underlying the drying of hops are similar to those for barley and malt (see Chapter Four). Drying was traditionally performed in oasthouses (Fig. 5.6). In the late twentieth century these charming buildings are far more likely to be employed as homes than for drying hops, which these days takes place in modern kilns. Using temperatures between 55° and 65° C, the moisture content is reduced from 75% to 9%. Traditionally in the United Kingdom hops are delivered to the Brewer compressed in jute (now polypropylene) sacks about 7 feet deep. These are

Figure 5.4. Hop cones.

Figure 5.5. Inside a hop cone. The central axis, like a stem, is called the strig, attached to which are the bracteoles. The paler regions, where the bracteoles meet the strig, are the lupulin glands where the resins are located. (*Photograph courtesy of Horticulture Research International.*)

called *pockets*, and each holds approximately 75 kg [or one-and-a-half Zentners, for the Zentner (50 kg) is the traditional unit for quantifying the weight of hops]. In the United States, hops are packed into bales measuring 20 × 30 × 57 inches, and weighing 200 pounds (91 kg or 1.8 Zentners). As we shall see, though, the use of hop cones without some form of modification is now rare.

HOP ANALYSIS

As for all raw materials used in the brewing process, the specifications applied to hops must be met if a transaction is to be conducted between the hop merchant and the Brewer. It is fair to say that hop analysis remains somewhat more primitive than the analysis of other brewery ingredients. Many of the assessment criteria for hop quality depend on noninstrumental judgment by experts. First, the sample of hops is inspected visually for signs of deterioration, infestation, or weathering. Then the assessor rubs a sample between the palms of her hands before sniffing the contents. She is looking for any smells associated with deterioration and, just as impor-

Figure 5.6. An oasthouse. (*Photograph courtesy of Tim Bailey.*)

tantly, is determining whether the "nose" is consistent with that which is expected from the variety in question.

The prime quantitative parameter upon which hop transactions are made in the United Kingdom is the lead conductance value. Lead acetate is added to an extract of hop resins in methanol, and the conductivity of the mixture is measured. The lead ions react with the resin α-acids (which are the precursors of the bitter compounds). Once all of the lead has complexed and surplus lead is present, the conductivity starts to increase. The more lead acetate needs to be added before the conductivity increases, the more α-acid is present. In the United States α-acids are measured spectrophotometrically; the extent to which an extract of hops absorbs ultraviolet light indicates the amount of resins present.

TYPES OF HOPS

There is an increasing tendency to classify hops into two categories: aroma hops and bittering hops. In reality they are merely variations on a theme. All hops are capable of providing both bitterness and aroma. Some hops, however, such as the Czech variety Saaz, have a relatively high ratio of oil to resin, and the character of the oil component is particularly prized. Such varieties command higher prices and are known as *aroma varieties*. They are seldom used as the sole source of bitterness and aroma in a beer; a cheaper hop with higher α-acid content (a *bittering variety*) is used to provide the bulk of the bitterness, with the prized aroma variety added late in the boil to contribute its own unique blend of oils. Those Brewers requiring hops solely as a source of bitterness may well opt for a cheaper variety, ensuring its use early in the kettle boil so that bitterness is maximized and unwanted aroma is driven off.

Brewers show fierce loyalty to one or a few of the many varieties of malting barley, and they approach hop selection with equal seriousness. In some countries one variety prevails, as in Australia, where Pride Of Ringwood has held center stage for many years. This situation can be compared with that in the United States, where a bittering variety, Cluster, has been in use since 1800, but aroma varieties like Mount Hood have emerged only in the last 10 years. The U.S. market is an interesting mix of modern and traditional, for prized aroma varieties like the English Fuggles and German Tettnang have been in use for over a century.

The history of Fuggles is a good example of the pressures that drive the hop market. It was introduced in Kent in 1875, and a half century ago it accounted for 75% of the English hop crop. Its problem is an acute susceptibility to *Verticillium* wilt. Breeding programs have delivered just one variant of Fuggles (Progress) that shows a sufficiently improved resistance. Accordingly, programs have sought other varieties with the necessary blend of quality and disease resistance characteristics. As yet, no single variety displays a comprehensive resistance to all hop diseases along with high bitterness potential and good aroma.

The most famed hop-growing region is the Hallertau, to the north of Munich, Germany, where a hop garden was first reported in the year 736. Western Czechoslovakia, a region known as Bohemia, is also feted for its hops. "Good" King Wenceslas introduced the death penalty for anyone who exported hop cuttings from Bohemia!

HOP CHEMISTRY

Hops contain a range of chemical species, including cellulose and lignin as structural components, proteins, lipids and waxes, oils, and tannins. We need consider only two of these constituents: the resins and the essential oils.

Resins

The resin fraction of the hop consists of several components. The chemistry is rather complex, but most Brewers consider only one type of component as significant: the α-acids. These molecules, also known as the humulones, can account for as little as 2% of the dry weight of the hop or as much as 15%. Clearly a high-α variety, such as Target in the United Kingdom or Nugget in the United States, is a richer source of bitterness. Less is needed to impart a given bitterness level to beer, but it also makes a proportionately lower contribution of the essential oils, that is, less aroma potential. Conversely, a low-α hop such as Fuggles or Tettnang is needed in larger proportions to afford a desired bitterness, which leads to greater potential aroma delivery. It is used at the risk of introducing other undesirable materials, such as the tannins, which promote haziness in beer.

α-Acid structure is shown in Fig. 5.7, which also shows the three amino acids (valine, leucine, and isoleucine) from which the α-acids are synthesized in the growing hop. You will note that there are three variants of the acids (cohumulone, humulone, and adhumulone), differing ever so slightly in the structure of the side-chain, which comes off the ring in the top right-hand corner. These differences reflect directly the structure of the three precursor amino acids. Received wisdom contends that better hops have a relatively low proportion of cohumulone.

When wort is boiled in the kettle (see Chapter Six), the α-acids are rearranged to form iso-α-acids in a process referred to as *isomerization* (Fig. 5.8). The products are much more soluble than the humulones and are more bitter. At the end of boiling, any unisomerized α-acid is lost with the spent hop material, and the iso-α-acids remain. The process is not particularly efficient, with perhaps no more than 50% of the α-acids being converted in the boil and less than 25% of the original bittering potential surviving into the beer. Each iso-α-acid exists in two forms, *cis* and *trans*, which differ in the orientation of the side chains (Fig. 5.8). The six iso-α-

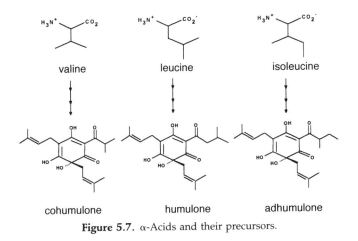

Figure 5.7. α-Acids and their precursors.

acids differ in the quality and intensity of their bitterness (see Chapter Three).

Essential Oils

The oil component of hops ranges from just 0.03% to 3% of the weight of a hop. Seedless hops tend to contain more essential oil. The oils are

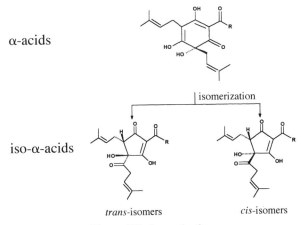

Figure 5.8. Isomerization.

produced in the hop late in ripening, after the majority of the resin has been laid down, which highlights the need for harvesting hops at the appropriate time.

The oil is a complex mixture of at least 300 compounds. Nobody can yet claim to have established a clear relationship between the chemical composition of the essential oils and the unique aroma characteristics they deliver. The science is enormously complicated, as a glance at the sorts of compound that contribute to hop aroma will prove (Fig. 5.9). It is most likely that *late hop character* (i.e., that aroma associated with lagers from mainland Europe, which is introduced by adding a proportion of the hops late in the boil) is due to the synergistic action of several oil components, perhaps modified by the action of yeast in the ensuing fermentation. *Dry hop character* (a feature associated with traditional English cask ales, afforded by adding a handful of whole hop cones to the vessel) is no less complicated. Generally, it would be held that myrcene, the major hydrocarbon component, is an undesirable feature of the oil, whereas compounds such as linalool and geraniol, which are present in far lower concentrations, offer attractive aroma notes. To a greater or lesser extent the individual essential oil components are lost from wort during boiling. The delivery of a given hop character, then, depends on the skill of the brewster in adding the hops at exactly the right time to ensure survival of

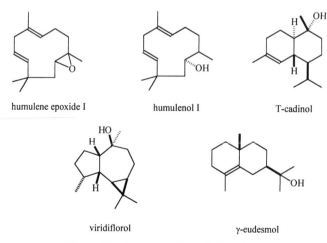

Figure 5.9. Some essential oils from hops.

the right mix of oils that imparts a given character to her product. No instrumental method is available as yet to assist in this process.

HOP PREPARATIONS

The use of whole cone hops is comparatively rare nowadays. The most common procedure for hopping is to add hops that have been hammer-milled and then compressed into pellets. In this form they are more stable, more efficiently utilized, and they do not present the Brewer with the problem of separating out the vegetative parts of the hop plants.

Nevertheless, because of the inefficient utilization of the α-acids during wort boiling, even from pellets, and as a result of vagaries in the introduction of defined hoppy aromas into beers, a wide selection of hop preparations has reached the marketplace. We can actually trace proposals for making hop extracts back to 1820, when lupulin glands were extracted with lime, alcohol, and ether! These days extracts are mostly based on the prior extraction of hops with liquid or supercritical carbon dioxide.

Over 25 years ago, the Brewing Industry Research Foundation (now Brewing Research International, my own organization) first showed that the resins and oils of hops could be extracted by using as a solvent carbon dioxide that has been liquefied at high pressure and low temperature. The resultant extracts can be fractionated into resin- and hop oil-rich fractions, with the resin portion added to the kettle as a source of bitterness in place of whole hops or pellets and the oil part providing an opportunity for controlled addition of hop character, either by dosing late in the boil for a late hop character or into the finished beer for a dry hop note.

It is possible to carry out the isomerization of the α-acids in the liquid CO_2 extracts by chemical means or by the use of light. The resultant pre-isomerized extracts can be used to add bitterness directly to the finished beer, which makes far better use of the bitter compounds because the extent of isomerization of α-acids is greater and because bitter substances are no longer lost by sticking onto yeast cells. A sizable quantity of beer, worldwide, has its bitterness introduced in this way.

Recent years have been marked by an enormous increase in the use of such preisomerized extracts after they have been modified by a process known as reduction. One of the side chains on the iso-α-acids is susceptible to cleavage by light; it then reacts with traces of sulfide materials in beer to produce methyl butene thiol (MBT), a substance that imparts an intensely unpleasant skunky character to beer. If the side chain is reduced, it no longer produces MBT. For this reason, beers that are destined for packaging in green or clear glass bottles are often produced using these modified bitterness preparations, which have the added advantage of possessing increased foam-stabilizing and antimicrobial properties.

Late hop aroma can be introduced through the use of extracts, too. It has been shown that the essential oils can be split into two fractions, one of which is spicy and the other floral. By adding them to bright beer in different proportions it is possible to impart different late hop characters, again offering tremendous opportunities for new product development. This mechanism makes it possible to introduce, under controlled conditions, a range of flavor characteristics and potentially to create a selection of different products by downstream adjustment of a single base beer.

*   *   *

We can see that the extraction of hops to make products such as preisomerized extracts, reduced iso-α-acids, and late hop essences has introduced enormous opportunities for a Brewer. Each of these materials is added as late as possible in the process. Still, though, most of the hopping of beers is carried out in the brewhouse, which is where we turn now.

ENDNOTES

1. Reynold Scot, *A Perfite Platforme for a Hoppe Garden, London: 1574,* as quoted in H. S. Corran, *A History of Brewing,* Newton Abbott: David & Charles, 1975, p. 45.
2. Ibid, p. 53.
3. A. Boorde, *Compendyous Regyment or Dyetary of Health,* London, 1542.

Chapter Six

COOKING AND CHILLING

The Brewhouse

The production of beer can be conveniently split into a hot end and a cold end. The former takes place in the brewhouse (Fig. 6.1), the latter in the fermentation cellar and all points downstream therefrom. Strictly speaking, *brewing* is what happens in the brewhouse and is a process designed to convert malt and any adjunct materials into a liquid called *wort*, which forms the feedstock that yeast converts into alcohol. Traditionally (and still extensively) it is in the brewhouse that the hops are introduced into the process.

CHEMISTRY AND BIOCHEMISTRY IN THE BREWHOUSE

Wort requires various features. First, it must contain sugars that the yeast is capable of fermenting into alcohol. These sugars are the energy source that the yeast needs to support its growth. It is not a question of any old sugars: The balance of different types can profoundly affect the way that a yeast performs and the efficiency with which it converts them into alcohol. Moreover, the type of sugar influences the balance of flavor compounds that the yeast produces and, therefore, the flavor of the beer.

Second, the yeast requires from wort the building blocks that it will use to synthesize its proteins. These are the amino acids and peptides (usually referred to as free amino nitrogen, or FAN), which in turn are produced during malting and mashing by the breakdown of barley proteins. Once more, they must be in balance. The relative proportion of the

117

Figure 6.1. A modern brewhouse. This is the brewhouse at Morland PLC, Abingdon, Oxfordshire, England. The brew length (that is, the size of a "run" through the brewhouse) is 240 U.K. barrels (equivalent to 279 U.S. barrels). (*Photograph courtesy of Briggs of Burton, who installed the brewhouse.*)

different amino acids influences yeast behavior, as does the relative balance of sugars to amino acids.

The balance of sugars and FAN is determined by what happens in the brewhouse. It is also within the brewhouse that the brewer establishes the right salt balance in the wort, whether or not the wort will contain the necessary levels of sulfur and other elements that the yeast depends on, and whether the beer will contain the necessary levels of foaming materials. And it is here that a range of undesirable materials is eliminated, including unpleasant flavors and materials that can promote turbidity in beer.

With the development of products such as preisomerized hop extracts, it is no longer the case that bitterness is necessarily determined in the brewhouse, although this is still the practice in a great many breweries. Color, too, can be modified downstream, but for as long as the brewhouse is a standard feature of brewery operations, it will have a major impact on all aspects of downstream performance and product quality.

We are about to embark on a simple description of the enzymic processes involved in mashing (which have to some extent already begun in malting). Appendix One may prove useful to those for whom enzymology is a mystery.

The Breakdown of Starch

As we have seen in Chapter Four, efficient brewhouse operation generally requires a malt to have its cell walls comprehensively degraded, as well as perhaps half of its protein. It is essential, however, for the bulk of the starch within the endosperm to survive, for it is this that the brewster will be using as a source of fermentable sugar to feed her yeast. The remarkable fact is that this is seldom a problem and that starch by and large does survive the malting process, even though the enzymes needed to disrupt it are plentiful. This tells us that starch is a relatively tough nut to crack. If it is to be broken down in the relatively short time frames available to a Brewer (frequently no more than an hour in the mash), then it must first be gelatinized. When starch granules are heated, the molecules of which they are composed "melt," and the granular structure disaggregates. This melting occurs at different temperatures, depending on the origin of the starch. Barley starch exists in two populations: large granules, which are generally between 15 and 20 μm in size (a micrometer is a thousandth of a millimeter), and small granules, which are less than 6 μm in diameter. Although there are 5 to 10 times more small granules than large ones, the latter account for more than 85% of the total starch by weight. The large granules gelatinize at 58° to 62° C, whereas the temperature must be raised to 68° C to melt the smaller granules. If the small granules are not degraded, they cause substantial problems for the brewer. In practice they don't survive in significant quantities into a well-modified malt, showing that despite their higher gelatinization temperature they are more readily consumed in germination.

To achieve gelatinization, then, mashing usually includes a "conversion" stage at 65° C for 50 to 60 minutes. The starch is gelatinized almost immediately, rendering it accessible to attack by the amylase enzymes, which rapidly hydrolyze it.

Rice starch gelatinizes over the range 64° to 78° C and corn starch at 62° to 74° C. These cereals, if they are used as adjuncts in the brewery, must therefore be "cooked," and the brewhouse that uses them will have a cereal cooker alongside the mash vessel. Wheat starch gelatinizes at temperatures similar to barley starch, and therefore wheat flour can be used directly in the mash.

Within the starch granules there are two other populations of starch: amylose and amylopectin. Both of these molecules are polymers of glucose units linked together in chains. They differ in that amylose, which is typically 25% to 30% of the total starch, is a straight chain of perhaps 1,800 glucoses, whereas amylopectin has branch points. The significance of this is that they require different enzymes to chop them up.

The major starch-degrading enzyme in malt is α-amylase. It's very similar to the enzyme found in human saliva; indeed, in some societies, fermentation of alcoholic beverages starts with the starch being digested by a generous donation of saliva from the brewer. I'm not aware of any beer brewers presently applying the technique! α-Amylase attacks at random in the middle of the amylose and amylopectin, releasing some small sugars but primarily short-chain molecules called *dextrins*. The next enzyme is the β-amylase, which starts at one end of the dextrin molecules, chopping off two glucoses at a time. (Two glucoses joined together represent the sugar maltose, so-named because it is the major sugar found in mashed malt.)

With amylose, the combined action of these two amylases leads to a mixture of sugars that is completely fermentable. Such is not the case with amylopectin. Its branch points are not chopped up by either of these amylases and, when β-amylase encounters them, it can't get past them. A third enzyme is needed, one whose role is to hydrolyze the branches. It is called *limit dextrinase*, but it is only produced late in the germination process. Moreover, it is bound up with other components of malt, which limits its activity. The outcome is that conventionally mashed malt doesn't produce a totally fermentable wort, with perhaps 20% of the sugar being tied up in a dextrin form. Most beers worldwide contain residual dextrin for this reason, and the belief is that these dextrins contribute to the body of beer. The so-called diet or lite beers, however, contain no residual sugar. The brewer will have added heat-stable enzymes (from microbial sources such as *Aspergillus*, a food-grade organism used, for example, in brewing sake) that are capable of chopping up the branch points in amylopectin. As a result of the combined efforts of the malt-derived and the exogenous enzymes, all of the starch is converted into fermentable sugar.

Some of the low-alcohol beers in the market, containing perhaps 1% to 2% alcohol by volume, are produced using a technique called high-temperature mashing. If the malt is mashed at a higher than normal temperature, say 72° C, then the β-amylase is quickly destroyed, and far less maltose is produced in the wort. Most of the starch is converted only as far as nonfermentable dextrins, so the resultant wort contains much less sugar convertible by yeast into alcohol.

The Breakdown of Cell Walls

Most Brewers look to the Maltster to provide them with malt that has had its cell walls comprehensively removed. In practice this is seldom the case: There is always some cell wall material remaining, either intact or partially degraded, and this can cause problems.

The cell walls of barley contain two major polysaccharides: the β-glucans and the pentosans. The former, which account for some 75% of the wall, is a straight-chain polymer of glucose, just like amylose. The difference is in the way that the glucoses are joined together. This means that the properties of β-glucans and starch are very different and also that a totally distinct set of enzymes is needed to break down the two materials. Pentosan is also a sugar polymer, but this time the backbone is a chain of xylose units and side chains consisting of another sugar, arabinose.

It is generally believed that the pentosans don't get substantially degraded during malting, and neither do they get extracted into wort during mashing. It is the β-glucans about which the Brewer is paranoid.

The β-glucan molecule gives very viscous solutions. If it is not broken down in malting or mashing, it will be extracted into wort to cause all manner of problems for the Brewer because of the viscosity effect: It will slow the rate at which the wort can be separated from the spent grains (see page 128) and, because it will survive fermentation intact, it will get into beer and greatly reduce rates of beer filtration. As beer is filtered around 0° C and viscosity increases as temperature is lowered, this is a particular problem. Not only this, but the solubility of β-glucan is reduced as the temperature falls. If this material survives into beers, there is the risk that sediment will form in beers stored in refrigerators. This is a particular problem with stronger beers: Because they contain more alcohol, they are likely to have been made from more concentrated worts (in other words, more malt per unit volume). In turn, this greater malt contribution will yield higher levels of molecules such as β-glucans to the beer. The situation is compounded further by the fact that alcohol itself acts as a precipitant, increasing the likelihood that the β-glucan will collect in the bottom of the bottle as a fluffy sediment.

The most important enzyme from malt that degrades this trouble-some polymer is β-glucanase. It is produced in ample quantities early on in germination and, providing it gets distributed through the starchy endo-sperm in malting, it is capable of removing most of the β-glucan. Most, but not all. The major problem with this enzyme is that it is extremely sensitive to heat. At 65° C (the temperature used to gelatinize starch), this enzyme is totally destroyed in a couple of minutes. For this reason many Brewers commence their mashing operation at a relatively low temperature (say 50° C) to enable the β-glucanase to act and then, after 20 minutes or so, the temperature is ramped up to 65° C. Alternatively, a heat-resistant food-grade β-glucanase, perhaps from *Bacillus subtilis* or *Penicillium funicu-losum*, can be added at the conversion temperature.

The Breakdown of Protein

Just as for cell walls, it is the malting operation that is most significant for protein hydrolysis (or proteolysis). Unlike the case for β-glucans, the brewster does not want total degradation of protein, for some of the protein is needed to form the backbone of the foam on her beer. However, she does need to generate low-molecular-weight products, primarily the amino acids, which the yeast requires to synthesize its own proteins. Proteolysis is also necessary to get rid of proteins that contribute to haze formation in beer.

Barley contains a range of protein types, broadly classified by their solubility properties. Primarily they can be divided into the water-insoluble, storage proteins called *hordeins*, which are the major storage proteins, and into the water-soluble albumins, among which are the enzymes.

Proteolysis in the context of malting and mashing is primarily in-volved with the degradation of hordeins. Two types of enzyme are in-volved. The proteases attack these proteins in the middle of the molecule, releasing shorter polypeptide chains of amino acids linked together in just the same way the glucose units are linked together in amylose or β-glucan. These shorter chains are then the substrate for a second enzyme, called carboxypeptidase, which starts at one end of the chain, chopping off one amino acid at a time.

Carboxypeptidase is quite heat-resistant, but the proteases aren't. Once again, then, Brewers may start their mash at a lower temperature to deal with protein, as well as β-glucan. This period of mashing is frequently referred to as a *proteolytic stand*.

Water

Malt is only one part of the equation in mashing; the other is water. It, too, must be right. The brewing process demands substantially more water than that which ends up in the beer. Large amounts are needed for cleaning purposes and for raising steam, which is the major heating element in most breweries. Most Brewers have made tremendous steps in reducing their water consumption, but the poor performers may still use as much as 20 liters of water for every liter of beer they produce.

Quite apart from the obvious requirements, such as an absence of taints and of hazardous components and an adherence to all requirements for a potable supply (to satisfy all of which a Brewer may treat all water by procedures such as charcoal filtration and ultrafiltration), the water must have the correct balance of ions. Traditionally, breweries producing top-fermented ales were established in areas such as Burton-on-Trent in England, where the level of calcium in water is relatively high (about 350 ppm). This compares with a calcium level of less that 10 ppm in Pilsen, a place famed for its bottom-fermented lagers. In many places in the world the salt composition of the water (some Brewers call it liquor) is adjusted to match that first used by the monks in Burton in the year 1295. This adjustment process is called Burtonization. Often the Brewer will simply add the appropriate blend of salts to achieve this specification. To match a Pilsen type liquor it is necessary to remove existing dissolved ions from the water by deionization.

Water may originate from the Brewer's own well or from a municipal supply. The former is more likely to have a composition that marries with the nature of the beer brewed in a long-standing brewery.

Calcium in brewing water plays several roles. First of all, it promotes the action of α-amylase. It reacts with phosphate in the malt to lower the pH to the appropriate level for brewing. Also, it precipitates another natural component of malt, oxalic acid, which otherwise would come through into the beer and cause problems such as the blocking of dispense pipes (beer stone). Calcium also promotes the flocculation of yeast.

Two other significant ions contributed by water are chloride and sulfate. They are particularly important for the palate of the finished beer. Sulfate provides dryness to a product, whereas chloride affords body and fullness. Many Brewers specify the chloride-sulfate ratio of their beers.

Adjuncts

A Brewer may substitute a proportion of malt for various reasons, the substitute sources of extract being referred to as adjunct. Some adjuncts are used because they introduce necessary characteristics to a beer. For instance, the intense flavor of Guinness reflects the use of roasted barleys and malts in their grist. At the other extreme, some of the delicate character of Budweiser clearly originates in the rice that it contains. Some Brewers use adjuncts such as wheat flour because they believe they provide foam-enhancing substances to beer.

As often as not, though, adjuncts are employed for reasons of economy: If the unit cost of fermentable carbohydrate is lower in an adjunct than it is from malt, then it makes sense to replace a proportion of the malt, provided it doesn't jeopardize any element of product quality, notably flavor. Some Brewers use corn products in the brewhouse. As we have seen, corn and rice starch have higher gelatinization temperatures than does barley starch and they will need to be cooked. Most commonly, hydrolyzed corn syrup or sucrose, both of which comprise ready-formed sugars that don't require an enzymatic stage in the brewhouse, are used to supplement wort at the boiling stage in the kettle. In all cases the brewer must perform his calculations carefully: If an adjunct is intended simply as a cheaper source of extract, it mustn't be forgotten that the additional processing costs for handling a more intransigent material may offset any potential savings.

In the United States adjunct usage is some 38% of the total grist bill. Almost half of the adjuncts used are corn grits, and just under a third is rice. Syrups and sugars amount to just over a fifth of the total. In the United Kingdom, malt usage is higher, at some 80% of the total grist. Hydrolyzed corn syrup is the most frequently used adjunct in the United Kingdom.

THE BREWHOUSE

Milling

Most frequently, malt is ground using roller mills, with the malt being passed through one, two, or three pairs of rollers. The aim is to produce a particle distribution that is best suited to that particular brewhouse and for the type of malt used. For example, if the husk of the malt is required as a filter bed for the separation of the wort, it will be necessary to have a setup that enables survival of this tissue while milling the starchy endosperm to a consistency fine enough to allow easy access of water for its solvation. If the malt is relatively well modified, it will need less intense milling than would a relatively undermodified malt to generate the same particle size distribution.

Generally speaking, the more rolls there are on a mill, the greater will be its flexibility. The Brewer will inspect the milled grist, using a sieve to screen it into its various-sized components; the roll settings will be adjusted if its particle distribution is felt to be suboptimal.

Some Brewers employ wet milling, in which the malt is steeped in water before milling begins. It is believed that the hydration of the husk lessens the risk of its damage during milling. Increasingly common is the use of hammer-milling, but only with modern mash separation processes such as the mash filter, which don't require the husk as a filter bed.

Mashing

Mashing is the enzymatic stage of the brewhouse operation. The milled malt is mixed intimately with the water, which enables enzymes to start acting. Essential requirements of this stage are the efficient hydration of particles and careful control over times and temperatures. It is by manipulating these factors that the Brewer is able to influence the efficiency with which the malt is extracted.

Modern mashing vessels (still sometimes called *mash tuns* or *mash mixers*) are fabricated from stainless steel. This is the norm for all brewery vessels, as it makes for robustness and for ready cleaning by *cleaning-in-place* (CIP) systems. To achieve intimate mixing of the milled solids and the water, the milled grist and the hot liquor are mixed on their way into the mash conversion vessel (Fig. 6.2). Mixing within the mash vessel (Fig. 6.3)

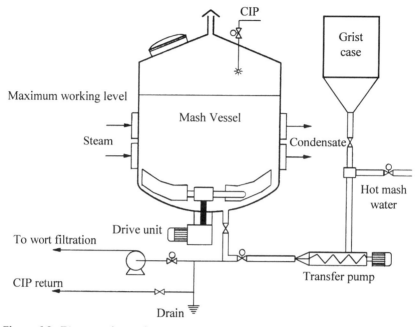

Figure 6.2. Diagram of a mash conversion vessel. (*Drawing courtesy of Briggs of Burton.*)

is provided by rousers. It isn't simply a matter of thrashing the mixture about. On the one hand, excessive physical damage to particles slows down the subsequent wort separation stage and leads to unacceptably turbid worts, and on the other it causes far greater uptake of air into the mash. It is now realized that this can promote staling of the beer.

Modern mash mixers are jacketed, with steam being used to heat up the contents of the vessel. As we have seen, mashing may commence at a relatively low temperature (say 45°C) to enable the more heat-sensitive enzymes such as β-glucanase to do their work. Once this rest is complete, the steam is turned on to bring up the temperature, perhaps at 1°C per minute, to that required for gelatinization of starch.

Typical practice may be to introduce a proportion of water, sufficient to cover the agitator, into the mash tun before running in the grist/liquor mix via the premasher. Grist entry is likely nowadays to happen near the base of the vessel, to minimize oxygen uptake. Various additions may be made. For instance, certain salts may be added if there is a need to adjust the chloride-sulfate balance. Calcium may be added to lower the pH of the mash (see Appendix One): Ideally a mash should be of pH 5.4 to 5.6 for

Figure 6.3. Inside a mash conversion vessel. The agitator is designed to ensure efficient and homogeneous mixing. (*Photograph courtesy of Briggs of Burton.*)

the appropriate balance to be struck between the various reactions that are occurring. Alternatively, acids may be used directly or introduced indirectly; for instance, in Germany lactic acid bacteria (named for their main excretion product) are used to "naturally" acidify mashes. Extra enzymes may be introduced, most often a heat-resistant β-glucanase to supplement the more sensitive enzyme from malt.

Cereal cookers used to gelatinize the starch in certain adjuncts are operated analogously to mash tuns, though of course the temperatures employed are higher.

Wort Separation

Once the enzymes have completed their job in the mash, it is time to separate the resultant wort from the residual (spent) grains. In many ways this is the most skilled part of the brewing operation. The aim is to produce a wort referred to as bright—in other words, one not containing lots of insoluble particles, which may present great difficulties later on. The challenge is to achieve this without sacrificing wort, thereby limiting yields. Furthermore, this has to be achieved within a limited time period, for a Brewer will want to put several brews through his brewhouse each day.

The majority of breweries in the world use a lauter tun for this purpose (Fig. 6.4). In newer brewhouses, though, you are likely to find a mash filter.

The science of wort separation is fascinating and is based on an equation developed by Darcy:

$$\text{rate of liquid flow} = \frac{\text{pressure} \times \text{bed permeability} \times \text{filtration area}}{\text{bed depth} \times \text{wort viscosity}}$$

Fundamentally, this means that the wort will be recovered more quickly if the vessel used for separation has a large surface area and is shallow (i.e., the distance through the bed is short). Low viscosities (i.e., low β-glucan levels) help, as does the application of pressure. The "permeability" depends on the particle characteristics of the bed. The best

Figure 6.4. A lauter tun. (*Photograph courtesy of Briggs of Burton.*)

analogy is sand and clay. Sand consists of relatively large particles, whereas the particles of clay are far smaller. To pass through clay, water has to take a far more circuitous route than it does through sand. Thus big particles tend to present less of an impediment to liquid flow than do small ones. At the end of mashing and during sparging, relatively high temperatures (e.g., 76° to 78°C) are maintained. In part this is because of the inverse relationship between temperature and viscosity, but it is also known that smaller particles agglomerate to form larger ones at higher temperatures.

Lauter Tun. Generally the lauter tun is a straight-sided round vessel with a slotted or wedged wire base and run-off pipes through which the wort is recovered. Additionally, within the vessel there are arms that can be rotated about a central axis (Fig. 6.5). These arms carry vertical knives that are used, as appropriate, to slice through the grains bed and facilitate runoff of the wort. The brewer first runs hot liquor (at about 77°C) into the vessel so that it rises to an inch or so above the false bottom. This ensures that no air is trapped under the plates, and it also serves to cushion the

Figure 6.5. The gear inside a lauter tun. (*Photograph courtesy of Briggs of Burton.*)

mash. The mash is then transferred carefully from the mash tun to the bottom of the vessel, again to minimize oxygen uptake, and the knives are used to ensure that the bed is even. Hot liquor is used to rinse out the mash tun and delivery pipes. The depth of the grain bed is unlikely to be more than 18 inches (see the Darcy equation above).

After a rest of perhaps 30 minutes, the initial stage is to run off from the base of the vessel and recycle this wort into the vessel, so it can be clarified. After 10 to 20 minutes of this so-called vorlauf process, the wort is diverted to the kettle and wort collection proper is started. This wort is at its most concentrated.

The remainder of the process is an exercise in running off as concentrated a wort as possible within the time frame available. More hot (77° C) liquor (the sparge) is sprayed onto the grains to ensure that the sugars and other dissolved materials are not left trapped in the spent grains. The knives are used as sparingly and carefully as possible so as not to damage grains and thereby make small particles that will clog the system or render the wort turbid or dirty.

Another factor that the brewster must consider is the strength of the wort that is needed in the fermenter. If she is intending to brew a very strong beer, then clearly the wort must be rich in sugars. This limits the amount of sparge liquor that can be used in the lauter tun. Some brewers collect separately in one kettle the initial stronger worts running off from the lauter tun, using this for stronger brews, before collecting subsequent weaker worts in a second kettle.

When the kettle is full, there may still be some wort left with the grains. Time permitting, this will be run off for use as "mashing-in" liquor for subsequent brews, a process referred to as *weak wort recycling*. The brewer needs to be careful, though; when the worts are very weak there is an increased tendency to extract tannins out of the grains, and these can cause clarity and astringency problems in beer.

At the completion of lautering, grain-out doors in the base of the vessels are opened, and the cutting machinery is used to drive the grains out. Almost without exception, spent grains are trucked off site as fast as possible (they readily spoil) for direct use as cattle feed.

Mash Filters.　Mash filters operate by using plates of polypropylene to filter the liquid wort from the residual grains. Accordingly, the grains serve no purpose as a filter medium, and their particle sizes are irrelevant. The high pressures used overcome the reduced permeability due to smaller particle sizes (the sand versus clay analogy I used earlier). Furthermore, the grains' bed depth is particularly shallow, being nothing more than the distance between the adjacent plates. The chambers of the press are first filled with liquor, which is then replaced by mash with filling times of less than 30 minutes. During this time the first worts are recovered through the plates. Once full, the outlet valves are closed. The filter is then given a gentle compression to collect more wort. This is followed by sparging to get a uniform distribution of water across the filter bed, then with a further compression to force out the remaining wort. Using mash filters, wort separation can be completed in 50 minutes rather than the periods of up to 2 hours needed for lautering.

Wort Boiling

The boiling stage serves various functions. First, the intense heat inactivates any of the more robust enzymes that may have survived mashing and wort separation, and it sterilizes the wort, eliminating any organisms that might jeopardize the subsequent good work of the yeast. Second, proteins tend to coagulate when strongly heated, as anyone who has boiled an egg will appreciate, and so, in wort boiling, proteins are removed that might otherwise precipitate out in the beer as haze. They cross-link with tannins (polyphenols) from malt and hops and produce what is known as *hot break*. Third, the α-acids from hops are isomerized into the bittering principles, and other flavor changes take place, including the driving off of undesirable characters originating from hops and malt. The color of wort increases during boiling through melanoidin reactions (see Chapter Three). Finally, as water is of course driven off as steam during boiling, the wort becomes more concentrated.

Most Brewers tend to use a boil of between one and two hours, evaporating some 4% of the wort per hour. Clearly this is a most energy-intensive stage of the brewing process, and every effort is made to conserve heat input and loss. Kettles come in a myriad of shapes and sizes, but in modern breweries they are stainless steel, straight-sided, and curved bottomed and are very likely to be heated using an external heat exchanger called a calandria (Fig. 6.6). Efficient boiling demands turbulent conditions

Figure 6.6. A kettle (right) with external wort boiler (left). (*Photograph courtesy of Briggs of Burton.*)

in the vessel and thorough mixing; the calandria, which employs convective mixing of the system, enables this (Fig. 6.7).

The significance of the boiling stage for beer flavor should not be underestimated. Apart from the driving off of unpleasant grainy characters that originate in the grist, certain other substances are actually produced during boiling and, at least in part, they can be desirable. Perhaps the best-studied of these materials is dimethyl sulfide (DMS).

As we saw in Chapter Three, opinion is divided on whether DMS is desirable in beer. I know one Brewer who firmly believes that a level of 50 to 60 ppb DMS makes a substantial contribution to lager quality, but another gets paranoid if the level rises about 20 ppb, which is below the level of detection by the nose. The challenge therefore is to deliver the desired level of DMS to the appropriate beer.

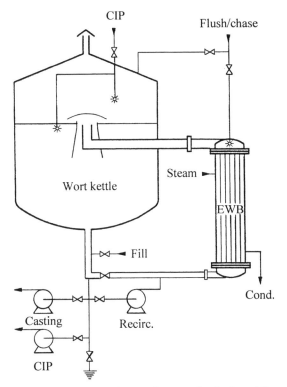

Figure 6.7. Diagram of a wort kettle, showing how good agitation of the wort is achieved using the external wort boiler (EWB, i.e., the calandria), and a spreading plate inside the kettle. (*Drawing courtesy of Briggs of Burton.*)

All of the DMS in beer originates from a precursor in the germinating embryo of malted barley. This precursor, sometimes called DMSP (P for precursor) or SMM (because the material is known to be S-methylmethionine), is increased to a greater extent if embryo development is substantial. Thus, if a malt is well modified (see Chapter Four), it will tend to contain more precursor. The most significant property of SMM is that it is quite sensitive to heat; when it breaks down it produces DMS. And so, whenever there is a heating stage during malting and brewing, SMM is degraded.

The first heating stage in the conversion of barley into beer is the kilning of malt: The more intense the kilning, the greater the breakdown of SMM. The DMS produced is largely driven off with the flue gases. For this reason, there is more SMM in lager malts than ale malts, because the latter are kilned more intensely. In other words, the DMS potential entering into lager brews is greater than in ale brews, and so lagers tend to contain DMS, whereas ales don't.

The next significant heating stage is what we have reached now: the boil. Of course, the mashing and wort separation stages involve quite a bit of heating, but it's only when the temperature gets much above 80° C that SMM breakdown occurs. In the boil, though, breakdown of SMM (which will have been extracted from the malt in the mash) is quite rapid. The more vigorous and extensive the boil, the more SMM breaks down and the DMS released goes up the chimney.

Brewers not wanting DMS in their lagers not only ensure that the malt has low DMS potential (see Chapter Four), but they also tend to demand a prolonged and vigorous boil. Those requiring some DMS ensure that there is ample SMM in the malt and throttle back the boil to ensure that some of the precursor survives to the next stage in the process. That's where we will go now.

Removing Trub

Various devices have been used to separate the trub and other residual solids from boiled wort. In the days when it was the norm to use whole-leaf hops, this stage was completed using a hop back, analogous to a lauter tun, in which the residual plant material formed a filter bed. Such approaches are not applicable when hop pellets and hop extracts are used. Centrifuges have been used to remove wort solids, but much more common is the whirlpool. These are cylindrical tanks, approximately 5 m in diameter, into which wort is pumped tangentially through an opening between 0.5 and 1.0 m above the base. The wort is set into a rotational flux, which forces the trub into a conical pile at the center of the vessel. After a period of perhaps one hour the wort is drawn off through pipes at the base of the vessel, so as not to disturb the collected trub.

The precipitation of insoluble materials in the brewhouse is sometimes promoted by the addition of materials called carrageenans, which are extracted from red and brown seaweeds. Carrageenans are polysaccharides (polymers of sugars) that stick onto the solids in beer, increasing their size and thereby making them more sedimentary.

For those Brewers aiming for some DMS in their lagers, the whirlpool stage is critical. The precursor that they ensured survived the boil continues to be broken down here. Temperatures are high enough for the SMM to degrade, but the conditions are far less turbulent. The DMS released is not driven off but remains dissolved in the wort. During fermentation (see Chapter Seven), much of this DMS will be driven off with the carbon dioxide produced by yeast, but some will survive. The trick is to ensure that the right amount of SMM survives the boil, to convert it all into DMS in the whirlpool, and to bring into the fermenter the level of DMS in wort that will leave the desired quantity of DMS in the beer after the proportion that will be lost with CO_2 has been accounted for. (Actually, the story isn't quite as simple as this—and we'll touch on it again in Chapter Seven.)

Wort Cooling

The whirlpool may be insulated, but if not the wort temperature may fall to 85° C or less. Even so, that is far too hot for yeast to survive. For this reason, the final stage before fermentation must be cooling. Customarily this is achieved using plate heat exchangers. The wort flows turbulently on one side of the plates, with a cooling medium (chilled water, brine, ammonia, or glycol solution) on the other. When wort is chilled, more solids may precipitate out, the so-called cold break. These solids consist of protein but also some lipids. Opinion differs among Brewers on the relative merits of this material (see Chapter Seven).

The final stage in wort production en route to the fermenters is the introduction of oxygen, which yeasts require for healthy growth, as we shall discover in the next chapter.

* * *

The sequence of events in the brewhouse, then, is complex and is geared toward generating, in the highest possible yield, a nutritious wort that the yeast will grow on to make the beer that the Brewer wants. The composition of that beer, and its quality, inherently depends on the behavior of the yeast, which in turn reflects the quality of the wort, as we shall see in the next chapter.

Chapter Seven

GODDISGOODE

Yeast and Fermentation

The common denominator in the production of all alcoholic beverages is fermentation. For beer this involves the conversion of sugars, derived primarily from malt, into ethanol (ethyl alcohol or, for most people, just alcohol) by the yeast *Saccharomyces cerevisiae*, the mysterious properties of which in medieval times prompted it to be known as goddisgoode. The nature of any alcoholic drink is determined by the yeast strain used to produce it and also on the substrate (feedstock) the yeast is converting. Thus wines have the character they do because of the strains of yeast used in wineries and because of the grape-based substrate. Wines are prized (or otherwise) because of the vintage they may enjoy. Beers, too, have the character they do because of the subtle interaction between carefully selected brewing strains of yeast and the malt and hops that come together as wort.

BREWING YEAST

Saccharomyces cerevisiae, then, is a busy beast. Apart from being the workhorse of the brewery, it is responsible for the production of cider, wine, spirits, and some other alcoholic beverages. And as every cook knows, it is essential for the production of life's other staple food, bread.

The reader needs to be aware that it is not the same strains of *S. cerevisiae* that do all these tasks. Just as it takes humans with all manner of skills to make up society, so is it a collection of strains of *S. cerevisiae* that tackle the range of tasks referred to above. Yes, brewing strains can be used to ferment grape must and make passable wine, and wine yeasts can be used to ferment wort with some interesting products. The fact remains, though, that the character of a beer is in large part established by the yeast that is used to make it. That is why Brewers guard their strains carefully—just as any skilled workman looks after the tools of his trade.

The Structure of Yeast

Yeast is a single-celled organism, about 10 μm in diameter (Fig. 7.1). Bacteria also comprise one cell, but yeast is substantially more complex and, like all eukaryotic organisms, the cell is divided up into organelles, each with its own job.

The heart of a cell is its nucleus, within which is stored much of the genetic information held in deoxyribonucleic acid (DNA). In turn the DNA is coiled up into chromosomes, of which *S. cerevisiae* has 16. The strains of this organism that have been used for much of the laboratory research over the years contain just one copy of each chromosome; they are said to be haploid. Other yeasts are diploid, with two copies of the genome. Brewing yeasts are aneuploid, containing approximately three copies of each chromosome. I say "approximately" because the exact number of copies of individual chromosomes present may differ. The fact that brewing yeasts contain more than a single copy of each gene makes them quite stable: They can afford to lose one of the copies of a gene simply because they fall back on the other copies. This is good news for Brewers, as their yeasts are consistent for many generations.

The yeast cell is surrounded by a wall, within which is a membrane, the plasma membrane. The wall offers strength to the cell, protecting the rather more delicate membrane beneath it. It also plays a major role in cell–cell interactions: It is through links between walls and calcium that cells flocculate and migrate either to the surface or base of a fermenting vessel. This has major implications for brewing practice; for instance, the mechanism that the brewer will use to separate the yeast from the "green" beer at the end of fermentation.

The function of the membrane is to regulate what does and what does not get into the cell. Although a yeast has its intracellular food reserves, it depends on materials in its growth medium (in the case of beer, the growth medium is wort) for its survival and growth. The composition of the membrane influences what (and how readily) molecules such as sugars and amino acids move into the cell. The membrane has a similar influence on what leaves the cell.

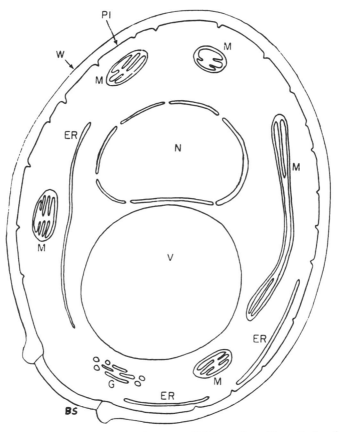

Figure 7.1. A schematic cross-section of a yeast cell. N = nucleus; M = mitochondrion; V = vacuole (contains enzymes used to recycle cell components); ER = endosplasmic reticulum; G = Golgi apparatus (sites involved in the synthesis of proteins); Pl = plasma membrane; W = cell wall; BS = bud scar (which is the remnant of where a daughter cell separated).

One other organelle worthy of mention is the mitochondrion. This is the part of a eukaryotic cell largely responsible for energy generation by respiration. However, the requirement for mitochondria by yeast in brewery fermentations is the subject of controversy. We know that when yeast converts sugar into alcohol it is an anaerobic process. Yeast, though, can also use sugar via a respiration route. Only in the latter case should active mitochondria be needed. But what if those organelles have some other function apart from energy generation? In fact, they do serve some other roles; for instance, they are involved in the synthesis of certain amino acids. And so they are to be found in brewing yeast when it ferments wort, albeit in a shape somewhat different from that of yeast growing in the presence of oxygen.

Like other single-celled organisms, brewing yeast reproduces by cell division. The daughter cell grows from the mother cell as a bud before separating off as a distinct cell, leaving a bud scar behind on the mother cell. Figure 7.2 shows yeast viewed under an electron microscope; budding cells and bud scars are readily seen. An indication of the age of a yeast cell is obtained by counting the number of bud scars, which can be as many as 40 or 50.

Classification of Brewing Yeasts

Until relatively recently, brewing yeasts were divided into two species: *Saccharomyces cerevisiae* and *Saccharomyces carlsbergensis*. The latter was named, of course, by the pioneer of pure yeast use, Emil Christian Hansen (see page 25). Carlsberg, the company into which he introduced

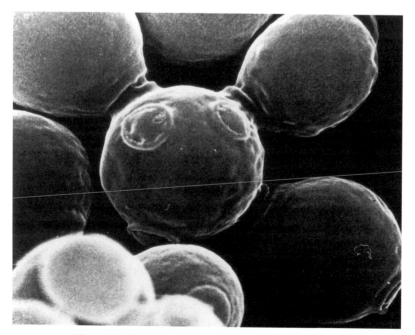

Figure 7.2. Yeast as seen under an electron microscope.

this technology in 1883, still proudly uses this terminology. Most others have used the term *Saccharomyces uvarum* for those yeasts that do their job at relatively low temperatures (typically 6°C to 15°C), which, after flocculating, drop to the bottom of the fermenter and which are traditionally used to make lager-style beers. The name *S. cerevisiae* was reserved for yeasts that make ales at temperatures in the range 18° to 22°C and that collect at the surface of the fermenting vessel. It is indeed possible to differentiate between yeasts in either category, notably by the fact that yeasts classified as *S. uvarum* can grow on the sugar melibiose, whereas *S. cerevisiae* can't.

Since the early 1980s, though, taxonomists have declared that all brewing yeasts should be classified as *S. cerevisiae* on the basis of their DNA properties. Sure, there are many different strains within this classification, ergo the variety of products we can enjoy.

Because brewing strains differ so much in their properties and behavior, it is important that a brewer know which strain he is dealing with. For instance, a company may brew the same brand in several different breweries and distribute the relevant yeast from a central repository. The sender and the recipient should both run checks to make sure that the yeast is the right one. Within a given brewery, too, several yeast strains may be used to make a range of products. It is critical to be able to distinguish them. Good housekeeping only goes so far. From time to time a check needs to be run to confirm that the correct yeast is being used. This problem is particularly acute when a brewery performs franchise brewing. I know of one major brewery, for instance, that brews at least four major international lager brands for four different companies. Not only is that brewery trusted with custodianship of the respective yeasts, but they are also under intense pressure to make sure that there are no mix-ups or cross-contaminations.

There are those who downplay the significance of yeast strain and, indeed, there is clear evidence that certain brands can be successfully made with yeasts associated with a totally distinct brand. Indeed there are opportunities for rationalization of yeast strains, but this demands rigorous trials to ensure that the desired beer is produced (and will continue to consistently display the required quality characteristics) and that there are no "funnies" in production. Such rationalization is far easier to achieve for the brands within a company. By and large, Brewers who franchise out a brand demand that their specified process is adhered to, using their specified raw materials—and that includes yeast.

Identification of brewing yeast strains is nowadays achieved using DNA fingerprinting in a technique exactly analogous to that employed in

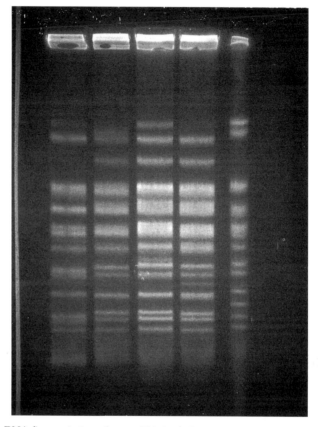

Figure 7.3. DNA fingerprinting of yeast. This is analogous to the protein fingerprinting of barley (see Fig. 4.2), except that here the chromosomes of yeast have been extracted and separated by electrophoresis. Each lane represents a different yeast strain.

a criminal investigation (Fig. 7.3). One might almost say that the rogue under pursuit is the yeast strain different from that which should be used to make the beer brand required.

THE USE OF WORT BY YEAST

Like any other living organism, yeast needs certain essentials to enable it to grow and survive. It needs vitamins; it needs a source of nitrogen (amino acids from the breakdown of barley protein during malting and mashing), which it will use to make protein; it needs a few trace elements. Most of all, yeast requires sugars, which it will chop up to release energy and to make smaller molecules, which it will use alongside the nitrogen source to fabricate its cellular components.

Yeast can use sugars in one of two ways. If it encounters high levels of sugar, such as are found in wort, then yeast will use them by a fermentative (anaerobic) process. They are converted into ethanol and carbon dioxide, which releases energy:

$$C_6H_{12}O_6 \rightarrow 2C_2H_5OH + 2CO_2 + \text{energy}$$
$$\text{sugar} \qquad \text{alcohol}$$

However, if the sugar content is low and if oxygen is available, then the sugar is used by respiration:

$$C_6H_{12}O_6 + 6O_2 \rightarrow 6CO_2 + 6H_2O + \text{energy}$$

In fermentation about 14 times less energy is captured for each glucose molecule broken down than is the case in respiration—but it's still enough for the needs of the yeast because of the high availability of its sugar feedstock.

This biochemistry is the basis of differentiation between yeast operating in a brewery and yeast being produced commercially for use in baking. In the latter case it is economically desirable to produce large amounts of yeast from as little sugar as possible. Therefore yeast is grown in a so-called fed-batch process in which the sugar source (usually molasses) is dosed in a bit at a time, so that at any point its concentration is low and the yeast is switched on to using it by respiration. Plenty of oxygen is introduced, and the yield of yeast is high. A Brewer, on the other hand, is interested in alcohol production. Sugar concentrations therefore are high in wort, oxygen levels are low, and the yeast metabolizes the sugars by fermentation. Indeed the Brewer wants very little yeast production, because the more sugar ends up in new yeast cells, the less has been converted into alcohol.

A more comprehensive equation that describes a brewery fermentation would be:

$$\text{maltose} + \text{amino acid} \rightarrow \text{yeast} + \text{ethanol} + CO_2 + \text{energy}$$
$$\text{100 g} \qquad \text{0.5 g} \qquad \text{5 g} \qquad \text{48.8 g} \qquad \text{46.8 g} \qquad \text{50 Kcal}$$

Even for the brewing of beer, yeast needs a little oxygen. Earlier we saw that the yeast membrane is important for a healthy yeast. This membrane contains various components, among which are sterols and unsaturated fatty acids. Yeast uses oxygen in the synthesis of these materials. So the Brewer carefully introduces just the right amount of oxygen into wort to enable the production of the appropriate amount of membrane material. Too little, and the yeast won't ferment the wort efficiently. Too much, and yeast growth will be excessive, and alcohol yield will be lowered.

Yeasts can be classified in yet another way, according to the amount of oxygen they require before they will ferment wort efficiently. Some are satisfied when the Brewer air-saturates the wort, that is, he bubbles air into the wort after cooling, which will introduce approximately 8 ppm of oxygen. Other strains demand oxygen saturation (16 ppm), while yet more aren't even satisfied with this amount of oxygen.

SETTING UP A BREWERY FERMENTATION

Getting the right level of oxygen into wort prior to pitching the yeast is but one of the conditions that has to be right.

First, the wort itself. It needs to have the correct strength in terms of level of sugar. Increasingly, fermentations are performed at so-called high gravity, in which case the concentration of wort (and, proportionately, of oxygen and yeast) is higher than needed to give the desired final alcohol content. This maximizes fermenter capacity. At the end of the process the beer is diluted with deaerated liquor (water) to the required alcohol content.

Irrespective of whether fermentation is at high or at "sales" gravity (i.e., fermentation of wort at the strength that gives the required beer without dilution), the concentration of sugars is measured by specific gravity (which is the weight of a volume of the wort relative to the weight of the same volume of water). The units most frequently used to quote specific gravity are "degrees Plato," 1°Plato equalling 1 g sucrose per gram of water. So, if a wort has a specific gravity of 10°Plato, it has the same specific gravity as a 10% solution of sucrose.

The wort also needs to have the required level of solid material suspended in it. This is the so-called cold break, rich in lipids, and produced in the brewhouse (see Chapter Six). Brewers differ hugely in their opinions on whether the presence of this material is a good or a bad thing. Some, for instance many German brewers, are adamant that cold break causes only problems and that it is a serious cause of poor foams and staleness in beer. The converse view is that some solids in wort are good news, because they promote a vigorous fermentation. This may be because they provide useful lipids and, perhaps, trace metals to the yeast, but is more likely to be because the particles form nucleation sites for gas release (see Chapter Three). This keeps yeast in suspension and therefore in contact with wort for fermentation as well as preventing the accumulation of carbon dioxide that tends to inhibit yeast metabolism.

The next essential is to use the correct level of yeast that is in the proper state of health and purity. The process of adding yeast to wort is called pitching. As a rule of thumb, 10 million yeast cells will be added per milliliter of wort at 12°Plato, with proportionately more added if the wort is stronger than this, or less if the wort is weaker. To measure the amount of yeast, most Brewers count the number of cells seen under a microscope in a drop of the yeast suspension placed on a special slide divided into grids. This device is called a hemocytometer because it was originally developed for counting red blood cells in clinical labs. By knowing how much suspension was put onto the slide, the Brewer can calculate the cell concentration. Some Brewers are rather more sophisticated than this and automatically dose yeast on the basis of measurements made with probes put directly into the pipeline that leads from the yeast storage tank to the fermenter. These probes work on various principles, among which are light scatter. Suspensions of particles, such as yeast, scatter light in proportion to the number suspended per unit volume.

The number of yeast cells added is important. So too is the health of the yeast. Dead cells won't ferment wort into beer. Just as significantly, the products of their decay can cause problems to the Brewer. The most common means for measuring the viability of yeast involves a dye called methylene blue. Living yeast is capable of decolorizing this dye, but dead cells aren't; as a result, they stain blue.

Even if a cell is living, it doesn't necessarily mean that it is in a fit state for carrying out an efficient fermentation. When a yeast is in a healthy and vigorous condition, ready to do its job, it is said to have vitality. The analogy would be the average couch potato compared with a championship athlete. It is the latter who possesses vitality, even though both blokes are living. Measurement of vitality is not a straightforward issue, and there is no agreement on the best way of assessing it. Most brewers recognize that the most appropriate course of action is to look after their yeast and ensure that it doesn't encounter stresses such as heat shock or those that arise from leaving it in contact with beer long after fermentation is complete.

The only other ingredients likely to be included in a brewery fermentation are a yeast food, most frequently a zinc salt, and antifoam. Zinc is a key component of one of the enzymes that yeast requires to carry out alcoholic fermentation. Other yeast foods are more complex mixtures of amino acids and vitamins, but many folk would have it that this solid addition merely acts as a nucleation site in just the same way as cold break.

Antifoam is required if a fermentation is characterized by high levels of head formation. This occurs particularly with certain types of yeast and for fermentations carried out at the higher end of the temperature range. Such overfoaming has two consequences. First, the capacity of the vessel is reduced. The Brewer is obliged to put less wort into the fermenter; otherwise, it will overflow during the process. Second, any foaming during the process reduces the amount of material that will survive to support the head on the finished beer in the glass. To minimize this foaming, many brewers add antifoam agents, most frequently those based on silicone. It is essential to remove them efficiently in the filtration operation; otherwise they will damage the head in the beer itself.

THE FERMENTATION CELLAR

Many types of fermenter exist in breweries across the world. Basically, though, they can be divided into two categories: square (Fig. 7.4) and cylindroconical (Fig. 7.5). The original commercial fermenters were open squares, and these are still used extensively for the production of ales in the United Kingdom. These days they are fabricated from stainless steel, but through the years they have been constructed from oak, slate, copper, and reinforced concrete. They come in a vast range of sizes, and vessels capable of holding over 13,000 hl have been used. More commonly "squares" are between 150 and 400 hl. Squares are highly suited to fermentations with top-fermenting yeasts, with the yeast periodically skimmed from the surface of the vessel. Clearly, there is a substantial risk of contamination, and, if you lean over such a tank and inhale, the vast quantities of carbon dioxide that are evolved will literally take your breath away. (Incidentally, in case the reader was worrying that the Brewer is carelessly pumping greenhouse gases into the atmosphere, it should be stressed that

Figure 7.4. A traditional square fermenter.

Figure 7.5. Modern cylindroconical fermentation vessels at the Bass Brewery, Cape Hill, Birmingham, England. (*Photograph courtesy of Briggs of Burton.*)

the amount of carbon dioxide produced in the world's brewery fermentations is minor compared with the amount of CO_2 that you and I and the rest of the world's animal population breathe out every second of every day. Not only that, remember that it takes a lot of carbon dioxide to support the growth of barley and hops by photosynthesis—rather more, in fact, than is produced during fermentation of beer.)

Many Brewers seek to collect the carbon dioxide from fermenters to put it, for instance, into cylinders for use as a motor gas in pub dispense systems. CO_2 collection is possible from closed fermenters. Some of these vessels are little more than open squares with a lid on, but for the most part fermenters these days are cylindroconical tanks, which are seldom of a capacity less than 600 hl but which can be as large as 7,000 hl. Once, the trend was to install bigger and bigger vessels; indeed, such vessels do make sense in breweries with limited ground space and that produce large volumes of one or a very few brands. There are, however, potential problems insofar as yeast behavior varies, depending on the hydrostatic pressure it encounters, and it may change its output of flavor materials, leading to a perceptibly different character in the beer. In particular, though, for breweries that are producing a diversity of brands it makes more sense to use smaller fermenters.

Cylindroconical vessels were originally developed by Nathan at the turn of the twentieth century and have the advantages of better mixing due to convection currents set up by rising gas bubbles, ease of temperature control through thermostatted jackets, and easy and hygienic recovery of yeast from the base (cone). These vessels are also easily cleaned using a water spray, followed by either dilute (1%) caustic or phosphoric acid and another water rinse, usually prior to a sterilant rinse with hypochlorite or peracetic acid. These various treatments are sprayed into the empty tanks from a spray ball (nozzle). (Incidentally such cleaning in place is also employed at other stages through the brewery between brews to ensure cleanliness in all types of vessel and pipeline.) It is possible to deliberately apply a pressure to cylindroconical vessels during fermentation; the formation of esters, for instance, is suppressed at higher pressures.

Whichever type of fermenter is employed, the principles of what happens during the fermentation are similar. Yeast takes up sugar (and the other materials) from wort and converts it into alcohol and CO_2. Most commonly, the progress of fermentation is monitored by measuring the decline in the specific gravity of the wort (Fig. 7.6). This decease occurs because the specific gravity of a solution of ethanol is vastly lower than that of a mixture of sugars. Alongside the fall in specific gravity is a drop

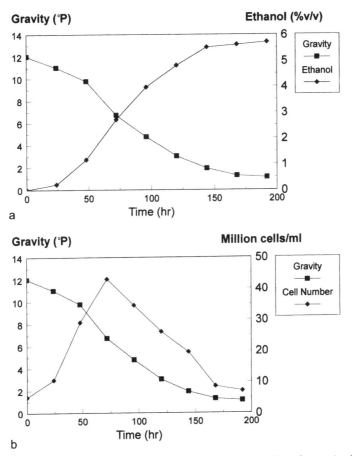

Figure 7.6. Changes marking the progress of a fermentation. (a) Specific gravity falls because sugars (with a much higher specific gravity than water) are converted into ethanol (which has a lower specific gravity than water). (b) The number of cells in suspension increases as the yeast grows by dividing; thereafter the yeast count falls because cells flocculate and leave the body of the beer.

in pH, as yeast secretes certain organic acids (such as citric and acetic acids, the acids found in lemons and vinegar respectively—happily, there is rather less of either in beer) and also digests materials from the wort that act as buffers. During the fermentation a range of molecules leak out from the yeast cell, among which are substances having distinctive flavors. They include esters and higher alcohols (which collectively are sometimes referred to as fusel oils), certain sulfur-containing molecules, and a particularly noxious material called diacetyl, which has a distinct butterscotch character (see Chapter Three).

Typically, lagers are fermented at temperatures between 6° C and 14° C, with the chosen temperature being controlled very carefully by the Brewer. The more traditional the Brewer, the lower this temperature is. Clearly, rates of fermentation are slower at lower temperatures. This leads to a different balance of flavor substances released by the yeast. Traditionalists contend that the best flavor balance is achieved if the process is painstaking—at lower temperatures. Others insist that perfectly good beer is produced by fermentation at the higher end of this temperature range. Such differences of opinion mean that fermentation of lager can take as little as three or four days, or as much as two weeks.

Ales have always been fermented at higher temperatures (15° to 20° C) than lagers, with the result that they tend to contain more flavor volatiles, such as esters, than do lagers. These fermentations also tend to be faster.

The vast majority of Brewers agree that diacetyl is an undesirable substance to have in the beer. This substance leaks out of yeast during fermentation but is subsequently taken up again by the yeast at the end of fermentation. The process must be continued until the diacetyl has been lowered to below 0.1 mg/liter, and this depends on there being enough healthy yeast present at the end of fermentation. Some Brewers allow the temperature to rise at the end of the primary fermentation to allow this mopping up operation to occur more rapidly.

Once fermentation and diacetyl removal are complete, yeast is separated from the beer. If yeast is allowed to remain in contact with beer for too long, materials can leak from the cells that can damage the beer. As we have seen, much of the yeast can be readily separated from the beers, either by skimming in the case of a top-fermenting strain working in an open square or through the collection of a bottom yeast in the cone of a cylindroconical vessel. If any further help is required it comes in the form of a centrifuge.

There are three possible fates for the yeast. Prior to another fermentation, it can go to a chilled storage tank for a few days, but seldom as long as weeks. Alternatively, it may be used immediately for pitching into another vessel; this practice is often called cone-to-cone pitching, as it involves the pumping of yeast from the cone of one vessel in which fermentation is complete into the cone of a vessel containing fresh wort. The third option is for the yeast to be disposed of. A proportion may go off to a distiller for whiskey fermentation. Some will be treated with propionic acid prior to ending up as pig slurry. The majority, though, goes off for autolysis to become yeast extract that will end up spread on somebody's toast!

Storage of yeast prior to repitching is itself a process demanding great care. The yeast is kept well mixed (roused), and a little oxygen may be introduced to keep the cells healthy. The tank is also likely to be thermostatted to 0° to 4° C. The yeast may also have picked up some contaminants in the fermenter, which must be gotten rid of. This can be achieved by washing the yeast for an hour or two in a solution of phosphoric acid at pH 2.2. Yeast survives this treatment quite happily, but bacteria don't.

YEAST PROPAGATION

Some Brewers have kept the same yeast going for years and years, a proportion of the yeast produced in a fermentation being used to pitch the next batch of wort, and so on. However, it is a fact that the yeast genome (despite the aneuploidy mentioned above) is not stable, and it is desirable to repropagate each yeast strain after every 10 to 15 batches of wort have been fermented.

Propagation is from a stock yeast, which may be held in various ways but which is increasingly likely to be either a deep-frozen culture or even one which has been freeze-dried. When it is time to propagate, this culture is used to inoculate a small amount of wort (perhaps 10 ml) with growth of the yeast being in progressively increasing amounts of wort (100 ml, 1 liter, 5 liters, until the final propagator, which may have vessels ranging in capacity from 10 to 300 hl). Rigorous conditions of sterility are essential, as is a plentiful supply of sterile wort and oxygen. The aim of propagation is to produce large quantities of yeast that is in good condition for subsequent brewery fermentations. As respiration yields far more energy than does fermentation and ethanol is not a desired product of propagation whereas yeast biomass is, highly aerobic conditions should be maintained in a propagator. The most efficient way to grow yeast is in fed-batch mode, which the purveyors of baker's yeast have long since appreciated (see page 143).

WHAT YEAST EXCRETES

Beer is, of course, a delicious and wholesome product. The fact remains, though, that it is merely the spent growth medium of a fermentation process. Beer is the way it is because of the things that yeast takes away, the substances that it excretes, and the stuff that it leaves well alone. Yeast "eats" sugars, taking away excessive sweetness and simultaneously producing its most significant excretion product, ethanol. It doesn't metabolize the proteins or the bitter compounds, although both can adsorb onto the yeast wall. And, importantly for the flavor of beer, yeast releases flavor compounds.

We have already heard about diacetyl, which is extremely undesirable, except in an occasional ale, which might benefit from a low level of the substance. Two categories of substance that are desirable when present in the appropriate quantity for a given beer are the higher alcohols, but more particularly their equivalent esters. The flavors associated with these esters are listed in Table 3.1. The levels obtained in beer depend on fermentation conditions: Levels increase at higher fermentation temperatures, if less yeast is pitched into the fermenter and if insufficient oxygen is used. Increasing the top pressure in fermentation can suppress the tendency of esters to be produced. Of particular significance, however, is the yeast strain, some strains producing more esters than others.

Yeast secretes a range of sulfur-containing compounds into beer, including hydrogen sulfide, dimethyl sulfide, and sulfur dioxide. Sulfur dioxide is produced by yeast from the sulfate present in wort. While not itself as flavor-active as other sulfur compounds, sulfur dioxide can suppress the deleterious flavors due to other compounds that can arise in beer. Notably, sulfur dioxide acts as an antioxidant and helps prevent stale flavors developing in the product.

By and large, the other sulfur compounds present in beer are strongly flavored at extremely low levels (see Table 3.2). Despite their individual pungency, if they are present at relatively low levels and in the correct balance, they contribute beneficially to the flavor of many beers, especially lagers. Just as for other products of yeast metabolism, there are substantial differences between yeast strains in their ability to form the various sulfur compounds. A major factor, therefore, in controlling the flavor of beer is to ensure use of the correct yeast strain, and only when it is in good condition.

In Chapter Six we encountered dimethyl sulfide (DMS) and found how its level could be controlled in wort and, therefore, beer. We said that much of the DMS is purged from wort during fermentation by the vast volumes of carbon dioxide produced by yeast. There is a complication: All brewing yeasts, to a greater or lesser extent, can *produce* DMS. Almost 20 years go, Brian Anness and I showed that they do this by converting a substance called dimethyl sulfoxide (DMSO). We found that the DMS precursor from malt (SMM) is not only broken down to DMS by heat on the malt kiln, but also some DMSO is produced. DMSO gets extracted into the wort and under certain conditions is changed into DMS by yeast. One of the most important of those conditions is fermentation temperature: If lager is produced in the traditional way at low temperatures (e.g., below 8°C), the tendency is for yeast to produce more DMS than at higher fermentation temperatures. A research group in Belgium recently suggested that the majority of the DMS found in one outstanding brand originates from this route.

The immediate precursor of ethanol, acetaldehyde, is another potent flavor compound that, if present, gives a green apple-type flavor to beer. Ideally, it shouldn't be present, but if too much oxygen is present during fermentation, it can occur. It can also be symptomatic of the presence of spoilage organisms, in this case *Zymomonas*. Indeed, abnormal levels of other flavor constituents of beer, including some of the sulfur compounds, may also be due to infection.

Organic acids (including succinate, lactate, and acetate) are normal products of the metabolism of brewing yeast. Their secretion results in the characteristic fall in pH that occurs during fermentation—from over 5.0 to as low as 3.8. Finally, yeast can produce medium-chain-length fatty acids, such as octanoic and decanoic acids, that provide a goaty flavor to beer.

MODERN FERMENTATIONS

Traditionally, fermentation was performed at sales gravity, in other words, the strength of the finished beer was in direct proportion to the concentration and the fermentability of the sugars in the wort. This is still the norm for many Brewers, particularly those producing smaller volumes of beer. These Brewers are more likely, too, to adhere to other traditional elements of the fermentation process, such as low temperature and fermentation at atmospheric pressure. Other Brewers, meanwhile, have considered and, in many cases, implemented procedures that will greatly enhance the productivity of their plant.

High-Gravity Fermentations

Many Brewers perform their fermentations at concentrations of wort that give alcohol yields in excess of target. Following fermentation and conditioning, the beer is diluted to the specified alcohol content by the addition of water (which must be deaerated to prevent oxidative damage to the beer and preferably carbonated to the level of the beer it is diluting). Thus, for a beer that might traditionally have been fermented from a wort of 10°Plato to give 4.5% alcohol, in high-gravity fermentations the yeast might be pitched into 16°Plato wort, and the ensuing beer of 7.2% alcohol diluted 10 parts beer to 6 parts deaerated water to produce the desired final beer strength.

Commercially, 20°Plato appears to have been as high as anyone has successfully fermented high-gravity brews. Providing sufficient fermentation and downstream facilities are available, it will be seen that high-gravity brewing presents tremendous opportunities for enhancing brewery capacity and maximizing the amount of beer produced per unit of expenditure on items such as energy. To be successful, of course, there must be the wherewithal to produce such concentrated worts. Also, sufficient control must be exerted to ensure that the finished beers are indistinguishable from those produced at sales gravity. High-gravity worts going to the fermenter can be produced by mashing at lower liquor-grist ratios, restricting such worts to the concentrated flows emerging early in the wort separation stage (see Chapter Six), or, most typically, by boosting the levels of fermentable sugar by adding syrups to the kettle boil. Several problems must be overcome. Hop utilization is inferior at higher wort strengths; brewhouse yields are, of course, poorer; and yeast behaves differently when confronted with extra sugar, finishing the fermentation in a less healthy condition and producing disproportionately high levels of certain flavorsome substances, notably esters. These problems are not insurmountable, and the combined use of higher yeast pitching rates and proportionately more oxygen for the yeast to use for membrane synthesis means that large quantities of the world's beer are now produced most successfully in this way.

Accelerated Fermentations

Another way to enhance capacity would be to increase the turnover of fermenters, that is, to speed up fermentations. This can be achieved by increasing the quantity of yeast pitched into the fermenter (with oxygen enhanced proportionately), maintaining yeast in contact with the wort rather than allowing it to flocculate, and by elevating the temperature. In each case there is invariably an effect on flavor, which will need to be addressed, perhaps by increasing the top pressure on the fermenter if this is feasible.

Continuous Fermentation

Many industrial fermentations are performed continuously. With a solitary exception, this is not the case for brewery fermentations, despite the obvious potential advantages for turnover and capacity. At times over the past 30 years various breweries did install continuous fermentation processes, notably employing tower fermenters with upflow of the liquid stream through a heavily sedimentary yeast capable of forming a plug at the base of the vessel. By adjusting the yeast content and the rate of wort flow, Brewers could produce green beer in less than a day. With that solitary exception, these fermenters have been stripped out, the main reasons given being inflexibility (most breweries produce a range of beers that demand diverse fermentation streams) and infection problems. It's bad enough having contamination in a batch fermenter, but substantially more inconvenient if the fermentation is continuous. There is also the matter of beer flavor. It is an undeniable truth that virtually any change in fermentation conditions, be they temperature, yeast concentration, or, in this case, continuous processing, leads to flavor shifts.

These problems are certainly not insurmountable—as has been proved by Dominion Breweries in New Zealand, who for many years have used continuous fermentation to produce some excellent beers. Indeed, there is a resurgence of interest from others in this area, including the use of so-called immobilized yeast, where the yeast is attached to a solid support and the wort is flowed past. One Dutch Brewer employs this process in the production of a low-alcohol beer, while others are experimenting with such fermentation systems for making full-strength beers on a boutique brewery scale. Furthermore, a Brewer in Finland employs immobilized yeast in an accelerated process for eliminating diacetyl at the end of fermentation.

*   *   *

Fermentation is now done, and the contemptible diacetyl destroyed, but the Brewer's job is far from over. The green beer produced still needs to be refined in flavor and appearance. Chapter Eight will tell us how that is achieved and how the beer is sent into the marketplace.

REFINING MATTERS

Downstream Processing

When a beer leaves the fermenter, it is not the finished article. It is highly unlikely to be sufficiently clear, or bright, and will certainly contain substances that will come out of solution in the ensuing package. Its flavor may still require some refining. All Brewers recognize the need to attend to the raw, or green, beer, but they differ in their opinions about quite how intense and involved this processing needs to be.

FLAVOR CHANGES DURING THE AGING OF BEER

As we saw in Chapter Seven, a rate-limiting step for moving beer onward from the fermenter is the time taken to mop up diacetyl and its precursor. Some people refer to this as warm conditioning. Many Brewers would consider this to mark the end of the useful flavor changes that they can dictate in the brewery. The traditionalists would contend that the beer still needs to be stored. There is, however, very little published data to indicate what, if any, further changes take place in the flavor of beer when it is aged in the brewery.

Some major brewing companies insist on holding lager for a prolonged period at low temperatures (decreasing from 5° to 0°C). This process (lagering) is a leftover from prerefrigeration days, when the removal of bottom-fermenting yeast demanded that the beer be held for a long time, with chilling perhaps facilitated by blocks of ice. Traditionally, beer from an already relatively cool fermentation (<10°C) was run to a cellar at a stage when there was still about 1% fermentable sugar and sufficient yeast left in it. The yeast would consume traces of potentially destabilizing oxygen and, by fermenting the sugar, release carbon dioxide, which would remain in solution to a greater extent at the lower temperatures. In this way the beer might be held at 0° C for perhaps 50 days. Yeast would settle out by the end of this time, together with protein and other material that otherwise would "drop out" as an unsightly haze in the finished beer in the customer's glass.

These days the technology exists to cover all these requirements for prolonged storage, including the use of clarifying agents, filters, stabilizing agents, carbonation systems, all allied to the use of refrigeration, as we will see in this chapter. This doesn't stop some major players in the brewing world from insisting on the costly process of holding beer in tank for many days. They are convinced it is right and as one of them so famously remarked, "If it ain't broke, don't fix it."

THE CLARIFICATION OF BEER

Cold Conditioning

Two types of particle need to be removed from beer at the end of fermentation: yeast and cold break. In addition, substances that are at this stage present in solution but will tend to form particles when beer is in the trade must also be eliminated. We'll come back to that later.

The first mechanism by which particles will separate from beer is simple gravitational pull. Most Brewers ensure that their beer is chilled to either 0° C or, better, −1° C after it has enjoyed the degree of fermentation and maturation that they deem it requires. Particles progressively sediment at this temperature in proportion to their size; furthermore, materials are brought out of solution, substances that might otherwise emerge as unsightly haze in the packaged beer.

To facilitate the sedimentation of particles, many Brewers add isinglass finings. These are solutions of collagen derived from the swim bladders of certain species of fish from the South China Seas, the dried bladders being referred to with such colorful titles as Long Saigon, Penang, and Brazil lump. Collagen has a net positive charge at the pH of beer, whereas yeast and other particulates have a net negative charge. Opposite charges attracting, the isinglass forms a complex with these particles, and the resultant large agglomerates sediment readily. Sometimes the isinglass finings are used alongside auxiliary finings based on silicate, the combination being more effective than isinglass alone.

Rather less widely used, but still an integral part of the process of the world's biggest Brewer, are wood chips. Over the years these have been mostly derived from well-seasoned beech and, individually, are a few inches wide and as much as a foot long. They therefore present a very ample surface area upon which insoluble materials can stick.

Filtration

After a period of typically three days minimum in this cold conditioning, the beer is generally filtered. Diverse types of filters are available, perhaps the most common being the plate-and-frame filter, which consists of a series of plates in sequence, over each of which a cloth is hung. The beer is mixed with a filter aid—porous particles that both trap particles and prevent the system from clogging. Two major kinds of filter-aid are in regular use: kieselguhr and perlite. The former consists of fossils or skeletons of primitive organisms called diatoms (Fig. 8.1). These can be mined and classified to provide grades that differ in their permeability characteristics. Particles of kieselguhr contain pores into which other particles (such as those found in beer) can pass, depending on their size. Unfortunately, there are health concerns associated with kieselguhr, since inhalation of its dust adversely affects the respiratory tract.

Perlites are derived from volcanic glasses crushed to form microscopic flat particles. They are easier to handle than kieselguhr but are not as efficient filter-aids.

Filtration starts when a precoat of filter-aid is applied to the filter by cycling a slurry of filter-aid through the plates. This precoat is generally a coarse grade, whereas the filter-aid (the bodyfeed) dosed into the beer during filtration proper tends to be a finer grade. It is selected according to the particles within the beer that need to be removed. If a beer contains a lot of yeast, but relatively few small particles, then a rather coarse grade is best. If the converse applies, then a fine grade with smaller pores is used.

The principles of beer filtration are similar to those we encountered when considering lautering (Chapter Six). Long filtration runs depend on the conservative application of pressure and are easier to achieve if factors

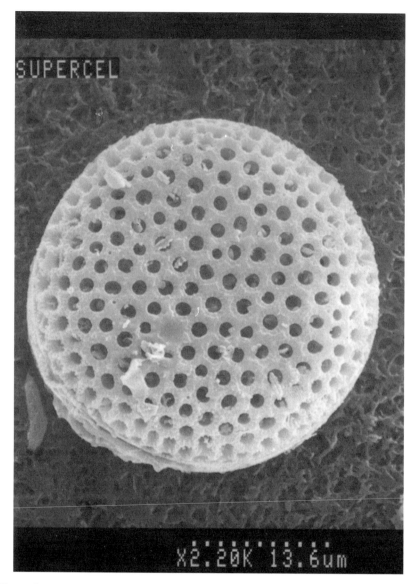

Figure 8.1. A particle of kieselguhr as seen by electron microscopy. (Magnification is × 2000.)

such as viscosity are low. As viscosity is substantially increased by lower temperatures and as beer should be filtered at as near $0°C$ as possible, it is particularly beneficial if substances like β-glucan are removed prior to this stage.

Stabilization

Apart from filtration, various other treatments may be applied to beer downstream, all with the aim of enhancing the shelf life of the product. There are three principal ways in which beer could deteriorate with time: by staling, by throwing a haze, and by becoming infected. The last of these will be covered in the next section.

As we have seen in Chapter Three, the flavor of beer changes in various ways in the package. The most significant of these changes are due to oxidation. It is now recognized that oxidation reactions can take place throughout the brewing process and that the tendency to stale can be built into a beer long before it is packaged and dispatched to trade. However, no Brewer would deny that the oxygen level in the beer as it is filled into its container should be as low as possible. The freshly filtered beer, which is called bright beer, should have an oxygen content below 0.1 ppm. In part this is achieved by running the beer from the filter into a tank that has been equilibrated in carbon dioxide or even nitrogen. The flow of beer into the vessel will be gentle. And if, once the vessel is full, the oxygen content of the beer exceeds specification, then the vessel is purged with carbon dioxide or nitrogen to drive off the surplus oxygen. Some Brewers add antioxidants such as sulfur dioxide or ascorbic acid (vitamin C) at this stage, but they are seldom especially useful at this point.

Brewing scientists have a long way to go before they fully understand the very complex area of beer oxidation. They understand much more about colloidal instability, that is, the tendency of beer to throw a haze. As a result, much more robust treatments are available to ensure that beer does not go cloudy within its shelf life.

A haze in beer can be due to various materials, but principally it is due to the cross-linking of certain proteins and certain tannins (or polyphenols) in the product. Therefore, if one or both of these materials is removed, the shelf life is extended.

As we have already seen in Chapter Six, the brewhouse operations are in part designed to precipitate out protein-tannin complexes. Thus, if these operations are performed efficiently, much of the job of stabilization is achieved. Good, vigorous, rolling boils, for instance, ensure precipitation. Before that, avoiding the last runnings in the lautering operation prevent excessive levels of tannin from entering the wort.

We have also seen that cold conditioning has a major role to play by chilling out protein-polyphenol complexes and enabling them to be taken out on the filter. Control over oxygen and oxidation is just as important for colloidal stability as for flavor stability, because it is particularly the oxidized polyphenols that tend to cross-link with proteins.

For really long shelf lives, though—and certainly if the beer is being shipped to extremes of climate—additional stabilization treatments will be necessary.

In the 1950s it was shown that nylon could efficiently remove polyphenols from beer. Nylon has rather more stylish applications in society these days, leaving an altogether more efficient if less glamorous material with the job of taking tannins out of beer: polyvinylpolypyrrolidone, which happily is usually abbreviated to PVPP. This can be dosed into tanks as a solid prior to filtration or can be impregnated into filter sheets. After use it can be regenerated by treatment with caustic soda.

Ironically, one of the foremost treatments used to eliminate haze-forming proteins from beer is to *add* more tannin in the form of tannic acid, which is extracted from gallnuts. Although this process boosts polyphenol levels, this is not a concern, because the proteins they react with will be removed in the brewery. Indeed, there is a school of thought that better beers contain higher levels of polyphenol, because these molecules contribute to body and also protect against staling through their role as antioxidants. Tannic acid is added at the cold conditioning stage.

Silica hydrogels and xerogels are increasingly used to remove haze-forming proteins from beer. These are matrices literally produced from a fundamental component of sand but in forms that have porous structures able to absorb macromolecules such as proteins. A range of these products is available, varying in their ability to take up proteins of different sizes. Most importantly, it is claimed that use of these materials does not eliminate the class of proteins that contribute the foam to beer.

A third opportunity to remove haze-forming protein is to add a protein-degrading enzyme to the beer. Most commonly, Brewers use papain, from the pawpaw fruit (the same enzyme that is used in meat tenderizer), but it is known that foam suffers as a result.

To reinforce beer foam, particularly to help its resistance to the damaging effects of oils and fats (see Chapter Three), some Brewers add propylene glycol alginate (PGA) to their beer. Like any material used in the brewing industry, PGA has been rigorously evaluated for its wholesomeness; like the carrageenans used in the brewhouse, it is derived from seaweed. The reader will be struck by the natural origins of the materials used in beer, not only the major raw materials but also the processing aids. Apart from PGA and carrageenan, we have isinglass finings (fish), kieselguhr (skeletons of diatoms), tannic acid (gallnuts), and beechwood chips.

Removing Microorganisms

Although beer is relatively resistant to spoilage (see Chapter Three), it is by no means entirely incapable of supporting the growth of microorganisms. For this reason, most beers are treated to eliminate any residual brewing yeast, infecting wild yeasts and bacteria before or during packaging. This can be achieved in one of two ways: pasteurization or filtration.

Pasteurization. Pasteurization can take one of two forms in the brewery: flash pasteurization for beer prepackage or tunnel pasteurization for beer in can or bottle. The principle in either case, of course, is that heat kills microorganisms. The higher the temperature, the more rapidly are microorganisms destroyed. A 7° C rise in temperature leads to a tenfold increase in the rate of cell death.

In flash pasteurization, the beer flows through a heat exchanger (essentially like a wort cooler acting in reverse; see Chapter Six), which typically raises the temperature to 72° C. Residence times of between 30 and 60 seconds at this temperature are sufficient to kill off virtually all microbes. Ideally there won't be many of these to remove: good Brewers ensure low loadings of microorganisms by paying attention to hygiene throughout the process and ensuring that the previous filtration operation is efficient. The configuration of the flash pasteurizer is such that heat from the beer leaving the device is used to warm that entering. It is essential to have the oxygen level of the beer as low as possible (preferably below 0.1 ppm) before pasteurization, because when temperatures are high, oxygen is "cooked" into the product, giving unpleasant flavors.

Tunnel pasteurization employs large heated chambers through which cans or glass bottles pass over a period of minutes, as opposed to the seconds employed in a flash pasteurizer. Accordingly, temperatures in a tunnel pasteurizer are lower, typically 60° C for a residence time of 10 to 20 minutes.

Sterile Filtration. An increasingly popular mechanism for removing microorganisms is to filter them out by passing the beer through a fine mesh filter. The rationale for selecting this procedure rather than pasteurization is as much for marketing reasons as for any technical advantage it presents: Many brands of beer these days are being sold on a claim of not being heat-treated and therefore free from "cooking." In fact, provided the oxygen level is very low, modest heating of beer does not significantly affect the flavor of many beers, although products with relatively subtle, lighter flavors will obviously display "cooked" notes more readily than will beers that have a more complex flavor.

The sterile filter must be located downstream from the filter used to separate solids from the beer. Sterile filters may be of several types; a common variant incorporates a membrane formed from polypropylene or polytetrafluoroethylene with pores of between 0.45 and 0.8 μm in diameter.

Gas Control

Downstream, apart from stabilization, final adjustment is made to the gas level in the beer. As we have seen, it is important to have the oxygen level in the bright beer as low as possible. Unfortunately, whenever beer is moved around and processed in a brewery, there is always the risk of oxygen pickup. For example, oxygen can enter through leaky pumps. A check on oxygen content is made once the bright beer tank is filled and, if the level is above specification (which most Brewers set at 0.1 to 0.3 ppm), oxygen must be removed. This is achieved by purging the tank with an inert gas, usually nitrogen, from a sinter in the base of the vessel. It is not a desirable practice, because whenever a purging process takes place, the beer foams. The foam sticks to the side of the tank and dries, and the resulting flakes fall into the beer to form unsightly bits.

The level of carbon dioxide in a beer may need to be increased or decreased. The majority of beers contain between 2 and 3 volumes of CO_2, whereas most brewery fermentations generate "naturally" no more than 1.2 to 1.7 volumes of the gas. The simplest and most usual procedure for introducing CO_2 is by injection as a flow of bubbles as beer is transferred from the filter to the bright beer tank. If the CO_2 content needs to be dropped, this is a more formidable challenge. It may be necessary for beers that are supposed to have a relatively low carbonation (beers such as the nitrokegs or draft-beers-in-can discussed in Chapter Two). As for oxygen, this can be achieved by purging. However, concerns about "bit" production have stimulated the development of gentle membrane-based systems for gas control. Beer flows past membranes made from polypropylene or polytetrafluoroethylene, membranes that are water-hating and therefore don't "wet-out." Gases, but not liquids, pass freely across such membranes, the rate of flux being proportional to the concentration of each individual gas and dependent also on the rate at which the beer flows past the membrane. If the CO_2 content on the other side of the membrane is lower than that in the beer, the level of carbonation in the beer decreases. If the CO_2 content on the other side of the membrane is higher than that in the beer, the beer becomes more highly carbonated. Gases behave independently, so the membranes can be used simultaneously to remove CO_2 from a beer and also to remove any oxygen from it, providing the levels of both gases are lower on the other side of the membrane. This technique is also an excellent opportunity to introduce nitrogen into beer, a gas that we have seen (in Chapter Three) has tremendous benefits for beer foam.

Packaging

The final process stage, prior to warehousing, is to put the beer into its intended package. In Chapter One (Table 1.2) we saw the relative distribution of beer packaged for draft (large pack) dispense as opposed to small pack in different countries of the world. In the United States in 1995 the balance of packaging was 11% on draft, 53% into cans, 33% into nonreturnable glass bottles, and the remainder in glass bottles returned to the Brewer for washing and refilling. The equivalent percentages in the member states of the European Union are shown in Table 8.1. As we saw in Chapter One, Ireland and the United Kingdom sell large proportions of their beer on draft dispense. In most other countries the favored package is the bottle, usually those that are returned to the brewery for washing and reuse. In France and Italy, though, much of the beer is retailed in nonreturnable glass, while in Sweden the highest proportion of beer is sold in cans.

Table 8.1. Domestic beer sales by container type (1996)

Country	% Draft	% Can	% Nonreturnable bottle	% Returnable bottle
Austria	32	9	1	58
Belgium	39	5	3	53
Denmark	8	0	0	92
Finland	25	4	0	71
France	24	6	56	14
Germany	19	14	3	64
Greece	6	16	5	73
Ireland	80	11	5	4
Italy	16	10	62	12
Luxembourg	52	2	11	35
Netherlands	31	*	*	*
Norway	28	1	<1	71
Portugal	30	5	11	54
Spain	33	10	22	35
Sweden	13	58	1	28
Switzerland	33	4	21	42
United Kingdom	66	24	8	2

*Individual data for small pack products not available.

Time was when all beer was on draft, in that beer was purchased from the alehouse or even the brewery in earthenware and pewter jugs and diverse other receptacles. In the United Kingdom it was the removal of a tax on glass that stimulated the bottling of beer as the twentieth century dawned.

The first trials for putting beer into cans took place in post-Prohibition New Jersey, when the Kreuger Brewing Company of Newark first sold canned beer in January 1935. A packaging medium that was light, non-breakable, and protected beer absolutely from the adverse influences of light was an immediate success. Just one year later the Welsh Brewer, Felinfoel, emulated Kreuger, taking advantage of the presence of can-manufacturing capabilities of the nearby steel industry. Now canned beer accounts for a quarter of the beer production in the United Kingdom, a proportion that has increased substantially in recent years following the development of the widget (see Chapter Two) and the shift toward drinking at home. The earlier enthusiasm for purchasing beer in plastic bottles for home consumption has subsided considerably; although the barrier properties of plastics are improving, such bottles can have a tendency to allow air to enter, causing the beer to stale.

The traditional package for beer in the United Kingdom, of course, is the cask, originally made from wood by coopers but increasingly composed of aluminum or stainless steel. In the United Kingdom, there is still a healthy market for cask-conditioned ale, beer that is not pasteurized and that retains yeast within it that serves to naturally carbonate the product. The yeast is settled out from the beer using isinglass finings, and it is essential to handle the beer carefully to avoid disturbing the sediment, rendering the beer cloudy.

Although the remarkable growth of microbrewers in the United States has introduced this type of beer increasingly into the consciousness of the American drinker, by and large such ale has not always achieved total acclaim within this market. Certainly, the men of the U.S. Army Air Corps stationed in East Anglia, England, in World War II didn't care to have cloudy beer delivered to them as they returned from missions. A shortage of glass meant that bottled beer was out of the question. The quandary prompted Air Force General Curtis LeMay to approach a nearby Brewer, Greens of Luton, to see how they could overcome the problem. Over $150,000 was spent on developing the process of putting beer that was carbonated and sediment-free into metal barrels. Keg beer was born.

Filling Bottles. Glass bottles used for holding beer come in diverse shapes and sizes. Only recently I saw a bottle in the shape of a baseball bat! The glass may be brown or black, green or clear (which is usually referred to as flint glass). Marketing people are increasingly obsessed with packaging beer in colored glass—as long as it isn't brown! They should listen to their technical colleagues: As we saw in Chapter Three, unless precautions are taken, beer develops a pronounced skunky character within seconds of exposure to light. Brown (or black) glass minimizes the access of light to beer, whereas green or flint glass provides no protection whatsoever.

Bottles entering the brewery's packaging hall are first washed, whether they are one-trip (disposable) or returnable. The former receive simply a water wash, as the supplier will have been required to make sure they arrive at the plant in a clean state. Returnable bottles, after they have been automatically removed from their crates and delivered to conveyors, need a much more robust cleaning and sterilization, inside and out, involving soaking and jetting with hot caustic detergent and thorough rinsing with water. Old labels are soaked off in the process. The cleaned and sterilized bottles pass an empty bottle inspector (EBI), a light-based detection system that spots any foreign body lurking in the bottle. Now they're on their way to the filler.

The beer coming from the bright beer tanks (after filtration) is transferred to a bowl at the heart of the filling machine. Bottle fillers are machines based on a rotary carousel principle. They have a series of filling heads: The more heads, the greater the capacity of the filler. Modern bottling halls are capable of filling in excess of 1,200 bottles per minute. If you go into the bottling hall, you will see these mighty beasts whirling round with empty bottles chinking their way toward it and full ones whizzing away from it.

The bottles enter on a conveyor and, sequentially, each is raised into position beneath the next vacant filler head, each of which comprises a filler tube. An air-tight seal is made and, in modern fillers, a specific air evacuation stage starts the filling sequence. (We have already seen how damaging oxygen is to beer quality.) The bottle is counterpressured with carbon dioxide before the beer is allowed to flow, by gravity, from the bowl into the bottle. The machine will have been adjusted so that the correct volume of beer is introduced into the vessel. Once filled, the "top" pressure on the bottle is relieved, and the bottle is released from its filling head. It passes rapidly to the machine, which will crimp on the crown cork. En route, the bottle will have been either tapped, or its contents "jetted," with a minuscule amount of sterile water in order to fob the contents of the bottle and drive off any air from the space in the bottle between the surface of the beer and the neck (the headspace).

Next stop is the tunnel pasteurizer (see earlier) if the beer is to be pasteurized after filling—although as we have seen, more and more beer is sterile filtered and packaged into already sterilized bottles. In the latter case the filler and capper tend to be enclosed in a sterile room to which only necessary personnel are allowed access.

The bottles now pass through a scanner, which checks to see that they are filled to the correct level; to the labeler, where labels are rolled on to the bottles; and then perhaps to a device that will apply foil to the neck. Other specialized equipment may involve jetting on a packaging date or "best before" date. Finally, the bottles are picked up by a machine that places them carefully into a crate, or box, or whichever is the secondary package in which they will be transferred to the customer. Perhaps they will go straight from this operation onto a truck or rail car for shipping, but more often they will be stored carefully in a warehouse prior to release.

Canning.   Putting beer into cans has much in common with bottling. It is the container, of course, that is very different—and definitely one trip!

Cans may be aluminum or stainless steel and will have an internal lacquer to protect the beer from the metal surface and vice versa. They arrive in the canning hall on vast trays, all preprinted and instantly recognizable. They are inverted, washed, and sprayed prior to being filled in a manner very similar to the bottles. The lid is fitted to the filled can by folding the two pieces of metal together to make a secure seam past which neither beer nor gas can pass. (To get an idea of this process, bend the fingers of both your hands toward the palms, then put the right hand palm downward on top of the left hand palm up before sliding the right hand toward the right until the ends of the fingers on the right hand are tight underneath those on the left hand. Squeeze the fingers on both hands toward your palms. The tight fit you have created is exactly analogous to the seal between a can and its lid.)

Kegging.   Kegs are manufactured from aluminum or stainless steel. They are containers generally of 1 hl or less, which contain a central spear through which beer is introduced in the packaging hall or dispensed in the bar. Kegs, of course, are multitrip devices. On return to the brewery from an outlet they are washed externally before transfer to the multihead machine in which successive heads are responsible for their washing, sterilizing, and filling. Generally, they are inverted as this takes place. The cleaning involves high-pressure spraying of the entire internal surface of the vessel with water at approximately 70° C. After about 10 seconds, the keg passes to the steaming stage, the temperature reaching 105° C over a period of perhaps half a minute. Then the keg goes to the filling head, where a brief purge with carbon dioxide precedes the introduction of beer, which may take a couple of minutes. The discharged keg is weighed to ensure that it contains the correct quantity of beer and is labeled and palleted before warehousing.

*   *   *

Right to the last process stage, then, with the weighing of the kegs, the Brewer is conscientiously ensuring that the product is precisely right for the consumer. As we have seen in Chapters Four through Eight, the

Maltster and Brewer operate processes that are carefully controlled to ensure consistency. To help them achieve this, they need procedures for measuring the raw materials and the various streams and for analyzing the finished product to ensure that everything is in order. So far I have mentioned the sorts of measures that are taken to monitor the raw materials and the process. Now, in Chapter Nine, we will find out how the Brewer analyzes the beer itself.

MEASURE FOR MEASURE

How Beer Is Analyzed

A former colleague of mine used to talk of his boyhood and of his father coming home from the pub. "That was a good pint tonight," the father would announce, doubtless licking his lips. The inference was that, some evenings, it wouldn't be a good pint.

These days the production of beer is marked by strong quality control. Indeed, breweries are as aware as any industry of the merits of applying principles of quality assurance out of respect for an ethos of "right first time" and backed up by adherence to international quality standards such as ISO 9000.

As we have seen, malting and brewing are not simple processes. They are marked by a complex blend of vegetative and mechanical stages, during any of which there is plenty of opportunity for things to go wrong. That they seldom do is testimony to the skill of the Maltster and the Brewer—and to the availability of robust analytical methodology.

THE ANALYSIS OF BEER

A Brewer would not succeed if his or her measurements were made on finished beer alone. Throughout this book, I have drawn attention to the sorts of specifications that are placed on raw materials and in individual process stages. The establishment of specifications demands the availability of methodology to make the necessary measurements. Wherever possible, Brewers install sensors to make automatic measurements with associated control systems that respond to the values measured. If these values are out of specification, they adjust a relevant parameter to push the process back on track. For example, temperature is readily measured remotely during fermentation; if it rises, it can be automatically lowered by triggering the circulation of coolant through the jackets of the fermenters.

Temperature is one of the fundamental parameters that need to be measured, and thus controlled, throughout the malting and brewing processes. Others include rates of liquid flow, pressure, and fill heights in vessels. Table 9.1 lists the other parameters that are routinely checked in a brewery to confirm that the process is progressing according to plan at all stages.

This chapter concentrates on the analysis of the finished beer itself. The techniques used confirm that a batch of beer is acceptable for packaging and for subsequent release into the trade. Equally, some of the methods used in the trade confirm that the product is in good condition.

Table 9.1. Analyses that should be made and responded to
for the brewing process to be kept under control

Parameter	Methodology
Absence of taints in water supply	Taste it daily
Specific gravity of wort collected in brewhouse and when fermenter is filled	Hydrometer or 'vibrating' U-tube instrumentation
Dissolved oxygen in wort pre-yeast dosing	Oxygen sensor
Amount of yeast "pitched"	Sensors based on light scatter or permittivity
Vicinal diketones in freshly fermented beer	Spectrophotometry or gas chromatography
Alcohol content of beer for declaring duty and controlling dilution of high-gravity brews	Various, including distillation, gas chromatography, or near infrared spectroscopy
Gases (CO_2, O_2, N_2) in bright beer	Specific gas sensors
Clarity of bright beer	Hazemeter
Color of bright beer	Spectrophotometer, tintometer, tristimulus colorimeter
Bitterness of bright beer	Spectrophotometry, high-performance liquid chromatography
Parameters during packaging (alcohol, gases, color, contents, integrity of seams between can and lid)	Physical stripdown and visual examination for seam checks
Caustic strength of CIP detergent	Titration
Flavor acceptability	Taste contents of all packages

They can also be applied to assess a competitor's beers to see what "tricks" they are employing and to try to unravel some of the procedures they are using to make a particular beer. Despite the fierce competition that exists between Brewers, they do share a spirit of cooperation in establishing the methodology used to measure their products. The driving forces for this are severalfold. First, Brewers must clearly use methods for measuring alcohol that enable them to directly compare the strength of their products for duty declaration purposes and to identify the strength of the product for the consumer. Second, there is much cross-brewing of beers: Brewers may well franchise-brew the products of a competitor. There is obviously a need for a common language to describe the attributes of a beer.

For these reasons, Brewers come together through various forums. In 1886, the Laboratory Club first met at a coffee house in Fitzroy Square, London, to enable British Brewers to share experiences. It developed into the Institute of Brewing (IOB), which now serves this purpose internationally. Among its roles is the publication and development of standardized methods. Relevant methods are debated in committee before being written up in an understandable, standardized format that can be easily used by various laboratories. The method and samples for measurement are circulated to a wide range of laboratories who individually produce a set of data. These data are collated and analyzed statistically by the committee, which assigns values for repeatability (r_{95}) and reproducibility (R_{95}). *Little r* (as it is called) is a measure of how consistent the results are when a method is applied by the same analyst in a single location. *Big R* is an index of how good the agreement is when a method is applied to the same sample but in different laboratories with different analysts. Only if these values are acceptably low will any confidence be placed in a method for its ability to give reliable and reproducible values that can be used not only for process control but also as a basis for transactions. If values for r_{95} and R_{95} are good, the method will be added to the IOB Methods of Analysis.

Similar activities occur within the European Brewery Convention (EBC) and the American Society of Brewing Chemists. There are clear differences between the various sets of methods, but also lots of similarities, and measures have been taken to harmonize at least the methods of the IOB and EBC. Pressures to prevent this are largely founded in history, in that the IOB methods relate more closely to technology employed in the British Isles (and some of her old colonies!), whereas the EBC methods relate to Continental brewing techniques. As brewing companies become more international and individual brands break down national barriers, it is the state of origin of a beer that tends to dictate how it will be analyzed.

The methods can be classified in several ways. Perhaps the most useful for our purposes is classification by chemical analysis, microbiological analysis, and organoleptic analysis.

Chemical Analysis

Alcohol. Perhaps the most critical measure made on beer is of its alcohol content. In many countries (although the United States is not one of them) duty is levied on the basis of alcohol content. In the United Kingdom, for instance, the rate of duty collection is in proportion to how much alcohol there is. Effective January 1, 1998, every 0.1% (by volume) increment in alcohol fetches an extra £1.12 ($1.68) per hectoliter in excise duty. So a pint of beer containing 4% alcohol fetches duty of 25.32 pence (38 cents), whereas a pint of beer of 4.1% attracts duty of 25.95 pence (38.9 cents) per pint.

Clearly a Brewer in the United Kingdom needs to be able to declare the alcohol content at least within an accuracy of 0.1%. The methodology employed can vary: Her Majesty's Customs and Excise stipulate only that a chosen method should be proven to give sufficiently precise results. Most commonly, alcohol is measured by gas chromatography; other methods include refractometry and specific alcohol sensors.

Allied to the declaration of alcohol, the Brewer must also identify for customs purposes (and also to satisfy weights and measures legislation) the volume of beer that is being produced for sale. This is generally established on a container-by-container basis by weighing the vessel, be it a keg, can, or bottle. Application of statistical distribution analysis indicates whether the inevitable spread of weights across a population of containers is within acceptable limits.

Accurate measurement of alcohol is also necessary to control the strength of beer produced by high-gravity fermentation techniques. As we saw in Chapter Seven, it is frequent practice for fermentation to occur in a concentrated state, with the beer diluted just prior to packaging. This dilution is controlled on the basis of alcohol content, with deaerated water being added to bring the alcohol content down to that specified for the beer in question. In many breweries this control is carried out in-line. A sensor prior to the dilution point measures the alcohol content continuously and regulates the rate of flow for beer and water at the subsequent mixing point. The alcohol-measuring sensor may be based on one of several principles, one of the most common being near-infrared spectroscopy.

Carbon Dioxide.   Carbon dioxide is also produced in fermentation, so it is a critical parameter to be measured in the finished product. The level of CO_2 is measured in the bright beer tank, most frequently using an instrument that measures CO_2 on the basis of pressure. If the gas level is too low, CO_2 is bubbled in to meet the appropriate specification. If the level is too high, carbonation can be reduced to specification levels by sparging with nitrogen or by using hydrophobic gas control membranes (see Chapter Eight).

Original Extract and Residual Extract.   The term *original extract* is frequently encountered. Allied to the measurement of alcohol, it is an indicator of the strength of a product. If the alcohol content of a beer is known, it is possible to calculate the quantity of fermentable sugar that must have been present in the wort prior to fermentation. This can be added to the real extract (sometimes called the residual extract and which comprises nonfermented material, primarily dextrins) to obtain a value for the original extract. The real extract is determined as specific gravity using a hydrometer or, more commonly these days, a gravity meter. These operate by vibrating a U-tube filled with the beer. The frequency of oscillation relates to how much material is dissolved in the sample. The real extract tells the brewer whether the balance of fermentable to nonfermentable carbohydrate in the wort was correct and whether the fermentability of the wort was too high or too low.

pH.   Another indicator of fermentation performance is the pH of the beer. During fermentation, acids such as citric and acetic acid are secreted by yeast, and the pH drops. The more vigorous and extensive the fermentation, the lower the pH goes. pH has a substantial effect on beer quality (see Chapter Three), primarily by its influence on flavor and its ability to suppress microbial growth. pH is measured with a pH electrode. As yet, no pH probe is robust enough for placing in-line in a brewery.

Color.   All beers have their characteristic color, whether it is the pale-ness of lagers or the intense darkness of a stout. The most frequently used procedure for assessing color is by measuring the absorbency of light at a wavelength of 430 nm. For many products there is a reasonable correlation between this value and color, but the correlation is by no means absolute. The perception of color by the human eye depends on the assessment of absorption at all wavelengths in the visible spectrum. It is no surprise, then, that a panel of expert judges could distinguish beers displaying identical absorption of light at 430 nm but which had small but significant differences in hue. The modern standard for color measurement in many industries is based on tristimulus and chromaticity, which describe color in terms of its relative lightness and darkness and its hue. As yet, this tech-nique is not standardized, but it surely must be before long. The nearest thing to it is a technique employed by traditionalists for a great many years, namely the comparison of the color of the beer with those of each of several discs in a device called a Lovibond Tintometer.

Clarity.   Another key visual stimulus in beer is its brightness, or clarity. Although a very few beers are intended to be turbid to a greater or lesser extent, for most beers cloudiness is undesirable. Haze is measured in beer by assessing light scatter by particles. Traditionally, this was by shining light through the beer and measuring the amount of light scattered at an angle of 90°. The more light scattered, the greater the haze. For most beers there is good agreement between the amount of light scattered in this way and the perceived clarity of the product—but not for all. Sometimes a beer may contain extremely small particles that are not readily visible to the human eye but that scatter light strongly at 90°. The beer looks bright, but the hazemeter tells a different story. This phenomenon is called invis-ible haze or pseudohaze. It doesn't present a quality problem in the trade, but it is highly problematic for the Brewer, as he is forced to make a qualitative judgment as to whether a beer rejected instrumentally is satis-factory for release to trade. Nowadays there are hazemeters that read light scatter at 13° rather than at right angles, and these don't pick up invisible haze. Unfortunately, they also miss some of the bigger particles. Some Brewers measure light scatter at both angles, but all will ultimately look at the beer for the acid test!

Dissolved Oxygen.   Even though a beer is bright when freshly pack-aged, it may develop haze after a greater or lesser period of time in the trade. One cause of this could be a high level of oxygen in the package. An even more likely problem in the presence of high oxygen levels is staleness. Brewers therefore are rigorous about excluding oxygen from the packaged beer. To an increasing extent, they try to exclude oxygen further and further back in the process. Reliable measurement of oxygen is essential, and this is generally carried out using an electrode based on principles of electrochemistry, voltametry, or polarography. It must be carried out before any pasteurization, for the heating will "cook in" the oxygen.

Prediction of Stability. Oxygen is only one factor that will influence the physical breakdown of a beer. The most common building blocks of a beer haze are proteins and polyphenols (tannins). As yet, nobody has proved which of the proteins in beer are particularly prone to throw hazes and, until this is determined, the only way to test the level of haze-susceptible protein is to titrate them out. In some quality control laboratories, samples of beer are dosed with aliquots of ammonium sulfate or tannic acid. The more of these agents needed to precipitate out a haze, the less haze-forming protein is present. Many Brewers measure the other components of haze, the polyphenols. These can be quantified by measuring the extent of color formation when beer is reacted with ferric (iron) ions in alkaline solution. Although this measures total polyphenols, it is a very useful means for checking whether a polyphenol adsorbent such as PVPP has done its job or whether it needs to be regenerated. (Not all polyphenols are harmful; for instance, some are likely to be antioxidants.) Most frequently, beer stability is forecast with breakdown tests. Beer may be subjected, for instance, to alternate hot and cold cycles, to try to simulate storage in a more rapid time frame.

Bitterness. Most Brewers rely on a method introduced over 40 years ago by a famed American brewing scientist, Mort Brenner. It involves extracting the bitter iso-α-acids from beer with the solvent *iso*-octane and measuring the amount of ultraviolet light that this solution absorbs at 275 nm. The greater the absorbency, the greater the bitterness. There is much debate about the use of high-performance liquid chromatography (HPLC) for measuring the level of bitterness in beers. This technique certainly enables the quantitation of individual isomers of iso-α-acids, thus making possible a closer measure of the perceived bitterness of a beer.

Diacetyl.   All responsible Brewers measure the level of diacetyl in their beers. As we saw in Chapter Seven, diacetyl is produced in all brewery fermentations, which must be prolonged until the yeast has consumed it. A colorimetric method is available to measure diacetyl, but more frequently it is assessed by gas chromatography. It is important to measure not only free diacetyl, but also its immediate precursor, a substance called acetolactate. If any of the latter is left in the beer, it can break down to release diacetyl in the package, giving a most unpleasant butterscotch character to the beer. Before the gas chromatography, therefore, the sample of beer is warmed to break down any precursor to diacetyl.

Other Flavor Compounds.   Diacetyl is easily the most frequently analyzed flavor component of beer. Some Brewers measure others as well, but for all Brewers it is through smelling and tasting the beer that they make their key assessment of its acceptability for release to trade. Recently, trials have been undertaken with so-called artificial noses, sensors that are claimed to mimic the human olfactory system. They are far from ready for the job (doubtless to the satisfaction of Brewers everywhere!). Among the volatiles that the brewing quality control lab may be required to measure by gas chromatography are dimethyl sulfide and a range of esters and fusel oils. It is most likely that this will be on a survey basis, perhaps monthly, rather than brew by brew.

Foam Stability and Cling.   By measuring the carbon dioxide content, the Brewster has an index of whether a beer has sufficient capability to generate a foam. This will not evaluate foam *stability*, for which another type of analysis is necessary. This is a difficult task and there is much debate over the best way to measure foam stability. In the United States there is reasonable acceptance of the sigma value test (see Box on facing page) as the recommended method; however, the Institute of Brewing does not seem to believe that any method is worthy of recommendation. The two most frequently used procedures worldwide are those of Rudin and NIBEM (see Box).

If the measurement of head retention is challenging, then that of lacing is even moreso! (See Box on page 180.)

An alternative strategy for assessing the foaming potential of a beer is to measure the various components of the beer that promote foam and ensure that they are present. Equally important, one should monitor and ensure the absence of foam-negative components. By measuring CO_2 and

Measurement of Beer Foam Stability

One of the great truths of analytical science is that if there are many methods for measuring something, then none of them can be much good. And there are a lot of methods for measuring foam quality—at least 20!

In the United States, one of the most widely used procedures is the sigma value method. In this test, foam is produced by pouring the beer into a specially designed funnel. The stability of the foam is then calculated from an equation that compares the amount of beer that has drained from the foam in a period of 3 or 4 minutes with the amount of beer that is still held in the foam itself. This method therefore depends on measuring the rate at which beer drains from foam: The more slowly the beer reforms as a liquid, the more stable the foam.

Forty years ago, Derek Rudin developed another drainage procedure that employs a long thin glass tube. A little beer is introduced into the bottom of the tube before carbon dioxide is bubbled through it to convert it all into foam, which rises up the tube. When the top of the foam hits a line marked off on the glass tube, the gas supply is switched off. The foam, of course, starts to collapse, and as it does so, the beer starts to reform at the bottom of the column. The analyst, armed with a stop watch, measures the rate at which the beer reforms by timing the rise of the foam–beer interface in terms of the seconds or minutes it takes to pass between two more marks on the glass tube. The longer this period of time, the more stable the foam.

A third device, this one developed by a Dutchman named Walter Klopper in the 1970s and called the NIBEM method, works on a different principle. Here the beer is poured into a glass; a plate with needles on it is lowered into the top of the foam. These needles sense the conductivity of the foam (suffice to say that this enables the needles to differentiate the liquid in the foam from the air above the foam). As the foam collapses, the needles lose the conductivity signal, and they send a message to a motor, which lowers the needles until the foam is contacted again. This continues as the foam collapses; clearly, the more rapidly the needles lower, the less stable is the foam. The rate of lowering is flashed up as a digital readout in terms of seconds.

From personal experience, I would have to say that the last of these methods is the one that most frequently (but by no means always) correlates with the stability of the heads of beer in the marketplace.

Measurement of Beer Foam Lacing

Few Brewers attempt to make an objective measurement of lacing. Those that do have tried photography, light scanning of the foam coverage of the glass surface with measurement by a photocell, and also light scatter. I'll mention my preferred procedure—and not only because Gordon Jackson and I devised it!

There are a couple of variants of the test, but the easiest is to pour a glass of beer in the time-honored way and then to take out the beer progressively. As we saw in Chapter Three, it is only when foam has "aged" that it is capable of lacing a glass. This takes time. If you are thirsty and consume all your beer in one gulp, then there won't be any foam left sticking to the glass! If, however, you leave a minute or two between sips from the glass, then a nice pattern of cling should form on the glass (providing the beer contains enough protein and bitter compounds and the glass is clean).

In our test, then, we take the beer out of the glass in stages that are two minutes apart to mimic this drinking. (Technically speaking it would be possible to remove the beer by drinking, but that hardly allows more than a few assays!) The beer is in fact siphoned off through a very narrow tube lowered into the beer and the beer–foam interface successively lowered to a series of marks on the side of the glass.

When all the beer has been removed, 50 ml of water is used to dissolve the foam that is sticking as lace to the side of this glass, and the amount of ultraviolet light that this solution absorbs at 230 nm is measured in a spectrophotometer. The more UV light absorbed, the more foam is dissolved in the water, and the greater was the lacing on the side of the glass.

It's a robust—and a fun—method. Sadly, most Brewers like their QC methods to be a tad faster than this one!

bitterness, the Brewer already has a handle on two key components that promote foam. Recently, we recommended the use of hydrophobic interaction chromatography to measure the hydrophobic polypeptides that promote foam. And those Brewers who use nitrogen gas to promote excellence in their foams can measure it using an instrument relying on membrane separation and specific conductivity measurement. There is as yet, however, no satisfactory way of measuring foam-negative components in beer. Moreover, it is far more likely that these will get into the beer during the dispense and consumption of beer rather than in the brewery itself. No method for assessing foam quality can forecast all the perils that a beer must face and predict the ingress of materials that will destroy the foaming potential that the brewer has painstakingly introduced into his beer.

Metals and Other Ions.   Several inorganic ions are measured in the brewery, mostly on a survey basis. Iron and copper are very bad news for beer, as they promote oxidation (otherwise iron would be a useful foam stabilizer). They are measured by atomic absorption spectroscopy, as is calcium. Liquid chromatography is used to detect the levels of a range of anions, such as chloride and sulfate, the balance of which is defined beer by beer for the effect it has on palate. The level of oxalate is compared to that of calcium to ensure that there is not going to be a problem with beer stone in the trade.

Microbiological Analysis

A few years ago a keen young brewer was inspecting the open square fermenters in an old-fashioned English brewery when he spotted a thick crust caked onto the inside. He scraped a lump off with his hand and marched in to see the head brewer.

"What's that, lad?" said the old man.

"It's dirt from the top of a fermenter," replied the young fellow, proud of his discovery and firmly resolved to clean up the plant.

"Well put it back," stormed the boss. "Where do you think the character in our beer comes from?"

The story is apocryphal (I think!). It does, however, serve to remind us that, despite the fact that beer is relatively resistant to microbial infection, thanks to hops (see Chapter Five), there is still plenty of opportunity for organisms to infect the process and the product.

Traditionally, microbiological analysis in breweries consisted of taking samples throughout the process and inoculating them on agar-solidified growth media of various types designed to grow specific categories of bacteria or wild yeasts (i.e., any yeast other than the one used to brew the beer in question). When the plates were incubated for three to seven days, any bugs on them would grow to produce colonies. The more colonies, the greater the contamination. The problem is that by the time the results were made available and discussed with the Brewer, that particular batch of wort or beer would have long since moved on to the next stage. Any remedial procedures would only help subsequent brews.

Far-sighted Brewers now use a quality assurance approach to plant hygiene, allied to the use of rapid microbiological methodology. Much more attention is given to plant design for easy cleanability, checking of the efficiency of cleaning (CIP) systems (e.g., caustic checks), confirming that the pasteurizer is working by testing temperature, and applying various checks to test that heat-sensitive components are being destroyed.

Various rapid microbiological techniques have been advocated. The most publicized and most widely used is based on adenosine triphosphate (ATP) bioluminescence (Fig. 9.1). The method depends on the firefly, an insect that emits light from its tail as a mating signal. This reaction involves an enzyme called luciferase, which converts the chemical energy store found in all organisms (ATP) to light energy. The enzyme can be extracted and this reaction carried out in a test tube. The more ATP present, the more light is produced, and it can be measured using a luminometer.

The rapid test used by brewers requires scraping a swab across the surface that needs to be tested. The end of the swab is then broken off into a tube that contains an extractant, together with the luciferase. After a period that can be as short as a few minutes, the amount of light emitted is measured. The dirtier the surface (i.e., the more bugs and debris on it), the more ATP will have gotten onto the swab and, in turn, the more light will have been measured. And so, in real time, an indication can be obtained of the state of plant hygiene. The method has been extended to measuring very low levels of microorganisms in beer, enabling the brewer to release beer to trade with confidence just a few hours (or, at most, days) after it was packaged.

$$\text{D-Luciferin/Luciferase} + \text{ATP} + \text{Oxygen} + \text{Mg}^{2+} \longrightarrow$$

Figure 9.1. The principle of ATP bioluminescence as a method for detecting soil and microorganisms in a brewery. Swabs used to sample different parts of the brewery are broken off in a solution containing luciferin (a substrate), a little magnesium, and luciferase, an enzyme extracted from the tail of the firefly. If there are organisms or there is soil on the swab, the ATP therein reacts with the luciferin in the presence of luciferase to produce light.

Sensory (Organoleptic) Analysis

Although drinking beer is a complex sensorial experience, bringing into play diverse visual stimuli and environmental factors (see Chapter Three), ultimately it is the smell and taste of a beer that decide whether it will prove acceptable to the consumer. For this reason, much time and effort is devoted within the brewery to tasting beer at all stages in its production.

One of my past jobs was as the Quality Assurance Manager of a large English brewery, where the first job at break of day was to stand alongside Neil Talbot, the Head Brewer, and taste the previous 24 hours' production. (This is not as much fun as it might sound to some, believe me!) A sip of each beer would be taken and scored on a scale of 1 to 4. A value of 1 indicated that the beer was of the expected high quality; 2 meant a minor flaw, which would warrant a quick check of the records but the beer could go to trade, as any deficiency was predicted to be imperceptible in the trade; 3 indicated a serious shortcoming in the product that demanded serious investigation and holding the beer while a decision was made about what to do with it; and 4 meant there was a major problem requiring destruction of the beer and an urgent inquiry. Happily I don't recall any scores of 4 and very, very few 3s. We tasted beer at the cold conditioning stage, at the postfiltration stage, and after packaging. We also checked the water that was to be used to brew beer and dilute high-gravity beer.

The system was straightforward and highly effective as a screen to ensure that the highest quality standards were being maintained and that we had identified as early as possible whether things were going awry. For instance, by tasting beer prepackaging we could nip in the bud any faults before the expensive packaging process began. It demanded, of course, that Neil and I were sensitive to the flavors expected in each product. As a QA technique, it served the purpose for which it was intended.

Taste, though, is a complex sensation, which depends on the interaction of many receptors in the mouth and on aroma perception through the nasal system. Sweet, sour, salt, and bitter are the basic tastes contributed by any foodstuff, and there are receptors for each on the tongue. Sweetness is detected at the center of the tip of the tongue, with salt on the sides. Bitter registers right in the middle of the tongue, with sour on either side of it. There are, however, many other flavors in a product such as beer; they are all detected ultimately by receptors within the nose, despite the perception that they are tasted.

Because of this complexity, it is not surprising that drinkers differ considerably in their sensitivity to different flavors. People can be blind to certain characteristics or acutely sensitive to others. In either instance it can be a problem. It's just as well that Neil and I seemed to be fairly middle ground. Had either of us been acutely sensitive, for instance, to the butterscotch character from diacetyl (see Chapter Seven), we might have rejected beers that most of the population would have judged perfectly acceptable. Conversely, if we had been incapable of spotting diacetyl, we could have released to trade beer that most people would have deemed undrinkable.

For these reasons, beer tasting can be much more sophisticated than simply having a Head Brewer and QA Manager standing around a spittoon. It is essential to have reliable and statistically well-founded tests available that can provide authoritative and semiquantitative information that can be applied to make decisions about beer quality. Broadly, these methods can be divided into difference tests and descriptive tests.

Difference Tests.   As the name suggests, difference tests are intended to tell whether a difference can be perceived between two beers. For instance, the Brewer may be interested in checking whether one batch of beer differs from the previous batch of the same beer, or whether a process change has had an effect on the product, or whether batches of the same brand of beer brewed in two different breweries are similar, and so forth.

It is essential that the tasters are not distracted in this task. The environment has to be quiet, and they must not be influenced by the appearance of the product. The beer therefore is served in dark glasses and in a room fitted with artificial red light. The tasters have no opportunity to make contact with other assessors. It is important that the tasters' sensitivity is not influenced by their having recently enjoyed a cigarette or coffee or any strongly flavored food. Best to have the tasting session prior to lunch, especially if curry is on the menu.

The classic difference procedure is the three-glass test: a minimum of seven assessors is presented with three glasses. Two of the glasses contain one beer, the third the other beer. The order of presentation is randomized. All the taster has to do is indicate which beer she thinks is different. Statistical analysis will reveal whether a significant number of tasters is able to discern a difference between the beers and therefore whether, according to the law of averages, two beers will or will not be perceived as tasting different by the public.

Alcohol	ethanol, vinous, full
Astringent	mouthpuckering, harsh, tart
Bitter	tonic water, quinine
Body	Full: cloying, thick, chewy, creamy, viscous
	Thin: watery, characterless, dull, bland
Burnt	smoky, chocolate, licorice
Carbonation	High: grassy, CO_2, tingle, liveliness
	Low: flat, dill, lifeless
Cardboard	bready, papery, straw, sawdust
Cheesy	sweaty, old cheese
Cooked vegetable	cabbage, parsnip
Diacetyl	butterscotch, buttery, toffee, vanilla
DMS	tomato juice, black currants, sweetcorn, canned tomatoes, baked beans
Estery	bananas, pears, pineapple, solvent, winelike
Fatty acid	tallowy, waxy
Floral	roses, hyacinth, fresh hops, flowers
Fruity	citrus, grapefruit, orangy, lime
Grainy	husky, mealy, corn, grits
Grassy	green beans, mown grass, herbal
Hoppy	resinous, fresh hops, herbal
Lightstruck	skunklike, leeklike
Malty	bran, nutty, horlicks
Medicinal	TCP, disinfectant
Metallic	mouthcoating, rusty, tinny
Musty	moldy, earthy
Phenolic	hospital, disinfectant
Rancid	vomit
Ribes	tomcat, catty, black currant leaves
Soapy	oily, goaty
Sour	lemon juice
Spicy	cinnamon, cloves
Sulfidic	H_2S, rotten eggs
Sulfitic	SO_2, choking, striking match
Sweet	honey, syrupy, primings, cloying, sugar
Toffee	black treacle, cooked sugar, caramel
Worty	coconut, almondy, sweet, chewy
Yeasty	autolyzed yeast, yeast pressings

Figure 9.2. Terms used in the profiling of beer flavor.

Descriptive Tests.   The three-glass test can be carried out essentially by anyone. However, if a Brewer wants to have specific descriptive information about a beer, he must use trained tasters, people who are painstakingly taught to recognize a wide diversity of flavors, to articulate information about them, and to be able to profile a beer.

The terminology used is described in Figure 9.2. A group of individuals collect around a table and taste a selection of beers. They then score the individual attributes, perhaps on a scale from 0 (character not detectable) to 10 (character intense). Obviously it takes real ability to be able to separate out the various terms and recognize them individually, without allowing one parameter to influence another. Once the scoring is complete, the individuals discuss what they have found and agree on how the flavor of a beer should be summarized. The findings may be reported in the form of a spider diagram (Fig. 9.3).

This type of test is widely used to support new product development and brand improvement and, of course, to characterize a competitor's

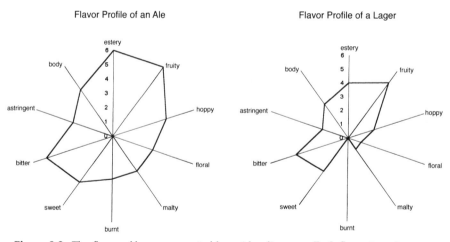

Figure 9.3. The flavor of beer represented by spider diagrams. Each flavor term is represented by a spindle. The more intense the score for a term, the higher is the score along the line. The individual scores are linked together to get a picture, the shape of which is characteristic for a product. Subsequent batches of that beer should have a pattern that essentially overlays that for the reference sample; if it doesn't, the specific flavor defect can be identified. Comparison of the two samples illustrated in this diagram shows that the ale has much higher flavor scores than the lager (i.e., its flavor is more complex and intense *for these particular flavor notes*). Had the spider diagram illustrated a term such as sulfury, the lager may well have registered a higher score than the ale.

beers. Once again, there are variants of this test, such as the trueness-to-type test. This procedure is well suited to assessing whether a beer brewed in one brewery is or is not similar to the reference (standard) beer brewed in another location. For each of various terms found in the flavor profile form, each assessor is asked to mark whether the sample has the same degree of that character (score = 0), slightly more (+1), substantially more (+2), slightly less (−1) or substantially less (−2). Obviously, the more flavor notes that are judged to have a score of 0, the more similar are the two beers.

Another test applied by Brewers is the evening drinkability or session test. This test is designed to assess whether a beer will prove satiating or whether the consumer will want to drink more than a single glass of it. One variant involves presenting the tasters (who don't necessarily have to be trained) with two or three beers whose drinkability is under assessment. The drinkers are asked to sip test each of them, pass comment on them, and then select one for continued drinking. They are able to switch to another beer at will. A careful record is made of how much of each beer is consumed—and the drinkers sent home by cab!

* * *

Such a test is, of course, somewhat primitive and unsophisticated, even if it can be rather informative. Many Brewers would value a straightforward test that will tell them in an uncomplicated way, Will the drinker *like* this beer? Alas, such a test must lie a good way into the future.

Which brings me now to ask: What does the future have in store for beer and brewing?

Chapter Ten

TO THE FUTURE

Malting and Brewing in Years to Come

The fundamental shape of the malting and brewing processes has remained similar for many years. The reader should not conclude from this that the industries are stagnant or primitive; rather, they should appreciate that the basic route from barley to beer, aided by hops and yeast, is essentially well fitted to the purposes for which it is intended. I hope, too, that a study of the previous chapters will lead the reader to conclude that an enormous amount of research has been devoted to unraveling the science of malting and brewing and to applying this knowledge—thus creating a living and thriving testimony to a time-honored biotechnology.

I do not foresee a dramatic change in the unit processes of malting and brewing in the near future, fundamentally for two reasons. First, the nature of beer is as it is *because* of these processes: Its flavor, its foam, its texture, its color, its wholesomeness all depend on the care and devotion invested by the Maltster, the Brewer, and the suppliers of hops and other ingredients. Which leads to the second justification for leaving the basic procedures as they are: Brewers *care*. They take a pride in their products and in their heritage and they are fundamentally convinced that the best interests of the consumer are served by ensuring that they adhere to professional standards. *Of course* the Maltster and the Brewer expect to operate efficient processes, using raw material and plant capacity resources economically. They know only too well, however, that their beers have the character they do because of a vast myriad of chemical and biochemical changes occurring during malting, brewing, fermentation, and downstream processing. It is a high-risk strategy to mess about with them. Accordingly, the far-sighted Maltster or Brewer listens attentively to suggestions for process adjustment and applies the science conscien-

189

tiously, but they resist absolutely any development that jeopardizes their product.

This book is filled with examples of how the malting and brewing processes have developed and have become vastly more efficient without fundamentally modifying the basic route from barley to beer. In Chapter Four we saw that interrupted steeping enabled the malting process to be foreshortened by several days and how the addition of extra gibberellic acid, a molecule naturally found in barley, can further speed up the process. Chapter Five tells that the essential bitter and aroma ingredients of hops can be introduced more efficiently into the process in a form free from the vegetative parts of the plant. Chapters Six and Seven show how the brewhouse and fermentation operations have been subtly altered to enormously improve efficiencies, without inherently changing the character of wort or beer; developments have included high-gravity brewing, pure yeast technology, and enhanced yeast-handling strategies. Chapter Eight indicates how enormous attention has been paid to stabilizing beer with beneficial effects on the consistency of beer quality. Advances here have included sterile filtration, use of nitrogen gas, and the application of stabilizing agents such as silica hydrogels. Finally, in Chapter Nine, we found how developments in analytical techniques are being applied by Brewers to achieve tight control over their process and product with genuine benefits for the consumer.

The future will see more improvements in the processes. Perhaps the most exciting opportunity centers on the use of gene technology.

GENE TECHNOLOGY

As I write, no Maltster or Brewer is directly using genetically modified raw materials. It may be that products *derived* from genetically improved organisms are used; for instance, some of the enzymes used to supplement those from the malt may be the products of gene technology but, of course, in this instance no genetic matter (DNA) per se enters the process.

The question is: Will Maltsters and Brewers take advantage of this exciting new technology? I believe the answer is *yes*, but only once they are absolutely convinced that there are real merits in so doing.

We have seen clear evidence of the readiness of these industries to embrace new technology, but there is also absolute caution applied by Maltsters and Brewers whenever change is suggested. Only when justification is 100% will a move be made. One has only to survey the history of brewing science to realize the truth of this statement. It is now over 20 years since the first research on genetic modification of brewing yeasts took place, and plenty of yeasts have been successfully modified. Even today, though, *none* of them is in commercial use.

Only one genetically modified brewing yeast has been cleared through all the necessary authorities, and this occurred in the United Kingdom. Should a brewing company wish to use it, they may. As yet, none has taken up the option. In part this seems to be because no Brewer wishes to be first into the marketplace with a beer labeled "product of gene technology." More importantly, however, none seems to be convinced that the merits of this particular organism outweigh the very real concerns that exist with the application of this science. The first Brewer to employ a genetically modified yeast will do so because it brings genuine benefit to the consumer. Perhaps the yeast will boost the levels of some component of beer that is beneficial to health (see Chapter Three). Or it might be a yeast that enables beer to be brewed substantially more cheaply (although I fail to see how the science of genetic modification can hope to address one of the most devastating cost components of beer in many countries: excise duty!).

The one yeast so far cleared for commercial use was "constructed" by John Hammond and his colleagues in our laboratories. A gene from another yeast has been introduced into a lager strain. This gene "codes" for an enzyme that will convert more of the starch into fermentable sugar, thereby enabling more alcohol to be made per unit of malt or, alternatively, enabling less malt to be used per unit of alcohol. As we saw in Chapter Six, not all of the starch from barley is converted into fermentable sugars in conventional brewhouse operations. To produce the diet beers that have more (even all) of these partial degradation products of starch (dextrins) shifted into alcohol, Brewers add an enzyme (called glucoamylase) that is capable of performing the extra conversion. What we did was to take the bit of the genetic code from *Saccharomyces diastaticus* that codes for this enzyme and transfer it to a conventional bottom-fermenting strain of *Saccharomyces cerevisiae*. This was done so efficiently that the extra DNA stayed in the yeast from generation to generation. Most importantly, we had transferred DNA from an organism that was extremely similar to the host organism: from one yeast to another one. And it worked! The host yeast was able to make the enzyme from the foreign bit of DNA and spew it into the wort, where it chopped up the dextrins. The fermentations were performed on scales as large 100 hl, and the beer produced was indistinguishable from that produced conventionally. The beer was produced, bottled, and labeled for research purposes only and was called Nutfield Lyte (Fig. 10.1).

The genetically modified yeast employed in making Nutfield Lyte was used as a test case for seeking approval from the necessary U.K. authorities. For approval to be granted, the yeast had to be cleared by *four* committees: the Advisory Committee for Novel Foods and Processes within the government's Ministry of Agriculture, Fisheries and Food; the Advisory Committee on Genetic Modification (part of the government's Health and Safety Executive); the Advisory Committee on Releases to the

Figure 10.1. Nutfield Lyte. A light beer fermented using a genetically modified yeast. It is brewed in the pilot brewery at Brewing Research International and is not available for sale. Its existence has, however, been widely publicized, for the most part with a positive or, at least, neutral reaction from the public in the United Kingdom.

Environment (Department of the Environment); and the Food Advisory Committee. Four different departments had a say—four separate elements to scrutinize every facet of the science, ethics, and safety of the project and who had to be satisfied before permission was granted. And *still* this yeast remains in the freezer awaiting application. Everybody is applying understandable caution, but all the evidence is that the technology is sound and safe, provided that a responsible attitude is adopted.

There is some way to go before suitable genetically modified barleys become available. They *will* be developed, perhaps with new properties such as enhanced disease resistance that will reduce the need to spray with pesticides. The Maltster will adopt the same cautious approach as the Brewer on whether to use them. Of course, both the Maltster *and* the Brewer have a stake in the use of barley: Indeed ultimately it will be the Brewer who will drive the use of genetically modified barley.

Gene technology, then, is an exciting concept and one that could provide genuine benefits. All the signs from the brewing industry are that the technology will only be used if those benefits accrue to the consumer.

WHAT WILL THE INDUSTRY LOOK LIKE IN TEN YEARS?

So how will our beer be made in the future? Can we anticipate a radically different approach to the traditional and semitraditional processes that have been used to make the world's favorite beverage for thousands of years? Or will the basic shape of the business stay as it is, with incremental improvements rather than radical alternatives continuing as the status quo?

I recently canvassed a selection of international experts from within the malting and brewing industries, asking them how they saw matters unraveling over a 10-year time frame.

Raw Materials

Nobody envisages a dramatic shift in the grist materials used for brewing. Indeed a number of Brewers have shifted back from sizable use of adjuncts to grists that are largely (if not entirely) of premium malted barley. They are convinced that this offers genuine quality, though there remains a clear justification for using other cereals when they offer unique attributes to, for instance, flavor or color.

The belief is that pressures will continue to minimize the use of additives in the growing of barley and its subsequent malting, yet everyone realizes that these agents can offer real advantages to the process and product: Better to use a pesticide in the production of barley and ensure its removal during steeping than to run the risk of a fungal infection of grain. Here, too, may be a major target for genetic modification: the construction of barleys that have inbuilt resistance to attack by undesirables.

There is concern that not enough premium malting quality barley will be available to meet the increasing demand for it. Leading hop varieties, particularly those with good aroma characteristics, will continue to be in heavy demand, and there may be shortages.

Brewing

The crystal ball suggests that brewhouse operations 10 years hence will not be radically different from those in place today. Already there has been an increase in the number of breweries incorporating mash filters rather than lauter tuns (see Chapter Six), and no successor to the mash filter seems to be emerging. Brewhouse operations may become continuous, to match continuous fermentation operations, yet few, if any, brewers seem to be convinced that continuous production of beer would be right for them.

Without doubt, though, Brewers, just like individuals in any other industrial sector, seek to lower their cost base. They all share the opinion, for instance, that processes will become far more automated, taking advantage of the rapid developments that are being made in the miniaturization, sensitivity, and flexibility of information technology. Automation has already happened to a considerable degree. The most impressive example of automation I have seen was in the warehouse operations of a major Japanese brewery. All but one of the forklift trucks was a robot, each busily shifting beer around the site according to a preprogram. And each truck played a tune as it trundled along—one was whistling *Yankee Doodle*!

Packaging

One brewer suggested to me that brewing could evolve to be a service to a distributed packaging industry, in just the same way that the soft drink industry operates today. It is certainly the case that approximately half of the cost of processing and, indeed, much of the innovation, is at this stage in the brewery operation. Therefore, issues such as reduced raw materials costs (for instance, use of aluminum), recycling, demanning of what tends to be a very labor-intensive function, and energy conservation are all to the fore.

The Product

The common theme, however, that ran through the replies on raw materials, brewing, packaging, and consideration of the beer itself is *quality*. In particular, Brewers anticipate beers having extended shelf lives to meet longer distribution chains, and there will be much more choice. The consumer is becoming more enlightened about issues of wholesomeness and quality. Brewers appreciate that they will have to meet drinker demand in this area, including the development of new beers with unique properties based on variables such as flavor, foaming, texture, and, in a very responsible manner, health attributes.

Research into consumer science areas is developing fast. In the future, it will be possible for producers of all types of foodstuffs, including beer, to be able to forecast with much more confidence which products will be enjoyed by the customer. Understanding the specific effects that different components of beer have on the sensory apparatus in the mouth and nose will enable the "design" of beers that are best suited to the enjoyment of the consumer.

Inputs and Outputs

Brewers will continue to strive toward minimizing inputs; for example, they will continue to develop processes that require less energy and less water. Consumption figures for efficient and inefficient breweries are shown in Table 10.1. Many breweries have a way to go to catch up with the pack. Even the leaders in the efficiency stakes are eager to improve.

The really energy-demanding operations in malting and brewing are malt kilning and wort boiling, and there is still some way to go in making substantial savings here without jeopardizing product quality.

Some concern exists for the ongoing availability of good-quality water for malting and brewing; this forces yet more attention on reducing water

Table 10.1. Inputs for the production of 100 hl of beer

Input	Efficient brewery	Less efficient brewery
Malt	1.5 tons	1.8 tons
Water	500 hl	2000 hl
Energy	15 gigajoules	35 gigajoules
Electricity	1000 kwh	2000 kwh

consumption in cleaning operations and on the need for more recycling. Concerning other outputs (other than the beer itself, of course), Brewers are adjusting their processing to reduce wastes such as spent grains, surplus yeast, and, of course, waste water. Naturally, the more efficiently a material such as malt is converted into beer, the less overflow there will be to spent grains. There is a long, long way to go, though, before malt will be entirely convertible into wort and thence beer. My own organization has gone further than any other conventional brewing operation toward introducing such changes. On a pilot scale, we have used acid hydrolysis of surplus grains to produce more sugars. The problem then became one of spent spent grains: The husk of barley is pretty resilient! Huskless varieties of barley are available, though they are susceptible to infection in the field. In terms of saving water, the focus has to be on the amount required for washing and cleaning purposes. Naturally, the smaller the plant relative to the output of beer, the less cleaning water is needed. Indeed, continuous processes run for days or weeks, potentially years, without stripping down and cleaning, and are therefore very economical in terms of water usage.

A former colleague was fond of drawing attention to the apparent illogicality of the malting and brewing processes: "We take moist barley from the field and, in drying, heat it to *drive off* water. Then we *add* water in steeping, germinate and then *drive off* water in kilning. To the brewery— and we *add* water in mashing. Then we *drive off* water in boiling." I took the point, of course, but reminded him that all of these stages are performed for very good reasons, which is not to say that there may not be radical alternatives in the future. Dry mashing, for instance?!

The Industry

There will be an ongoing drive toward international brands—recognized names that thrive far beyond home base. This will be achieved by acquisition, joint ventures (of the type seen in the construction and modernization of breweries in China), brand licensing, and contract brewing. Brewing companies will become further polarized, into the ever bigger at one extreme and the very small at the other. It will be those in the middle order that will find survival ever more challenging. More and more beer will be consumed at home, which is one of the justifications for increasing the shelf life of the product. Once a beer has been retailed, the Brewer has no further control over its handling. All he can hope to do is build robustness into the product.

*   *   *

"Robustness into the product." Those are apt words, indeed, with which to bring this book to a conclusion. Brewers (and their colleagues, notably Maltsters and hop suppliers) have devoted themselves for many, many years to delivering to the public a wholesome and flavorsome product, robust and so very consistent, glass to glass.

Beer has a long and proud tradition. Thanks to more than a century of dedicated research, brewing has developed into a tightly controlled, efficient technological process, albeit one, unavoidably and fascinatingly, subject to the vagaries of its agricultural inputs.

Brewing is very much a science. Engage a brewer in conversation, though, and see the twinkle in his or her eye and you will rapidly come to the conclusion that they love their brewing and their beer—just as all connoisseurs love their chosen art.

SOME SCIENTIFIC PRINCIPLES

I realize that not everybody reading this book will have enjoyed scientific training. To help such people I offer here a simple crash course in chemistry, biology, and biochemistry, with just a little physics thrown in.

ELEMENTS AND COMPOUNDS

All matter in this world, whether animal, vegetable, or mineral, consists of chemicals. One of the simplest of these—and yet one of the most important—is water. Most of us know it as H_2O, which means that it is made up of two hydrogen atoms and one oxygen atom. An atom is the smallest unit of an element, and it is from the elements that all matter is composed. At the last count there were over 100 elements. The simplest is hydrogen, which is given the symbol H. Other important ones include oxygen (O), nitrogen (N), sulfur (S), sodium (Na, after the Latin *natrium*), and chlorine (Cl). Perhaps the key element in life is carbon (C). Organic chemistry is the chemistry of carbon compounds. The key components of living organisms are organic compounds in that carbon is a key element in them.

A compound is a chemical entity, with its own individual properties, consisting of a collection of atoms of the same or different elements. The basic unit of a compound is a molecule. Water is a compound of hydrogen and oxygen. So, too, is hydrogen peroxide, H_2O_2. The latter molecule has just one extra oxygen atom, but this makes all the difference. Hydrogen peroxide is extremely reactive and finds uses as diverse as bleaching hair and sending rockets to the moon! Water is, of course, a wonderful solvent (a solvent is something in which a solute can dissolve. For instance, if you add sugar to water, sugar is the solute and water the solvent.) As we shall see, it is this ability to dissolve things that makes water so important to life—including the brewing of beer!

There are a great many organic compounds. Some are very simple; for example, natural gas consists of the simplest, *methane*, whose molecule consists of one carbon and four hydrogen atoms (CH_4). (Incidentally, carbon dioxide, CO_2, the compound that puts the fizz in beer, is *not* classified as an organic compound.) At the other extreme are very complicated molecules that consist of a great many carbon atoms and other atoms, too. Here I will refer to those compounds that are relevant to living systems such as barley, hops, and yeast.

CARBOHYDRATES

Starch is a carbohydrate, as is sugar. In fact the term *sugar* refers to a wide range of related substances, and not just sucrose—which is the granulated sugar that you stir into your coffee. The simplest sugar is glucose, which has the formula $C_6H_{12}O_6$. Like other sugars, it is very sweet. Its formula is often written out as shown in A (see facing page), although sometimes it is represented as in B.

This indicates that glucose (like other sugars) can exist in a ring form, the links (bar one oxygen atom) on the ring being carbon atoms, with the other atoms and groups of atoms protruding out. I show two ways of drawing glucose, in the second of which all but one of the carbon atoms have not been shown. This is standard practice when organic chemists draw formulae. You will find other examples in Chapter Five, where the formulae of hop acids and cannabis resin are shown. Every time you see two lines join or a line end without another type of atom (e.g., H) signified, there is a carbon atom at that point.

Sugars such as glucose are able to join together to make bigger molecules. They do this by splitting out a molecule of water between them. If two glucoses join together, they make maltose (see C).

Now if water is added to maltose, the *reverse* reaction can occur, and it will be split into two glucose molecules. When water is used to break up a molecule in this way, it is called *hydrolysis*. Usually this reaction doesn't happen spontaneously; for instance, if you dissolve maltose in water, very little of it is hydrolyzed to glucose. Maltose needs help to be broken down, and this help comes in the form of enzymes, which we will come to shortly.

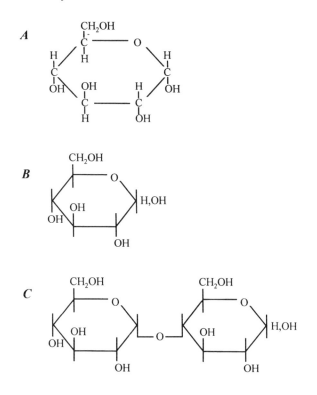

Maltose can pick up another glucose, and the resultant sugar is malto-triose (*tri* indicating that this molecule contains three glucoses). Add a fourth glucose and you have maltotetraose, and so on. Each of these molecules, with one, two, three, four, and so on glucose units has different chemical properties. For example, they are progressively less sweet.

Molecules containing relatively short chains of glucose units are known as *dextrins*. Sometimes they are called *oligomers*, and the basic building block, glucose, is called a *monomer* (mono = alone). When there are lots and lots of building blocks, in this case glucose linked together, we have a polymer. In the case of polymerized glucose, the best known molecule is starch, which is the major food reserve in the barley grain. Polymers of sugars are called *polysaccharides*; the building blocks (in this case glucose) are called *monosaccharides*; dextrins are *oligosaccharides*.

A molecule such as glucose can join together in different ways. If the links between the glucoses are in a certain configuration in three-dimensional space (the so-called α-conformation), the resultant polymer is α-glucan, or starch. If, however, the links have a β-conformation, then the resultant polymer is a β-glucan, which has a totally different set of properties from starch. β-Glucan is the main component of the barley cell wall, for instance, whereas starch is the food reserve packed within those cell walls.

PROTEINS

A different type of polymer found in living systems is protein. Here the monomer is not sugar, but rather amino acid. These are simple molecules that, unlike sugars, contain nitrogen atoms. There are 20 or so different amino acids, each of which has different properties. Just like sugars, they can link together, by splitting out water to form long chains. Again, as for polysaccharides, the reverse process can take place, and addition of water to a polymer of amino acids leads to hydrolysis to individual amino acids.

When a few (say 2 to 10, although the exact definition is somewhat arbitrary) amino acids are linked together, the molecule formed is called a *peptide*. A molecule containing say 10 to 100 amino acid monomers is called a *polypeptide*. Bigger molecules are called *proteins*.

Because there are different amino acids, they can be linked together in many different sequences. Thus there is tremendous diversity between proteins in their structure and properties. Egg white is composed of protein; so, too, are the nails on your fingers and the silk in your tie or your dress.

The proteins in nails or silk are structural proteins. Another very important class of proteins are the enzymes. These are found throughout biological systems and are catalysts. A catalyst is a compound that speeds up or enables a chemical reaction to take place. For example, we saw above that if two glucoses link together, they form maltose. This joining together doesn't happen spontaneously; it has to be catalyzed. There is an enzyme that does that job. There is also an enzyme, a different enzyme, that enables the reverse reaction, that is, the breakdown of maltose into glucose by the addition of water. Because it catalyzes a hydrolysis it is called a *hydrolase*. Wherever you see the suffix *-ase* it refers to an enzyme. Synthases catalyze synthetic reactions, such as the adding of two molecules together. Decarboxylases split carbon dioxide out of molecules. Oxidases add oxygen to molecules, whereas dehydrogenases take hydrogen out of molecules. There are many different enzymes, each of which has its specific job to do.

For the most part, an organism only produces an enzyme when it needs it to do a job. Take barley, for instance. When it is ready to germinate, it needs to break down the food reserves in its starchy endosperm. First of all, it needs to break down the cell walls that are the wrapping of the endosperm, so it needs first to make the enzymes that do this job. Key among these enzymes are the β-glucanases. So these are the first enzymes to be produced by the protein-synthesizing machinery in the aleurone tissue, which responds to a specific hormone trigger from the embryo (see Chapter Four). (Hormones are molecules, usually small ones, that signal that a specific change needs to take place in a living system. They don't effect that change themselves.)

Once the walls are gone, the barley needs the *proteases* to break down the proteins, exposing the starch, which in turn will be hydrolyzed by the amylases. (As we saw in Chapter Four, the key components of starch are amylose and amylopectin, hence the name of the enzymes that degrade them.)

β-Glucanases, proteases, and amylases are enzymes that have their own jobs to do. By ensuring such specificity in enzymes, living organisms can maintain control over their metabolism (an organism's metabolism is the sum total of all the reactions involved in its life cycle).

To act, enzymes need to get close to the molecules that they act on (the substrates). The reaction generally only occurs when there is water present in which the enzyme and substrate can move around. This is why water must be introduced into barley before its metabolism can swing into action and be driven off from malt in kilning when the maltster wishes to stop the modification process. It's also why you must add water to milled malt to get the starch and protein hydrolysis reactions going again.

All chemical reactions take place more rapidly at higher temperatures, the rule of thumb being that the reaction rate doubles for each $10° C$ rise in temperature. This applies to enzyme reactions, too, but there is a complication. Enzymes are, to a greater or lesser extent, inactivated by heat. Some are very sensitive and are rapidly killed at relatively low temperatures such as $50° C$. The β-glucanases are an example of this high lability. Other enzymes are more robust—for example, some of the peroxidases (enzymes that use hydrogen peroxide as a substrate) in barley happily survive $70° C$. These varying sensitivities to heat have major implications for the malting and brewing processes, as we saw, for example, in Chapters Four and Six.

OTHER POLYMERIC MATERIALS IN LIVING SYSTEMS

There are two other key classes of complex molecules found in all living systems, including barley, hops, and yeast: the nucleic acids and the lipids. Both are relatively complex substances, and it is not necessary to go into any detail here. It is sufficient to say that the nucleic acids are the molecules involved in synthesizing the proteins of an organism. They contain the genetic code that determines the nature of an organism, whether it is a man or an amoeba, a barley or a hop, a yeast or an organism intent on spoiling beer. There are two types of nucleic acid: deoxyribonucleic acid (DNA) and ribonucleic acid (RNA). The former comprises the genetic code, or blueprint; the latter provides the protein synthesizing machinery.

There are many types of lipids in cells. Most of them contain very long chains of carbon atoms linked to hydrogen, the so-called fatty acids. The only property that I want to mention here is that, by definition, they are not soluble in water but in other types of solvent. There is a saying in chemistry that like dissolves like. Lipids thus dissolve in organic solvents. This is essentially the definition of a lipid. I refer you to the home for the simplest explanation. Think of a sugar such as glucose. You have seen from its formula that it has lots of $-OH$ groups on it, rather like water, H_2O or, if you like, $H-O-H$. Glucose readily dissolves in water. Now think of a greasy spot on your clothes caused by butter. Butter is composed of lipid, and you won't get rid of that stain by washing with water. You will need a solvent that also has a long carbon chain, something like petroleum. Because of this insolubility, lipids tend to be associated with structural elements in a living organism and, in a process such as brewing, they tend to associate with particles such as the spent grains. Cooking fats, lipstick, glass-washing detergents: They are all lipids, because of their water insolubility, and if they get into beer they will tend to go into the foam rather than the liquid beer. Once in the foam they disrupt it and kill it (see Chapter Three).

CELLS

The fundamental unit of all living organisms is the cell. Some organisms, such as brewing yeast, are unicellular, in that they consist of just one cell. Organisms such as barley and hops are multicellular, with many different types of cells. Thus, in barley, there are embryo cells, aleurone cells, starchy endosperm cells, and so on. Collections of similar cells (for example, the aleurone) are called tissues.

The bacteria that can contaminate wort and beer are also unicellular, but they are even simpler than yeast. In a bacterium there is no division of the contents of the cell into compartments. All of the nucleic acids, carbohydrates, proteins, and other simpler molecules involved in the metabolism of the bacterium are in a watery soup called the cytoplasm. Such simple organisms are called prokaryotic.

The cells of yeast and other higher organisms (such as barley and hops) are *eukaryotic*: The cytoplasm is divided into distinct regions, called *organelles*. Just as the organs of the human body have their own roles, so organelles within a cell have their own functions. These are referred to for yeast in Chapter Seven (see page 138).

Living cells need a source of energy, which, when it's released, is used by them to survive, to grow, to divide, or to do the job allocated to that cell. A cell in the embryo of barley consumes energy in making the hormones that it sends out to the aleurone cells, which in turn consume energy in producing the hydrolytic enzymes that degrade the starchy endosperm. In organisms such as yeast and barley grain, the energy is obtained by "burning" sugars. In a series of enzyme-catalyzed reactions, the sugar is degraded and energy is progressively released. The standard equation for respiration is given in Chapter Seven, which also indicates the equation for the process when it is carried out in the absence of oxygen (fermentation). In both instances the energy is collected in the form of a chemical carrier called ATP, which is found in all living cells and is often called the universal energy currency. ATP is then used by the energy-consuming reactions, such as movement of cells, synthesis of new proteins and membranes, and so on.

FOOD RESERVES ARE POLYMERS—WHY?

Wouldn't it be easier if the cells of the starchy endosperm of barley were packed full of glucose and amino acids rather than starch and protein, meaning that all the embryo had to do was open up the wrapping cell wall and then bathe in the flood of goodies that surged out? Yes, it would, but it isn't possible, because cells must keep their food reserves in a polymeric form.

We have to understand the phenomenon of osmosis to appreciate the reason for polymeric storage. If you have two liquids, one a concentrated solution of glucose and the other a dilute solution of glucose, and you separate them by a membrane, water will progressively pass from the dilute solution to the more concentrated one, until the strength of the solutions is identical on either side of the membrane. This is osmosis. The numbers of glucose molecules on either side of the membrane is critical in this experiment. Now, if those glucoses were all linked together as starch (see above), instead of having many molecules of sugar in the concentrated solution, we would just have a single molecule. There is just the same amount of sugar, but far far less *osmotic pressure*. Herein we find the reason for the polymeric form of food reserves. If all the glucose and amino acids in the starch and protein food reserves of barley were monomeric, they would exert an enormous osmotic pressure in the cells, and water would flood into them and burst them.

pH

pH is a measure of the relative acidity or alkalinity of a solution. Although there are several definitions of an acid, for our purposes it's sufficient to say that it is a chemical substance that releases hydrogen ions. pH is a measure of the concentration of hydrogen ions. It might seem obtuse, but the lower the pH, the more hydrogen ions are present and the more acid is a solution. The symbol for the hydrogen ion is H^+. It has one positive charge. Ions are basically chemicals that have charges. They attract or repel other ions; one positive ion will repel another positive ion, but it will attract a negative ion. The saying goes: "Like charges repel, opposite charges attract."

One negatively charged ion is the hydroxide ion, OH^-. If a hydrogen ion and a hydroxide ion get together by attraction, they can go as far as to react with one another and make . . . yes, water!

$$H^+ + OH^- \rightarrow H_2O$$

Clearly, if all of the hydrogen ions in a solution are mopped up by hydroxide ions, the solution is neutral and not acidic. Its pH is 7.0. If there are more hydrogen ions than hydroxides, the pH is below 7 and is acidic.

The lower the pH (1.0 is the lowest value), the more acidic is a solution. If there are more hydroxide ions than hydrogen ions, the solution is alkaline and has a pH above 7.0, 14.0 is the highest pH, and such a solution would be extremely alkaline (caustic).

Beer is acidic, with a pH usually between 4.0 and 4.6.

Hydroxide isn't the only negatively charged species that the hydrogen ion can react with. Others include the bitter substances, the iso-α-acids, which can exist in a charged, negative state at higher pHs, but when the pH is low (H^+ is high) they pick up this ion, and the charges cancel out—they become uncharged. This type of interaction is tremendously important. In the case of hop compounds, it influences their bitterness and foaming properties. The uncharged forms are much more bitter, more foaming, and also better able to kill microorganisms than are the charged forms. It is for this reason, too, that enzymes are more or less active at different pHs, because they can have different structures depending on the extent to which their negative groups interact with the hydrogen ion.

Buffers are materials that can chemically soak up hydrogen ions and therefore stop a pH changing. They are very important in living cells, because the pH needs to be kept fairly constant, as the cell's machinery is designed to operate to best effect at that pH.

The starchy endosperm cells in barley and malt therefore have their preferred internal pH. A mash of malt will have a pH of around 5.5, due to an internal buffering system (including some of the soluble proteins, polypeptides, and peptides), which holds the pH at that value. Quite a lot of acid needs to be added to drop the pH from that value. The pH falls during mashing because the buffering system (peptides) is used up by the yeast and because the yeast releases acid.

One factor involved in lowering the pH in a mash is the level of calcium in the water (liquor). It does this by reacting with phosphate from the malt, releasing hydrogen ions:

$$3Ca^{2+} + 2HPO_4^{2-} \rightarrow Ca_3(PO_4)_2 + 2H^+$$

COLOR

The color of a liquid such as beer, or our clothes, or the cover of this book—of all things—is due to the extent to which our eyes detect different types of light.

Light can be thought of as a vast collection of different waves, each of which has a different size (wavelength), measured in nanometers (1 nm = one thousand-millionth of a meter). Visible light is a collection of light waves of anything between 400 nm and 800 nm. Blue light is at the shorter wavelength end, red light at the longer wavelength end.

If you have a light source equally strong at all of these wavelengths, the light you see is vivid white. Conversely, if there was no light whatsoever, you would see black. You would also see black if somebody put a filter between your eyes and that light source, a filter that screened out light at all the wavelengths. If, however, that filter sifted out only the longer-wavelength light, you would detect the light as blue, because the shorter wavelengths are reaching the eye. If the filter trapped the shorter wavelengths, you would see red light emerging.

This is the basis for seeing different colors. Paints and pigments are the color they are because they absorb a series of wavelengths of sunlight *other* than those associated with the color that they reveal to you. A green paint has the shade it has due to a selection of wavelengths of light that it doesn't filter out and that therefore enter your eye.

Many individual chemical compounds absorb light of specific wavelengths, and this is the basis for measuring them. Take our friends the iso-α-acids again: They absorb what is known as ultraviolet light, which is very short-wavelength light, beyond the blue light at the lower wavelength end of the spectrum, light that cannot be detected by the human eye. By measuring the amount of light that absorbed by a solution of the iso-α-acids, one can deduce how much of these materials are present, because the more of a chemical compound, present in a solution, the more light it will absorb. To measure these bitter compounds then, they are extracted into a solvent and light at a wavelength of 275 nm is shone through the solvent. This is done in a spectrophotometer, which is a device that can split up light into individual wavelengths and measure how much of each wavelength is "taken out" by a solution. Spectrophotometry, using a wide selection of wavelengths, each appropriate to the chemical to be measured, is extensively used in industry, including the brewing industry.

CHROMATOGRAPHY

Another analytical technique of enormous value in the brewery is chromatography. Fundamentally this involves the separation of mixtures by passing a mobile phase past a stationary phase. Substances differ in their preference for the two phases and are either held on the stationary phase or tend to move along with the mobile phase. When chromatography is complete, the individual substances are detected in some way, perhaps by measuring their absorption of specific wavelengths of light (see above), staining them with a dye, and so on. There are various types of chromatography: in gas chromatography the mobile phase is a gas mixture and the stationary phase some type of solid in a column. High-performance liquid chromatography differs in that the mobile phase is a liquid at very high pressures.

GLOSSARY

Term	Description
Abrasion	Damaging the part of the barley corn farthest from the embryo in order to stimulate activity of the aleurone and "two-way" modification
Abscisic acid	A plant hormone that counters the action of gibberellic acid
Accelerated fermentation	Fermentations carried out under conditions in which they proceed more rapidly, e.g., by operating at a higher temperature
Acid washing	Treating yeast with acid in order to kill contaminating organisms without destroying the yeast itself
Acrospire	The developing shoot in germinating barley
Adjunct	A source of fermentable extract other than malt for use in brewing
Aerobic	In the presence of oxygen
Aging	The holding of beer in order for it to be matured to suitable state for retail to the consumer
Agitator	A device for mixing the contents of a vessel, e.g., a mash mixer

Air rest	Period employed during the steeping of barley in which water is drained from the grain bed to allow the access of oxygen to the embryo
Albumin	Soluble protein class in barley
Alcohol	A class of organic compounds containing the hydroxyl ($-OH$) group; the principal product of fermentation by yeast is ethyl alcohol (ethanol); other "higher" alcohols are also produced in much lower quantities by yeast and are implicated in the flavor of beer
Alcoholic strength	The amount of alcohol in a beverage, frequently referred to as ABV (alcohol by volume), in which the ethanol content is quantified in terms of volume of ethanol per volume of beverage
Ale	A type of beer generally characterized by an amber color and traditionally produced using a top fermenting yeast (in medieval England, ale referred to unhopped beer, but this no longer applies)
Aleurone	A tissue 2–3 cells deep that surrounds the starchy endosperm of the barley corn and is responsible for making the hydrolytic enzymes (hydrolases) that degrade the barley food reserves
α-Acids	Resins from the hop that are the precursors of the bitter compounds in beer
Amino acids	Small molecules (there are approximately 20 different ones) containing nitrogen, which are the building blocks of proteins
Amylases	Starch-degrading enzymes
Amylose	A linear polymer of glucose that is a key component of starch

Amylopectin	The second key component of starch, differing from amylose in that it has branches
Anaerobic	In the absence of oxygen
Aneuploid	Indicates that an organism contains more than two copies of its genetic blueprint (haploid organisms contain one copy, diploid organisms contain two copies, polyploid organisms contain many; there is no agreed point at which aneuploidy becomes polyploidy)
Antifoam	A material added to fermentations to suppress excessive production of foam
Antioxidant	A material either native or added to a raw material that serves to protect against the damaging influence of oxygen
Aroma hops	Hop varieties said to give particularly prized aroma characteristics to a beer
Astringency	A drying of the palate
ATP bioluminescence	A technique for detecting microorganisms and soil by measuring the amount of light produced by the action of the enzyme luciferase acting on ATP present in the sample
Autolysis	The breakdown of a cell by its own enzymes
Auxiliary finings	Agents used alongside isinglass to facilitate the settling of insoluble materials from green beer
Awn	The beardlike projection on a barley corn
Barley	*Hordeum vulgare*; a member of the grass family and the principal raw material for malting and brewing worldwide
Barley wine	A very strong type of ale of long standing in England
Barrel	A volume measure of beer (United States = 31 U.S. gallons or 1.1734 hl; United Kingdom = 36 U.K. gallons or 1.6365 hl)

Beading	The formation of bubbles of carbon dioxide in a glass of beer and their rise to the top of the drink
Beer stone	A precipitation of calcium oxalate in beer dispense pipes
β-Glucan	A polymer of glucose that forms the bulk of the cell walls in the starchy endosperm in barley and that causes several serious problems to the Brewer if not properly broken down in malting and mashing
β-Glucanase	The type of enzyme that hydrolyzes β-glucan
Biological acidification	A practice common in Germany in which microorganisms (lactic acid bacteria) are encouraged to grow in the process in order to increase the acidity (lower pH)
Biological stability	The extent to which a beer is able to resist infection
Bitter	A type of ale that is not excessively colored
Bitterness	A flavor characteristic customarily associated with beer; also the term used to quantify the content of bitter compounds (iso-α-acids) in beer
Bock	A type of lager-style beer
Boiling	The process of vigorously heating sweet wort at boiling temperatures
Bottom fermentation	Traditional fermentation mode for lagers where yeast collects at base of fermenter
Bracteoles	The leafy parts of a hop cone
Breakdown	Deterioration of a beer
Break point	The stage during kilning of malt when the temperature of the air leaving the malt becomes identical with that entering the malt, because all of the free water that is not inside the malt has been driven off; whenever there is unbound

	water present, it will consume energy (latent heat) in order to escape, essentially as steam; if this free water is taking up the heat, then the air coming off the kiln remains relatively cool
Brewhouse	The part of the brewery in which grist materials are converted into wort
Brewster	A female brewer
Bright beer	Beer postfiltration
Bright beer tank	The vessel to which a beer is run after filtration and before packaging, sometimes called a fine ale tank
Bromate	Has been employed (as potassium bromate) in order to suppress rootlet development during germination of barley
Burtonization	Adjustment of the salt content of brewing liquor to render it similar to that of the water at Burton-on-Trent in England
Calandria	A device either internally or externally linked to a kettle and used for heating wort
Calcofluor	A substance that binds specifically to β-glucans and reveals them via fluorescence
Carbonation	The amount of carbon dioxide in a beer and also the act of increasing the level of carbon dioxide
Carboxypeptidase	An enzyme in barley that hydrolyzes proteins by chopping off one amino acid at a time from one end
Cardboard	An undesirable flavor note that develops in packaged beer on storage
Carrageenan	An extract of seaweed used to aid solids removal in the wort boiling stage
Cask	The traditional vessel for holding unpasteurized English ale
Cell	The basic unit of any living organism

Cellar	The part of a brewery containing the fermenters and the conditioning vessels, also the part of a retail outlet (e.g., bar) in which the beer containers are stored
Cell wall	The outside of a cell whose role is to maintain the shape of that cell
Charcoal	A material capable of adsorbing flavors and colors from liquids that it contacts; used, for example, to treat water coming into a brewery
Chilling	The cooling of liquid streams in a brewery, e.g., hot wort going to the fermenter, or green beer passing to conditioning and filtration
Chromosome	The form in which the genetic material of a cell (DNA) is held in eukaryotic cells
CIP (cleaning in-place)	An integrated and automated system of cleaning with caustic and/or acid installed in modern breweries
Cling	The adhesion of foam to the walls of a beer glass (also known as lacing)
Coalescence	The tendency of bubbles in beer foam to merge together and form bigger bubbles
Cold break	Insoluble material that drops out of wort on chilling
Cold water extract	A measure of modification of malt based on the small-scale extraction of milled malt in dilute ammonia
Colloidal instability	The tendency of a beer to throw a haze on storage
Color	The shade and hue of a beer
Conditioning	The maturation of beer in respect of its flavor and clarity
Continuous fermentation	A process in which wort is converted to green beer in a few hours by passage through a vessel holding yeast

Conversion	The stage in mashing when the temperature is raised to enable gelatinization of starch and subsequent breakdown of the starch by amylases
Cooker	A vessel in the brewhouse in which adjuncts with very high gelatinization temperatures are cooked
Cooler	A device (often called a paraflow) in which hot wort flows contra to a cooling liquid in order to bring it down to the temperature at which fermentation will be carried out
Copper	The vessel (often called the kettle) in which wort is boiled with hops
Corn	Maize, the word is also used to describe individual grains of barley
Crabtree effect	The control mechanism that dictates that yeast ferments sugar rather than metabolize it via respiration if the sugar concentration presented to the yeast is high
Cropping	The collection of the yeast that proliferates during fermentation
Crown cork	The crimped tops used on beer bottles
Culms	The rootlets of germinated barley that are collected after kilning and sold as animal feed
Curing	The higher temperature phases of kilning when flavor and color are introduced into malt
Cylindroconical vessels (CCVs)	Tall fermentation vessels with a mostly cylindrical body, but a conelike base into which the yeast collects after fermentation
Darcy's law	An equation that explains the rate at which liquid flows, e.g., in a lauter tun or a beer filter
Decoction mashing	Practice originating in mainland Europe in

	which a mash is progressively increased in temperature by taking a proportion of it out of the mix and boiling it prior to adding it back into the whole
Descriptive tests	Beer-tasting protocols in which trained tasters describe the taste and aroma of beer according to a series of defined terms
Dextrins	Partial breakdown products of starch that consist of several glucose units and that are not fermentable by yeast
Diacetyl	A substance with an intense aroma of butterscotch that is produced by yeast during fermentation but that is subsequently mopped up again by the yeast
Diatomaceous earth	The skeletal remains of microscopic organisms used in powder filtration of beer (also known as kieselguhr)
Difference tests	Blind tasting procedures in which tasters (including the untrained) are asked to differentiate samples of beer
Dimethyl sulfide	Compound that imparts a significant flavor to many lager-style beers
Dirty wort	Wort containing a high level of trub solids and which is therefore turbid
Disproportionation	The passage of gas in beer foam from small bubbles to larger bubbles, leading to a disappearance of the former and increase in size of the latter
Dissolved oxygen	The amount of oxygen dissolved in a wort prior to fermentation or, more commonly, the amount dissolved (and undesired) in beer
Dormancy	The control mechanism in barley that prevents the grain from germinating prematurely

Downy mildew	A disease of hops
Draft beer	Beer in either cask or keg, or sometimes unpasteurized beer in small pack
Drinkability	The property of beer that determines whether or not a customer judges it worthy of repurchase
Dry beer	Beer genre in which beverage contains relatively low residual sugar
Dry hopping	Traditional procedure in the production of English cask ales in which a handful of hop cones are added to the cask prior to shipment from the brewery
Duty	Excise tax on beer
Dwarf hops	Hops that grow to a lower height than traditional varieties
Ear	The head of a barley plant that holds the grain
Embryo	The baby plant in the grain
Endo enzymes	Hydrolytic enzymes that chop bonds in the inside of a polymeric substrate (examples are α-amylase and β-glucanase)
Endogenous enzymes	Enzymes in the malting and brewing process that are contributed by the raw materials (malt and yeast)
Endosperm	The food reserve of the barley plant
Enzyme	A biological catalyst, comprising protein
Essential oils	The aromatic component of hops
Ester	A class of substances produced by yeast and that afford distinctive, sweet aromas to beer
Ethanol	The principal alcohol in beer, which is the major fermentation product of brewing yeast and which affords the intoxicating property to the beverage, originally called ethyl alcohol
Evaporation	A measure of the water loss during wort boiling

Excise
Tax on alcoholic beverages levied by government agencies

Exo enzyme
Hydrolytic enzymes that chop bonds at the ends of substrate molecules, thereby yielding small products generally assimilable by organisms (examples are β-amylase and carboxypeptidase)

Exogenous enzymes
Enzymes added to the brewing process from outside sources (i.e., not from malt or yeast)

Feed-grade barley
Barley that yields a relatively low level of extractable material after conventional malting and mashing

Fermentability
The extent to which a wort can be used successfully by yeast to produce ethanol

Fermentation
The process by which sugars are converted into ethanol by yeast

Filtration
The clarification of beer (sometimes people refer to the recovery of wort from spent grains as filtration, but strictly speaking this is wort separation)

Fingerprinting
The differentiation of yeasts (or barleys) by analyzing the pattern of DNA fragments produced from them

Finings
Materials used to clarify wort and especially beer by interacting with solid materials and causing them to sediment

Flash pasteurization
Heating of flowing beer to a high temperature (e.g., 78° C) for less than a minute in order to inactivate microorganisms

Flavor profile
An expert semiquantitative evaluation of beer flavor made by trained tasters using defined taste and aroma descriptive terms

Flavor stability
The extent to which a beer is able to resist flavor changes (usually undesirable) within it

Flocculation	The tendency of yeast cells to associate
Foam	The head (froth) on beer
Foam stabilizer	Endogenous materials (e.g., proteins from malt) that stabilize foam or materials added to beer to protect foam (e.g., propylene glycol alginate)
Font	The unit on the bar that labels the draft beer being served from that tap
Franchise brewing	The brewing of one company's beer under license by another company
Free amino nitrogen (FAN)	A measure of the level of amino acids in wort or beer
Fungicide	An agent sprayed onto crops such as barley and hops to prevent the growth of fungi thereon and therefore ensure that those crops are healthy, high yielding, and don't introduce harmful materials into the brewing process
Fusarium	A fungal infection of barley that can cause a beer made from that barley to gush
Gallon	A standard unit of beer volume (a U.S. barrel = 0.8327 U.K. barrel)
Gelatinization	A disorganization and loosening of the internal structure of starch granules by heating, rendering the starch more amenable to enzymic hydrolysis
Genetic modification	A process of modifying the genome of an organism by introducing specific pieces of DNA from an exogenous source
Genome	The information code of a cell, held within DNA, that determines the nature and behavior of that cell
Germination	The process by which steeped barley is allowed to partially digest its endosperm and the embryonic tissues to partially grow
Gibberellins	Plant hormones, produced within the embryo of barley, that migrate to the aleurone and trigger enzyme synthesis

Gravity   The strength of wort in terms of
                           concentration of dissolved substances,
                           as measured traditionally using a
                           hydrometer
Green beer   Freshly fermented beer prior to
                           conditioning
Green malt   Freshly germinated malt prior to kilning
Grist   The raw materials (malt and other cereals)
                           that will be milled in the brewhouse;
                           more loosely applied also to those
                           adjunct materials that don't require
                           milling (e.g., syrups to be added to the
                           kettle)
Gushing   The uncontrolled surge of the contents of a
                           beer from the package after opening
Hammer mill   A mill that grinds malted barley down to
                           extremely fine particles that are suited
                           to a mash filter for subsequent wort
                           separation, but not a lauter tun
Haze   Turbidity
Hazemeter   An instrument for measuring the clarity of
                           beer: operates on the principle that
                           since particles scatter light; the more
                           light scattered, the more particles are
                           present. Some hazemeters measure the
                           amount of light scattered at right
                           angles (90°) to the light beam shone at
                           the particles. Other meters (forward
                           scatter meters) measure the light
                           deflected at 13°. The former type is
                           sensitive to extremely small particles,
                           the latter to big particles.
Heat exchanger   Device for rapidly cooling down liquid
                           streams, e.g., boiled wort. The hot
                           liquid flows countercurrent to a cold
                           liquid on either side of thin walls.
                           Heat passes from the hot to the cold
                           liquid.

Hectoliter	100 liters
Hemocytometer	Microscope-based chamber for counting yeast cells
High-gravity brewing	Technique for maximizing vessel utilization whereby the wort being fermented is more concentrated than necessary to make the desired strength of beer; after fermentation, the beer is diluted to the required alcohol content
High-performance liquid chromatography	Analysis technique involving separation and measurement of components of a mixture on the basis of their affinity for a high-pressure liquid stream or a solid support
High-temperature mashing	Mashing performed at higher-than-normal temperatures to rapidly eliminate one of the starch-degrading enzymes (β-amylase) and produce a wort that contains fewer sugars that are fermentable by yeast and, hence, a lower-alcohol beer
Higher alcohols	Compounds similar to ethanol but that contain more carbon atoms; they may contribute to the aroma of beer (and certainly do after conversion into their equivalent esters); it has been suggested that they may be responsible for hangovers, although there is very little evidence for this
Hop	Plant that provides bitterness and aroma to beer
Hop back	Vessel rarely found these days that was used to separate boiled wort from residual solids by passage through a bed of waste hops
Hop cone	The flower of the female hop plant, which is the part of the plant used in the brewing process

Hop garden	Where hops are grown
Hop oil	The component of hops providing aroma (essential oils)
Hop pocket	A large sack packed with hops
Hop preparations	Extracts of hops, usually made with liquid carbon dioxide, which can be used at various stages in the brewing process to introduce bitterness or aroma to wort or beer more efficiently
Hop resin	The precursors of bitterness in beer (α-acids)
Hopped wort	Wort after the boiling stage
Hordein	Insoluble storage protein in barley broken down during malting and mashing
Hormone	Small molecule that switches on or off events in a living organism; e.g., gibberellins are hormones that switch on enzyme synthesis in barley
Hot break	Insoluble material that drops out of wort on boiling
Hot water extract	A measure of how much material can be solubilized from malt or an adjunct obtained by carrying out a small-scale mash of the material and measuring the specific gravity of the resultant wort
Husk	The protective layer around the barley corn
Hydrogel	Material derived by acid treatment of silica that is used for the removal of potential haze-forming materials from beer ("chillproofing")
Hydrolyzed corn syrup	Material produced by the acid or enzymic hydrolysis of corn starch and that can have different degrees of fermentability; added to the wort kettle, thereby providing an opportunity to extend brewhouse capacity by avoiding the need for mash extraction and separation stages

Hydrometer	Device operating on a principle of buoyancy for measuring the specific gravity of a solution; the higher it floats the more material is dissolved in the solution
Hydrophobicity	A measure of the extent to which a molecule moves away from water; grease and fats are hydrophobic, whereas salt is hydrophilic ("water-loving")
Ice beer	Beer produced with a process including ice generation
Immobilized yeast	Yeast attached to an insoluble support (e.g., glass beads) that can be used in continuous processing whereby wort or beer flows past it
Indirect heating	Heating of a material without direct application of heat, but rather via a heat exchanger
Infestation	Condition whereby a raw material in the maltings or brewery has animal life within it, e.g., insects in badly stored barley
Inorganic	Any chemical species other than those containing carbon (carbon dioxide, despite containing carbon, is regarded as inorganic)
Insecticide	Material sprayed onto crops during growth or storage to eliminate insect infestation
Invisible haze	Haze that registers on a hazemeter but that is not perceptible to the eye; sometimes called pseudohaze
Iron	Inorganic element that can enter into beer from some raw materials (e.g., filter aids) and potentiate oxidative damage
Isinglass	Preparation of solubilized collagen from the swim bladders of certain fish; used for clarifying beer, normally referred to as finings

Iso-α-acid   Bitter component of beer derived from
                               hops
Isomerization   The conversion of hop α-acids into iso-α-
                               acids, achieved during wort boiling
Keg   Large container for holding beer, for
                               subsequent draft dispense by pump
Kettle   Brewhouse vessel in which wort is boiled;
                               also known as copper
Kieselguhr   Mined powder, derived from skeletons of
                               microscopic animals, used to aid the
                               filtering of beer
Kilning   Heating of germinated barley to drive off
                               moisture and introduce desired color
                               and flavor
Krausening   Traditional German fermentation practice
                               in which fresh fermenting wort is
                               introduced late during warm
                               conditioning to stimulate maturation
                               of beer
Lacing   Tendency of beer foam to stick to the side
                               of the glass (also known as cling)
Lager   A type of beer, traditionally pale, produced
                               by bottom-fermenting yeast and
                               produced in a relatively slow process,
                               which includes lengthy cold storage
                               (lagering); the word *lager* is derived
                               from the German "to store"
Large pack   Kegs or casks
Late hopping   Practice of adding a proportion of the hops
                               very late in the wort-boiling phase in
                               order to retain certain hop aromas in
                               the ensuing beer
Late hop essences   Extracts that can be added to beer to
                               introduce a late hop character
Lauter   The act of separating sweet wort from
                               spent grains and also the vessel used
                               to perform this duty
Lead conductance value   A method for assessing how much
                               bitterness precursor is present in hops

Light (lite) beer	Beers in which a greater proportion of the sugar has been converted into alcohol
Lightstruck	Skunky flavor that develops in beer exposed to light
Limit dextrinase	Enzyme in malt that breaks the branchpoints in the amylopectin component of starch
Lipid	A material that does not dissolve in water, but does dissolve in organic solvents
Liquid carbon dioxide	Solvent produced by liquefying carbon dioxide gas at low temperatures and high pressures; used for extracting materials from hops
Liquor	Water
Low-alcohol beers	Beers containing a low level of alcohol (e.g., less than 2% ABV), although the definition differs between countries
Lupulin	The glands in hop cones that contain the resins
Malt	Dried germinated barley
Malting	The controlled germination of barley involving steeping, germination, and kilning so as to soften the grain for milling, develop enzymes for breaking down starch in mashing, and to introduce color and desirable flavors
Malting grade	Score allocated to a barley variety that indicates whether it will give a high hot water extract after conventional malting and mashing
Masher	Device positioned before the mash mixer that facilitates intimate mixing of milled malt and hot water
Mashing	Process of contacting milled grist and hot water to effect the breakdown of starch (and other materials from the grist)
Mash filter	Device incorporating membranes for separating wort from spent grains

Mash tun	Vessel for holding a "porridge" of milled grist and hot water to achieve conversion of starch into fermentable sugars
Mashing off	Conclusion of mashing, when the temperature is raised prior to the wort separation stage
Maturation	The postfermentation stages in brewing, when beer is prepared for filtration
Mealy	Favorable texture of the starchy endosperm of barley that makes it easy to modify
Melanoidins	Color contributors in beer produced by the reaction of sugars with amino acids during heating stages in malting and brewing
Membrane	A sheet, either one found in a living system (e.g., the plasma membrane which surrounds a yeast cell) or one that has a specific job to do in a brewery (e.g., in a mash filter or a beer filter)
Metabolism	The sum of the many chemical reactions involved in the life of an organism such as barley or yeast
Micropyle	The area at the embryo end of a barley corn through which water can gain access
Milling	The grinding of malt and solid adjuncts to generate particles that can be readily broken down during mashing
Mitochondrion	The organelle in a eukaryotic cell responsible for generating energy in respiration
Modification	The progressive degradation of the cell structure in the starchy endosperm of barley
Moisture content	The amount of water associated with a material such as barley, malt, hops, or yeast

Mold	Infection of barley or hops
Mouthfeel	The tactile sensation that a beer creates in the mouth (also referred to as texture)
Near infrared	A region of the light spectrum where wavelengths are longer than those in the visible red region, but shorter than those in the infrared region; NIR spectrometers are increasingly widely used for making various rapid measurements in maltings and brewery
Nitrogen	There are two completely separate meanings for nitrogen in malting and brewing: (a) used to refer to the nitrogen atom as it is found in proteins; therefore its level in barley, malt or wort is a measure of how much protein they contain; (b) used to refer to gaseous nitrogen (N_2), which is sometimes introduced into beer to enhance foam; this process is called nitrogenation
Nonalcoholic beers	Beers containing very low levels of alcohol, i.e., less than 0.05% ABV (although the definition differs among countries)
Nonenal	Compound that contributes to the cardboard character that develops in stale beer
Nonreturnable bottles	Glass bottles that are not returned to the brewery for refilling; also referred to as one-trip bottles
Nucleation	Spontaneous bubble formation in a wort or beer
Nucleic acids	The complex polymeric molecules in living systems that are responsible for carrying the genetic message and translating it
Organelle	A distinct region within a eukaryotic cell with its own specific function

Organic   Refers to compounds containing carbon
                          (apart from carbon dioxide and
                          carbonates)
Organic acids   Carbon-containing acids such as citric and
                          acetic acid released by yeast and
                          largely responsible for pH fall during
                          fermentation
Organoleptic   Pertaining to taste and smell
Original extract   The amount of extract present in a starting
                          wort as calculated from the amount of
                          nonfermented extract left in a beer
                          together with the amount of extract
                          equivalent to the quantity of alcohol
                          produced in a beer; in some countries
                          this is known as original gravity
Osmotic pressure   The force that drives water to pass from a
                          dilute solution to a more concentrated
                          one through a semipermeable
                          membrane
Oxalic acid   An organic acid found in malt that must be
                          precipitated out in the brewhouse by
                          reacting with calcium to form the
                          calcium salt, otherwise it will
                          precipitate out in beer as "stone"
Oxidation   At its simplest, process of deterioration of
                          beer due to ingress of oxygen
pH   A measure of the acidity/alkalinity of a
                          solution
Pale ale   English-style ale usually in small pack
Papain   Protein-hydrolyzing enzyme from pawpaw
Pasteurization   Heat treatment to eliminate
                          microorganisms
Pentosan   Polysaccharide located in cell walls of barley
Peptide   Molecule consisting of perhaps 2–10 amino
                          acids linked together
Perlite   Volcanic ash used in the filtration of beer
                          as an alternative to kieselguhr

Pesticides	Agents used to protect crops from infection and infestation during growth and storage
Piece	The bed of grain in a maltings
Pils	A style of lager originating in Czechoslovakia
Pint	A measure of beer volume (473 ml in U.S.; 568 ml in U.K.)
Pitching	The introduction of yeast into wort prior to fermentation
Plate-and-frame	A type of beer filter
Plato	Unit of wort strength
Polypeptide	A partial breakdown product of proteins containing approximately 10–100 linked amino acid units
Polyphenol	Organic substance originating in husk of barley and also in hops and that can react with proteins to make them insoluble; also known as tannin
Polysaccharide	Polymer comprising sugar molecules linked together
Polyvinylpolypyrrolidone (PVPP)	Agent capable of specifically binding polyphenols and removing them from beer
Preisomerized extracts	Extracts of hops in which the α-acids have been isomerized
Primings	Sugar preparations added to beer to sweeten it
Propagation	Culturing of yeast from a few cells to the large quantities needed to pitch a fermentation
Propylene glycol alginate	Material added to beer to protect the foam from damage by lipids
Protease	Enzyme that breaks down proteins
Protein	Polymer comprising amino acid units
Proteolysis	The breakdown of proteins by proteases
Pseudohaze	Invisible haze

Purging   Elimination of an unwanted volatile
                                    material (e.g., a flavor or a high CO_2
                                    or O_2 content) by bubbling through N_2

Quality assurance   Approach to quality maintenance that
                                    involves establishing robust processes
                                    and systems designed to yield high-
                                    quality product

Quality control   Monitoring of a process to generate
                                    information used to adjust the process
                                    to ensure the correct product

Racking   The packaging of beer

Real extract   The amount of dissolved material in beer
                                    that has not been converted into
                                    alcohol

Reduced hop extracts   Preisomerized extracts that have been
                                    chemically reduced so that they are no
                                    longer light-sensitive and can be used
                                    to provide bitterness to beers intended
                                    for packaging in green or clear glass

Refractometer   Device for measuring the strength of beer

Repitching   Practice of taking yeast grown in one
                                    fermentation to pitch the next batch of
                                    wort

Resin   Fraction from hops that generates the
                                    bitterness in beer

Rough beer   Beer before filtration

Saccharomyces cerevisiae   Brewers' yeast

Saladin box   Type of vessel for germinating barley

Screening   Cleaning of unwanted debris from barley

Seam   The "join" between a beer can and its lid

Small pack   Cans and bottles

Soluble nitrogen ratio   The ratio of the dissolved nitrogen (protein)
                                    in wort and the total nitrogen (protein)
                                    in malt, which is in direct proportion
                                    to the nitrogen modification
                                    (sometimes called the Kolbach index)

Sparging   Spraying the spent grains with hot water
                                    during the wort separation process to

	facilitate extraction of dissolved substances
Specification	A parameter measured on a raw material of brewing, on a process stream or the finished beer, that must be within defined limits for the material to pass to the next stage in the process
Specific gravity	The weight of a liquid relative to the weight of an equivalent volume of pure water (also referred to as relative density)
Spectrophotometer	Device for measuring the amount of light absorbed by a solution
Spent grains	The solid remains from a mash
Spoilage organism	Microbe capable of infecting wort or beer
Square	Style of fermenter in that shape
Stabilization	Treatment of beer to extend its shelf life
Staling	Deterioration in the flavor of beer
Starch	Polysaccharide food reserve in barley
Steely	Texture of starchy endosperms of those barleys that are difficult to modify
Steeping	Increasing the water content of barley by soaking
Sugar	Small, sweet carbohydrate
Sulfur compound	Flavor-active material containing sulfur atom(s)
Sweet wort	Wort prior to boiling with hops
Syrup	Concentrated solution of sugars
Taint	Off flavor in beer or a raw material
Tannic acid	Material added to beer to precipitate out protein
Tetrazolium	Dye used to detect whether barley is alive
Three glass test	Procedure for blind tasting to discern whether two samples of beer can be differentiated
Tintometer	Device consisting of a series of colored discs for comparing with a beer to ascertain whether it has the correct color

Top fermentation	Fermentations in which the yeast collects at the top of the vessel
Total soluble nitrogen	A measure of the dissolved protein in wort
Trigeminal sense	Sensation of pain detected by the trigeminal nerve
Trub	Insoluble material emerging from wort on heating and cooling
Tunnel pasteurization	Pasteurization of small-pack beer by passage through a heated chamber
Ultrafiltration	Filtering out of material at the molecular level by passage through very fine membranes
Viability	Measure of how alive something is
Vicinal diketones	Butterscotch-flavored compounds formed during brewery fermentation
Vigor	A measure of the strength of growth of the barley embryo during germination
Viscosity	A measure of how much a liquid resists flow
Vitality	A measure of the healthiness of a living yeast
Volatile	A molecule in beer that contributes to aroma and is easily driven off
Vorlauf	Recycling of the first wort runnings from a lauter tun to ensure bright wort
Water sensitivity	Tendency of a barley's germination to be suppressed by the presence of excess water
Weak wort recycling	Use of the weaker worts from the end of wort separation to mash in the next mash
Whirlpool	Vessel for separating trub from boiled wort
Wort	Fermentation feedstock produced in the brewery
Wort separation	Act of separating sweet wort from spent grains
Xerogel	Colloidal stabilizing agent (similar to hydrogel) made from silica

Yeast   Living eukaryotic organism capable of
                               performing alcoholic fermentations
Yeast food   Source of amino acids and vitamins
                               sometimes used in brewery
                               fermentations
Zentner   Unit of hop mass (50 kg)

FURTHER READING

The reader will have found relatively few references in this book. This has been a deliberate policy, for in most instances the most relevant references are to scientific and technical journals, written for the specialist and unlikely to be readily digested by the layperson. Indeed, most of the books covering the brewing process are somewhat technical, but I am able to recommend some volumes which will appeal variously to those with different extents of scientific education.

The brewing scientist's "bible" remains *Malting and Brewing Science*, by J. S. Hough, D. E. Briggs, R. Stevens, and T. W. Young, which was published in 1982 in two volumes by Chapman and Hall, London (ISBN 0-412-16590-2). This is a very comprehensive treatise of malting and brewing, which the authors penned as an aid to teaching relevant Masters degrees.

One of those authors (Tom Young) also co-authored a more recent (1995) book from the same publisher, entitled *Brewing* (ISBN 0-412-26420-X). The other author was M. J. Lewis; Mike taught brewing for many years at the University of California, Davis. In many ways this latter book is a distillation of the above, but is targetted as an introductory guide for students entering the world of brewing and for those setting up small breweries.

A History of Brewing, by H. S. Corran (David and Charles, Newton Abbot, U.K., 1975, ISBN 0-715-36735-8) remains possibly the most instructive historical treatise on brewing. For those especially interested in the history of beer (and other alcoholic drinks) in the British Isles, then they should refer to an outstanding bibliography compiled by David W. Gutzke entitled *Alcohol in the British Isles from Roman Times to 1996: An Annotated Bibliography* (Greenwood Press, Connecticut, 1996, ISBN 0-313-29420-8).

INDEX

239